"It is terrific to have a book which so effectively addresses the unique challenges and opportunities of leadership in the nonprofit sector, replete with sound advice and concrete examples. Tom Adams brings a wealth of experience and savvy to the topic. Paid and volunteer leaders of nonprofits at all levels will benefit from reading it."
—**Irv Katz,** president, National Human Services Assembly

"Rich with innovative examples and advice, this book is grounded in the reality of nonprofits. It will be an extraordinarily useful guide to nonprofit organizations of all types and sizes."
—**Ruth McCambridge,** editor in chief, *Nonprofit Quarterly*

"Make no mistake: attracting and retaining top talent should be priority number 1 for the nonprofit sector. Adams's book offers practical advice for how to embed this priority into the sector's DNA. All who care about nonprofit effectiveness would be well served to give this book a close read."
—**Kathleen P. Enright,** president and CEO, Grantmakers for Effective Organizations

"Tom Adams has taken his considerable experience with executive transitions into new territory: leadership development set in the context of inevitable transitions, and he shares his new insights with us eager readers."
—**Jan Masaoka,** editor, *Blue Avocado,* former executive director of CompassPoint Nonprofit Services

"This guide is one of a kind in providing a realistic frame for the world of nonprofit leaders. It is long overdue in the sector as a real tool for leaders. Maybe even more important, it helps nonprofit boards of directors and philanthropic organizations to understand the connection between their investment in leadership and achieving organizational goals."
—**Diane Bell McKoy,** CEO, Associated Black Charities

"This amazing book provides the road map that community leaders have long sought. It is a practical, experience-based approach to developing leaders and building strong, lasting organizations that make a difference. As a Latina leader who has built an organization that I want to live on, I understand that knowing how to attract and develop a next generation of leaders from the communities we serve is essential. This guide is a must-read for anyone serious about that agenda."
—**Beatriz Otero,** president and CEO, CentroNía

"Two words come to mind after reading this book—it works! Tom Adams has a recipe for successful transitions of leadership. A must-read for anyone in the nonprofit business."
—**Capt. Hank Sanford,** USN (Ret), CFO & treasurer, U.S. Naval Academy Alumni Association & Foundation

"Maintaining a robust talent pipeline is a critical need that has rarely gotten the attention it deserves in the nonprofit sector. Tom Adams brings the issue front and center. His new book is a valuable road map for the funders, community organizations, and educators seeking to address the leadership needs of the sector."
—**Tim Wolfred,** senior project director, CompassPoint Nonprofit Services

"Tom Adams is a very wise guide to nonprofit staff and board leaders and those who support them. This book is chock-full of practical advice and helpful examples that will help nonprofit organizations strengthen their leadership and performance."
—**Paul Connolly,** senior vice president and director, TCC Group

"*The Nonprofit Leadership Transition and Development Guide* by Tom Adams is a must-read for anyone who is currently leading, or aspires to lead, a thriving nonprofit organization. With all the varied challenges that nonprofits face, excellent leadership is a key enabler of high-quality mission. The guide will help both new and experienced leaders reach that goal."
—**Peter Brinckerhoff,** president, Corporate Alternatives, Inc.

"Those who truly care about the well-being of our communities and the effectiveness of the nonprofit sector need this book. Nonprofit leaders—nonprofit CEOs, leadership staff, and board members alike—will treasure this book as an essential component of their toolkits for success. Managing change in key leaders is an essential competency and Mr. Adams's experience, wisdom, and practical approach provide a sure roadmap for success!"
—**Don Crocker,** executive director, Support Center for Nonprofit Management

"This practical and insightful view built upon a depth of experience makes this guide a valuable resource for anyone engaged in nonprofit organizational lasting performance. These sensible and thoughtful methods for successful transitions and leadership development set a plan that can be carried forward."
—**Bruce Gottschall,** executive director (founder), Neighborhood Housing Services of Chicago

"Tom Adams is an authority on transition planning and on leader development and recruitment. He is expert in managing change—for key leaders, as well as for boards of directors and top administrators in not-for-profits. I'm so happy that this will be in book form so that agency executives and boards of directors can readily profit from Tom's vast knowledge and experience."
—**Bob McMahon,** executive director, SCO Family of Services

"Tom's concept of a 'leaderful organization' provides a useful framework for nonprofit boards and executives who can benefit from his useful tips and tools on leadership development and effective leadership transitions. His ideas are drawn from years of practical experience, and this work should become required reading for the leaders—both paid and volunteer—of any organization concerned about long-term sustainability."
—**Cheryl A. Casciani,** director of community investment, Baltimore Community Foundation

"Especially during these times, Tom's experiences and perspectives on leadership and transition are exceptionally helpful. He effectively shares his practical wisdom in this book. As a foundation executive and former mayor, I am keenly aware of the difference leadership makes. This is must reading for funders and others who invest in mission-based organizations."
—**Jim Hoolihan,** president, Blandin Foundation

"How easy it is to hire the wrong person—out of idealism! This wise book will guide your search committee through the science and art of a leadership transition."
—**Char Mollison,** former senior executive, Independent Sector and the Council on Foundations

"Tom Adams's book makes an extraordinary service of helping boards of directors, executive directors, and nonprofit managers know how to develop a path for successful transition in leadership and to demonstrate the powerful relation between a leader and institutional results and impact."
—**Gustavo Torres,** executive director, CASA de Maryland

"Tom Adams's hands-on experience in working with scores of nonprofit organizations through the years makes this book a must read for nonprofit board members and senior staff. Adams's systemic approach reveals a practical path to strengthening, sustaining, and renewing internal organizational leadership over the long haul."
—**Nick Nyhart,** president and CEO, Public Campaign

"Tom Adams is the coach's coach. His book is a must-read for any board of directors or rookie executive director seeking to be the beacon for transformational leadership in their organization. Tom and TransitionGuides worked with the LEDC Board and me when I was hired. Since becoming executive director, I've continued to turn to TransitionGuides as a resource. He is an inspiration to everyone in the field of change-oriented leadership and exemplary nonprofit management."
—**Manny Hidalgo,** executive director, Latino Economic Development Corporation

"Tom's thoughtful advice on leadership transitions in mission-driven organizations comes from his lived experience—first as a leader and subsequently in helping many boards, leaders, and successors navigate the white water of transition. Combining attention to both leader transitions and leader development is powerful and the path forward for the sector. An invaluable resource."
—**Thomas Gilmore,** vice president, CFAR–Center for Applied Research, Inc.

"Tom Adams's keen insights force us to recognize leadership development and transition as critical to nonprofit performance and ability to sustain services. He provides a unique roadmap for funders, trustees, and all those who care about the vitality of the nonprofit sector and those they serve."
—**Cynthia King Vance,** nonprofit trustee

"Tom Adams has been at the forefront of new knowledge and practice in the field of leadership transitions for years. He shares his wealth of knowledge and experience in this guide. For nonprofit leaders and board members it is an essential read."
—**Deborah Linnell,** director of programs, Third Sector New England

TOM ADAMS

Foreword by Ralph Smith

Executive Vice President, The Annie E. Casey Foundation

--- THE ---

NONPROFIT
LEADERSHIP
TRANSITION AND
DEVELOPMENT
--- GUIDE ---

PROVEN PATHS FOR LEADERS AND ORGANIZATIONS

JOSSEY-BASS
A Wiley Imprint
www.josseybass.com

Transition
Guides

Published by Jossey-Bass

A Wiley Imprint

989 Market Street, San Francisco, CA 94103-1741—www.josseybass.com

Jossey-Bass books and products are available through most bookstores. To contact Jossey-Bass directly call our Customer Care Department within the U.S. at 800-956-7739, outside the U.S. at 317-572-3986, or fax 317-572-4002.

Jossey-Bass also publishes its books in a variety of electronic formats. Some content that appears in print may not be available in electronic books.

Library of Congress Cataloging-in-Publication Data

Adams, Thomas H., date.
    The nonprofit leadership transition and development guide: proven paths for
leaders and organizations/Tom Adams; foreword by Ralph Smith—1st ed.
      p. cm.
    Includes bibliographical references and index.
    ISBN 978-0-470-48122-6 (pbk.)
    1. Nonprofit organizations—Management. 2. Leadership. I. Title.
    HD62.6.A33 2010
    658.4′092—dc22
                                               2009054081

Printed in the United States of America

FIRST EDITION

PB Printing   10 9 8 7 6 5 4 3 2 1

CONTENTS

WEB CONTENTS

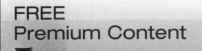

APPENDIXES

Appendix A: Executive Transition Management Tools and Worksheets
- A1. Executive Transition Management Process Overview
- A2. The Interim Executive Advantage: An Overview of the Benefits
- A3. Where to Find an Interim Executive
- A4. Sample Transition Timeline
- A5. Sample Chief Executive 90-Day Entry Plan
- *A6. Chief Executive's Position Profile and Job Announcement Templates
- *A7. Sample Interview Agenda and Questions

Appendix B: Finding and Choosing a Consultant
- B1. When to Use and How to Find a Consultant

Appendix C: Succession Planning Tools and Samples
- *C3. Sample Sustainability and Succession Report

Appendix D: Leader Development and Talent Management Tools and Samples
- D1. Examples of Leader Development Learning Opportunities
- D2. Talent Management Tools

Appendix E: Helpful Inventories
- E1. Leader's Personal and Professional Inventory
- E2. Questions About the Organization
- E3. Diversity Inventory
- E4. The Leader's Emotional Check-in Barometer
- E5. Action Planning Notes and Commitments

Note: Most of the online appendix files listed here are from the appendixes in this book. Asterisked files are supplemental material only on the Web site.

MORE ONLINE SUPPLEMENTS
- TransitionGuides Newsletter and Webinars
- Resiliency in Nonprofit Leadership Transitions: Three Kinds of Rituals That Really Work
- The Four Elements of a Sustainable Organization
- When Should You Consider an Outside Advisor for Your Transition?
- Departure-Defined Succession Planning Process Overview

PERMIT ME TO BEGIN THIS FOREWORD by recalling a meeting long past but not forgotten.

About a decade ago, I had occasion to talk with Karl Dennis, the founder and former executive director of Kaleidoscope, an organization that does outstanding work helping connect foster kids who have been labeled "hard to place" with a permanent and loving home.

Kaleidoscope was part of the inaugural group of the FAMILIES COUNT National Award Winners, a program that The Annie E. Casey Foundation created to recognize and honor organizations that demonstrate, day in and day out, our premise that children do well when their families are strong, capable, economically successful, and live in places that help them and their kids to thrive.

What I remember most about meeting Karl is not the conversation we had about how foster care reform advocates across the country were taking up Kaleidoscope's approach and promoting it at the state and national levels.

What I remember most is that he planned to retire in the next year. And what struck me was that, all too often, critical work to improve the lives and life chances of our most vulnerable populations hinges on an assumption that people like Karl Dennis will never leave their jobs.

It was a conversation that brought to mind the depressingly low survival rates of high-performing nonprofit programs cited by Lisbeth Schorr in *Within Our Reach* and *Common Purpose*. Again, all too often, the demise of these programs can be attributed to an institutional failure to prepare for and pay appropriate attention to leadership transition and development.

This was an epiphany of sorts—one of those moments when the obvious becomes unavoidable—and it was one we would have over and over again with the FAMILIES COUNT honorees. In fact, of the fifty organizations that received the award from 2000 to 2007, more than half have undergone a leadership change.

A desire to help those organizations with executive transition and succession planning led us to Tom Adams and the folks at TransitionGuides. This connection helped us to build a body of work, ably led by Donna Stark, now Annie E. Casey's vice president for human development and operations, to help our mission-critical grantees successfully operate through the departure of effective leaders and keep working to identify, recruit, and support new leaders.

In addition, through a series of monographs, seminars, and presentations, we have joined with Tom and his team at TransitionGuides to promote the practice of and investment in executive transition management services, leadership development, and financial sustainability planning in our own work and throughout the nonprofit sector.

With this book, Tom has taken the very practical advice that helped us and our grantees and has translated it into essential reading for the entire non-profit field. The pages that follow make an irrefutable case: nonprofit organizations that care about getting results and having an impact on the children, families, and communities they serve—especially in a time of shrinking resources and growing need—must be intentional, focused, and deliberate about leadership transitions and development. (Organizations that don't care about getting results will not be helped by this or any other book.)

The author punctures the rationalizations and half-truths that account for so much inaction by nonprofits on the leadership front, from lack of resources and procrastination to an overreliance on serendipity and passionate, committed staff.

He exposes some inconvenient truths, including the continuing state of denial among many funders and government agencies about what it really takes to run a high-performing organization and a tendency to present strong leaders as so exceptional that the job seems impossible for a mere mortal, even one who is more than willing, able, and ready to learn and lead.

And to his credit, the author chose not to duck, mumble, or posture about the diversity challenge. Instead, he offers practical, commonsense advice that can move us away from blaming and toward discernable results. Any reader of this guide will come away with the hard but certain realization that underinvestment in and lack of attention to leadership transition and development makes a fool's errand of even the best work in this field. This pattern undermines our efforts to improve the odds for children, families, and communities that are now at even greater risk of being left behind and counted out. Tom has illuminated a path to a better day. It's up to us to follow up and follow through.

January 2010

Ralph Smith
Executive Vice President
The Annie E. Casey Foundation

To the growing number of amazing and inspiring
leaders of organizations working for
a more just, caring, and sustainable world.

I AM NOT THE USUAL SUSPECT to write a book about nonprofit leadership. I identify more with the entrepreneurial founder leader who typically is focused on mission and results and has less appetite for leader development and internal systems.

I was privileged to become the first executive director of a start-up neighborhood housing organization in my late twenties. A yearlong organizational formation process resulted in a very talented and committed board. Our collective passion, expertise, and resources culminated in rapid growth and amazing results. This was my first experience of what I call a "humming organization." With some bumps and growing pains, we achieved an amazing harmony and capacity. We attracted the leaders (staff and board) we needed. We used our board and staff meetings and an annual retreat to sharpen our strategy. We were well connected to resources both locally and nationally. I experienced the powerful results that are possible when leaders, strategy, and resources are aligned.

During my six years there as we grew from myself as the only staff person to thirty staff members, I took my growing pains and many challenges as an inexperienced leader to a wonderful mentor and an organizational development consultant. The two of them began the slow process of teaching me that leading an organization was about more than passion and mission. They taught me about management teams and how to build and lead one. As we were invited to serve an African-American neighborhood, they taught me about differences in power and experience and to appreciate different points of view.

My next stop was to serve fifteen years with a national organization. I was asked to manage part of the field operations division and replied that I would prefer to lead a special projects unit focused on innovation. I ended up doing both. This experience broadened my understanding of the complexity of leadership in a larger national system. It also provided me with a place to begin what became a five-year research project about executive transitions within our member organizations. With more resources than are available to most thanks to the W.K. Kellogg Foundation and my employer, NeighborWorks America, I crafted an approach to nonprofit executive transitions.

Over my thirty-plus years of work with nonprofit organizations, I have continued to be a student of leadership and organizational development. I'm keenly aware that neither the world nor Amazon.com needs another "this is the magic bullet" leadership book. I have learned a lot from reading and studying about leadership and organizational effectiveness. I've learned as much and perhaps more from the opportunity to consult with hundreds of board leaders and executives to advance their mission through attention to the intersection of leadership and strategy.

America and the world abound with leaders passionate about causes and making a difference. That energy is the unquantifiable equity of the nonprofit sector. It is the reason the sector has grown and continues to grow.

Unfortunately, not all stories of passion and good work have happy endings. Like small businesses, too many nonprofits die with their founder's or key leaders' waning interest or energy. Other more established organizations—some of which had become household names—have faltered and died quickly or slowly because of the inability to manage leadership transition and commit to an ongoing investment in leader development.

While management companies develop complex analytical tools to improve for-profit corporations, I am convinced that for nonprofit organizations the focus is simpler. Where effective leaders are aligned around a mission and armed with a solid strategy, they are able to attract resources and achieve amazing results. There's a simple equation for this: leadership + strategy + resources = results.

Achieving this alignment of effective leaders who fit the mission and strategy is not a simple job. Humming organizations are the ones where leaders are aligned around strategy and have the capacity to execute it successfully.

Most organizations are somewhere on the continuum from humming to crisis. There is not and probably never will be sufficient support (time and dollars) for organizational capacity building to systematically build on each organization's strengths and move more organizations to the status of "humming" results producers.

In the absence of such a financial and time commitment, we as leaders of the sector are challenged to think deeply about where and how to make investments in the alignment of leadership, strategy, and resources.

After being nonexistent for most nonprofit organizations thirty years ago, strategic planning is continuing its evolution to become a more flexible and efficient tool for leaders to build consensus on mission, strategy, and results. Ten years from now, my hope is that attention to leader transitions and leader development is as firmly established as strategic planning is now.

However, leadership and leader development is a more complex and thorny question for our sector. While an organization can budget for a strategic planning effort annually, it has always been difficult and is getting more difficult to set aside time and money for leader development.

This book seeks to provide a point of view and tools to advance our attention to the leader portion of the leadership + strategy + resources = results equation. Simply said, while there are no easy answers, there are clear indications of the paths that lead to more effective leadership and therefore better results.

The nonprofit sector is overflowing with talent. Leaders and potential leaders come and go with varying stays lasting from a few years to decades.

This asset is underutilized and needs focused attention to increase results and overall sector effectiveness. While not everyone has the capacity or interest to be a nonprofit CEO, opportunities exist for all to lead.

Our sector's challenge is to move beyond episodic and scattered attention to leader transitions and leader development to a consistent and thoughtful ongoing strategy. Because of our limited resources and passion for mission, our approach tends to be scarcity-driven and either too narrow or too broad. For example, there is no question that the nonprofit executive position is one of the more challenging leadership positions in America. Yet very limited resources are devoted to consistently preparing and supporting executives and executive transitions.

However, some organizations debate the merits of investing in the executive and managers versus the entire staff. This debate is an important one. Unfortunately, it too often results in a compromise that doesn't serve the organization well over the long term.

To change our approach to leader transitions and leader development requires a big change for a generation of leaders, many of whom learned leadership and management on the job as their career and the organization they served grew. For some organizations and leaders the change is already under way. For others this book is an invitation to join and to expand attention to the leader portion of the leader + strategy + resources = results paradigm through the following means:

1. Laser-focused attention to the executive role and executive transitions: preparation, planning for succession, and transition. Underinvesting in executive leadership or settling for unacceptable performance for too long undermines the potential of the organization and the sector.

2. Consistent and rigorous commitment to learning how to most powerfully invest precious resources in leader development in your nonprofit organization. Too often competing demands for scarce dollars and time results in no action or watered-down initiatives with a little something for everyone and limited organizational benefit.

3. An expanded view of leadership and talent and thoughtful application of the best of the for-profit sector's talent management approach.

Such an effort at scale will better connect the many talented and diverse leaders with opportunities in which each can succeed and contribute to a changed world.

The practices described in the following chapters provide nonprofit leaders and supporters with a path to better-led organizations and more good for the world. Attention to these ideas in the sector historically is episodic. The 2008–09 recession is a reality and a factor in the plan and pace for change. The lessons from numerous studies and twenty years of field research make a compelling case for change. While it is counterintuitive to suggest commitments requiring resources in tough times, now is the time for change to happen.

If you are already a champion for attention to leader investments for enhanced results, I hope you will find value in a guide to practices that work. If, like me, you come to this topic with some skepticism, welcome. My hope is you will find an idea or two that will give you hope and a path to growth as a leader and as an organization that works for you. In the end, we need each other at our best to continue to harness the amazing energy and talents of our sector for good. The seeds of a campaign for change have been planted. My hope is that you will join this effort. Together we can grow America's and the world's leaderful organizations. The positive benefit for people and communities around the globe will drive this change.

Silver Spring, Maryland   Tom Adams
January 2010

ACKNOWLEDGMENTS

MANY LEADERS AND ORGANIZATIONS have helped shape the ideas and practices in this book. Each of the chapters is the result of the influence of these leaders and organizations, who have embraced new ideas and ways of thinking about leader transition and leader development. Without these early users and supporters, the ideas and learning would languish.

The notes in each chapter recognize other thought leaders whose experience informs this work. What follows are the organizations and individuals who have personally provided guidance and support.

My first leadership transition experience was my own from Neighborhood Housing Services of Baltimore. Elaine Lowery introduced me to organizational development and guided that process. Joe McNeely supported the early work and continues as a mentor.

Bill Whiteside, George Knight, and Margaret Frisbee of NeighborWorks America (then the Neighborhood Reinvestment Corporation) provided intellectual and financial support for the early executive transition management development. Margo Kelly and Ken Wade continued that work under their leadership. John Burkhardt and Rick Foster of the W.K. Kellogg Foundation partnered with NeighborWorks in the support of the Community Development Leadership project and the executive transition management research. Tom Gilmore of the Center for Applied Research and Katherine Farquhar of American University were pioneers in leader transition research and provided valuable guidance. Karen Gaskins Jones of JLH Associates served as a lead consultant and advisor in the NeighborWorks developments and has continued to serve as a thinking partner in the evolution of non-profit succession planning and leader development and a member of the TransitionGuides consulting team.

Cheryl Casciani of the Baltimore Community Foundation organized the first group of local funders to invest in an executive transition management initiative and collaborated with The Annie E. Casey Foundation in its lead role in the second phase of investment and research. Doug Nelson, Ralph Smith, Donna Stark, and Patrick Corvington at The Annie E. Casey Foundation have invested significantly in the refinement of executive transition management, the application of succession planning to nonprofit organizations, and field building to introduce these ideas to communities across America. Without the investments by the W.K. Kellogg Foundation, NeighborWorks America, and The Annie E. Casey Foundation and the local funders who joined them, the executive transition and succession planning practices for the nonprofit sector would not have evolved to their current level of sophistication. Among local funders, the Meyer Foundation and the Evelyn and Walter Haas, Jr. Fund have contributed to research and field building as well as supporting services for grantees.

To carry out The Annie E. Casey Foundation learning and field building and to grow the body of knowledge and its application, TransitionGuides was formed. Don Tebbe was a cofounder of TransitionGuides and is my business partner today. His commitment to learning and innovation has contributed significantly to the ideas and practices herein. Denice Rothman Hinden of Managance Consulting was part of the founding of TransitionGuides and a thought leader on succession planning and led the early executive transition survey work nationally.

At the same time that TransitionGuides was formed, a national group of consultants and management support organizations interested in this work came together. Tim Wolfred of CompassPoint Nonprofit Services joined the collaboration with Annie E. Casey at the outset and has partnered with me in shaping these ideas, introducing them around the country, and putting them in practice in our respective organizations. Jan Masaoka, Jeanne Bell, and the CompassPoint team all have supported and advanced this work.

The Alliance for Nonprofit Management has provided a home through its Executive Transition Management Affinity group for consultants, management support organizations, and funders to share lessons and learn. Ruth McCambridge and the *Nonprofit Quarterly* have provided a much-needed vehicle for sharing ideas and practices Ron Guisinger from the Benefactor Group ably assisted with the leader development section.

Sue Stevens focused attention on the importance of nonprofit founders and encouraged this focus for our practice. Ron Guisinger from the Benefactor Group ably assisted with the leader development section.

The chapter on diversity is shaped by years of relationships and learning. Most recently TransitionGuides is working with Diane Bell McKoy and A. Adar Ayira of Associated Black Charities and Beatriz "BB" Otero of Centro Nía to develop a collaboration of Baltimore-Washington nonprofit leaders to support and expand the role of leaders of color in the region's nonprofits. Ron McKinley, Tim Brostrum, and Mai Neng Moua of Fieldstone Alliance's Innovative Practice Fund have invested in this work, which builds on the Denver Foundation's Inclusiveness Project and the Third Sector New England Diversity Initiative. Brigette Rousson, a leader of the Cultural Competency Initiative of the Alliance for Nonprofit Management and coauthor of a newly published book on the same topic, provided thoughtful editing comments on the diversity chapter.

Closer to home, the TransitionGuides team has provided an amazing group of colleagues to shape and make real our collective ideas and dreams. Special thanks to my partner Don Tebbe, our operations team led by Karen Schuler and including Ginna Goodenow, Jackie Huber, Doris Kiser, and Melody Thomas-Scott, and our consulting team A. Adar Ayira, Catrese Brown, Victor Chears, Lisa Burford-Hardmon, Karen Gaskins Jones,

Katherine Morrison, and Heller An Shapiro. Our amazing intern Miriam Johnson has fact-checked each note and made the tedious part of writing a book possible and manageable.

Other generous contributors include Tim Wolfred and Don Tebbe, who edited many of the chapters, and Peter Brinckerhoff, who edited the generational diversity section of the diversity chapter. Frances Kunreuther also provided helpful guidance from her work on next-generation leadership.

I was delighted to have the opportunity to work with Vince Hyman as my editor. His experience in the nonprofit field and as an editor and publisher added immensely to the clarity of this book. Jesse Wiley and the Jossey-Bass/John Wiley publishing team have provided great support and guidance. Jesse made the process so easy and painless that sometimes I couldn't believe it. Each in their own way made a new challenge for me a manageable undertaking.

As the chapter on emotions notes, without resiliency rituals and attention to self-care leading becomes a burden. I am enormously grateful for the love and support of my wife, Geraldine. Her encouragement renews my spirit regularly and contributes much to my capacity to lead. My parents, siblings, children, and friends have all encouraged and supported me and this effort. Thanks to all for enriching my life's journey and work! Let's continue to learn and grow practices that unleash more leaders and organizations who are successfully working for a more fair, caring, and sustainable world!

—T. A.

TOM ADAMS is president and cofounder of TransitionGuides, a national consulting company based in Silver Spring, Maryland, that advises nonprofits on leadership succession, executive search and transition management, and related leader development and capacity-building initiatives. In 2008, Tom received the Innovative Practice Award for "innovation that has significantly changed the nonprofit capacity building field" from the Alliance for Nonprofit Management, the trade organization for nonprofit capacity builders. Tom and Tim Wolfred of CompassPoint Nonprofit Services were recognized for their national leadership in developing new and effective approaches to executive transition and succession planning for nonprofit organizations. From 2001 to 2005, Tom served as lead consultant and project advisor to The Annie E. Casey Foundation for their work on nonprofit leader transitions and succession. Tom and the TransitionGuides team have continued their role as innovators through leading the development of a collaborative of nonprofit leaders in the Baltimore-Washington area committed to increasing the number and roles of leaders of color in the nonprofit sector.

A national thought leader, speaker, and trainer on leadership and leadership transition topics, Tom has published extensively, including articles in the *Nonprofit Quarterly,* the *Stanford Journal for Social Innovation,* and three monographs (*Capturing the Power of Leadership Change; Founder Transitions: Creating Good Endings and New Beginnings;* and *Staying Engaged, Stepping Up: Succession Planning and Executive Transition Management for Nonprofit Boards of Directors*). *The Nonprofit Leadership Transition and Development Guide,* published in 2010 by Jossey-Bass/John Wiley, is Tom's first book. For additional articles and other resources, visit the TransitionGuides Web site at www.transitionguides.com.

TransitionGuides has assisted over three hundred nonprofit organizations, including local, regional, and national nonprofits from a wide variety of mission areas (advocacy, associations, environment, health, education, philanthropy, housing and community development, and children, family, and other human services, among others). TransitionGuides is a leader in developing educational workshops on leadership transition and succession planning topics for boards, executives, and funders. Over five hundred long-term and founding executive directors have attended the TransitionGuides flagship two-day Next Steps workshop, which provides executives an opportunity to learn and network with peers on this sensitive topic.

Prior to launching his consulting practice, Tom directed a five-year national field research project for Neighborhood Reinvestment Corporation (now NeighborWorks America), a national organization in the community development field, supported by the W.K. Kellogg Foundation and focused on executive and board leadership changes in community-based nonprofit organizations. As part of this project, he studied executive transition in over a hundred organizations in three regions of the country and performed hands-on comprehensive executive transition work with a dozen organizations. This resulted in the three-phase approach to executive transition that has evolved into Executive Transition Management. Earlier in his career, he was the first executive director of Neighborhood Housing Services of Baltimore.

Tom and TransitionGuides can be reached in Maryland at 301-439-6635 or at info@transitionguides.com.

1

The Leader's Way

THIS BOOK IS ABOUT the irrefutable connection between effective leaders and organizational results and impact. It challenges those who lead and care about the work of nonprofit organizations to appreciate our leadership advantage, to face some "ugly truths" about our current practices, and to consider the amazing gains in impact possible through focused and intentional attention to leader recruitment, development, and transition. It makes a powerful case for preparing for and successfully managing change in key leaders as an essential competency of successful leaders and organizations. It further offers a way for organizations to become more intentional about leader development despite limited resources. The results of adopting the practices suggested are a more leaderful organization that more consistently meets and exceeds its mission-driven goals.

Well-led organizations consistently outperform organizations that struggle to find and fully engage executive, board, and staff leaders needed to successfully carry out the mission. This is true for all sectors—for-profit, public, and nonprofit. While the case for the connection between leader effectiveness and organizational effectiveness is clear, how to consistently attract and retain the leaders needed for a particular organization and its work is more illusive.

The intent of this book is to contribute to the extraordinary work of America's nonprofit sector by offering practical specific actions that are proven to dramatically increase an organization's capacity to attract, develop, and retain the leaders needed to sustain success. Through attention to leader transitions, succession planning, and leader development, we will demystify the path to a more leaderful and effective organization.

A local advocacy group in the Midwest was founded by a teacher who grew up in Central America.* She was tortured for her role in fighting to end oppression and was forced to flee her country and come to the United States. She started a nonprofit and over a period of twenty years built an organization that provided education and health services to 2500 low-income immigrants each year. Finally, aging parents in her home country and her own health forced her to begin considering leaving the organization. The board had relied heavily on her and was a mix of professionals and recent immigrants served by the organization. In her final two years as executive, the organization did not meet its expenses and built up a $500,000 deficit. The board advertised and had difficulty finding candidates who met their requirements. They wanted someone with the same passion and commitment as their founder plus proven fund-raising and management experience. They did not find that person so they appointed a senior manager from the staff. He was quite skilled in working with the people the organization served, but had limited experience in raising money. In twelve months, the deficit grew to $1.5 million and the center was forced to lay off half its staff and severely reduce its services.

A human services organization in the Southwest was founded by five collaborating churches. During the period when the organization was forming and starting up, it served thirty families a week through volunteers and one part-time social worker. With success, the board decided to hire its first executive. Over the next four years, the organization had three executive directors, each less successful than the one before in achieving the goals set by the board. After the third executive resigned, the board decided to close the organization. The church leaders and volunteers were too exhausted from the efforts over the past four years to keep going.

*Note: All stories in this book are fictional, although derived from the author's consulting experience.

A community development organization in the Northeast was founded by three activists concerned about displacement as their neighborhood attracted upper-income buyers looking for a convenient urban neighborhood. The organization grew and was the city and region's largest owner of affordable rental housing. With a staff of twenty-eight and a talented six-person management team (three of whom were the cofounders) the organization thrived. Over a three-year period, four of the six leaders including two of the founders left the organization. Two left due to health issues and two for promotions to run larger organizations. No middle managers were ready to move up to the top leadership positions. Of the four senior managers hired from outside the organization, two left in the first year and one more in the second year. The organization struggled for the next five years, and when the last founder died, funding dropped by 30 percent and the organization lived largely on rental income from properties developed by prior leaders. The golden era was over and the community was disappointed and angry at the lack of growth in available affordable housing.

Unfortunately there are many stories like this. They are stories of organizations full of passion and leaders. The passion and compelling work is enough for a period of time, sometimes a long period. Ultimately, however, without deeper attention to the connection between sustained leadership and inevitable leader transition, the organization weakens and in some cases closes down.

This book is written in the midst of the 2008–09 recession. There are many points of view on its impact on the sector depending on the leader's background and role in the sector. Some point to the negative impact of failed leader transition or organizations struggling with leaders who cannot provide the skills and competencies required in a new resource environment. For a number of foundations, executives are dealing with losses of 20 to 40 percent of the value of their assets and significantly reduced annual contributions. Organizational priorities and whose work is most valued are under much closer scrutiny.

Some leaders of color see organizations that serve communities of color or are led by leaders of color as most vulnerable to reduced resources and forced merger or elimination in times of economic distress. Paul Light of the Brookings Institute predicts that one hundred thousand nonprofits will cease operation during the current economic downturn.[1]

Regardless of our philosophies or points of view about the sector and current economic conditions, the underinvestment in the leaders and infrastructure of nonprofit organizations is no longer acceptable. The cost of weakened and failed organizations like the three organizations above is too great for a wealthy democratic nation.

The idea that organizations with effective leaders achieve more and better results than organizations with ineffective leaders is self-evident. The deeper question that this book addresses is whether organizations can take actions that increase the effectiveness of their leaders and therefore their results. This question also seems straightforward. Certainly examples of for-profit companies, governments, and leading nonprofits exist who demonstrate this capacity.

In the for-profit world, companies such as GE and UPS stand out as often-cited examples of companies that consistently invest in leader development and as a result lead their industries. It is tempting to attribute the capacity to pay attention to leader transitions and development to size. Larger organizations in any sector have the resources for that, not midsize and smaller organizations. What follows argues strongly (and we hope persuasively) that attention to leader transitions and development is about commitment and action rather than about size and resources.

The nonprofit sector is building a habit of investing in leader transitions and leader development. As with any new habit, progress is uneven. I believe this habit will grow over the coming decades, because we are at the beginning of a major leadership turnover. Though nonprofit sector experts argue over the numbers involved, leader transitions are as certain as death and taxes, and they have the potential to have significant impact on organizational effectiveness. It makes sense for leaders and organizations to enthusiastically embrace practices that reduce the risks of a failed or poor transition and increase the odds of organizational progress and in some cases organizational transformation.

Once a leader and organization decide leader transitions are important, it is a small step to engage in succession planning. As we explain in greater detail later, a number of actions can advance succession planning. The important decision is the commitment to the habit of paying attention to succession all the time.

Any discussion of leader succession of necessity requires clarification of what it means to lead in a particular organization and who are the leaders. Most nonprofit organizations who have this conversation conclude that two types of leaders are important to their success: *positional leaders* (those who have a title and formal leadership role like executive director, development director, board chair, treasurer, and so on) and *informal leaders* (those whom the organization relies on to carry out much of its work—managers, staff, volunteers, and board members). When the positional leaders and an organization commit to investing in leader development of both positional and informal leaders, they make huge steps on the path to becoming a leaderful organization. The decision to invest in positional leaders or informal leaders achieves similar results. An organizational habit of paying attention to leader development is deepened.

What follows expands on the benefits, barriers, and changes that are necessary for the habit to take deeper root in the sector. In this process we will define further what is meant here by "leaderful organization" and other terms important to exploring these ideas.

For those of us who lead nonprofit organizations—on staff or a board—paying attention to the importance of leadership is challenging. While reading, you may even have a little voice reminding you of some of our many deeply engrained defenses or rationalizations for inaction, such as:

- "Sure, investing in leaders is important, but we don't have the resources."

- "I don't expect to leave any time soon, so why worry about executive change now?"

- "Sure, our management team is aging, but when we need to, we'll find great successors for ourselves. We always have."

- "We'll get to that as soon as we finish this big project."

- "We have too many people to serve to take the time to talk about leadership or to have our staff distracted from our mission."

- "We have all the talent we need. Every time I put an ad in *Idealist* I get more energetic people full of passion for our work than I need. Why should I spend precious time and dollars on leader development when I can hire a new leader whenever I need one?"

- "This sector is built on passion and commitment. That trumps leader development any day. As long as I have that in the staff, I can make it work."

This book challenges the reader to reexamine these and other half-truths that severely limit the impact of the nonprofit sector. It offers a set of practices that if adopted will increase the effectiveness of leaders and any organization's capacity to achieve the results it seeks. To explore this possibility, bring an open mind and a commitment to try out the practices that have worked for other leaders and organizations.

Besides offering a case that a commitment to leader development is both possible and makes sense, this book offers a framework and set of practices that serve as a guide to building a *leaderful organization*. Since resources are indeed scarce, we offer a point of view on how to make the most of any investment in leader development. This book offers concrete processes and examples to be used at two strategic points of investment:

1. Preparing for and making the most of leader transition when it occurs

2. Building attention to leader identification and development into the ongoing processes of the organization through leader development and talent management

Embracing this approach means letting go of some of our "either/or" choices that limit possibility. For example, given the two investment points above, either we invest in one or the other. "Either/or" thinking argues that investing in both leader transitions and a leader development system isn't possible. "Both/and" commitment says it is not only possible, but vital to success and sustainability.

A second "either/or" debate that frequently arises in considering leader development is "either we invest in our top leaders and managers or in our next generation." Yes, available resources will require choices. However, once there is a shift to a commitment to creatively exploring leader development with the same passion we bring to the results we want in the world, more possibilities open up.

To make these ideas concrete, contrast two organizations in your mind's eye for a minute. Think about your favorite "humming" organization—the one where the board and executive and staff have a clear agreement on their work and how it will contribute to good. There is great chemistry among the leaders. Ideas are explored, plans are made, the appropriate people and resources are in place, and the results are amazing. If you are fortunate, this is your organization or one you have been a part of. If you haven't personally experienced it, you've probably heard about such organizations and seen and felt their impact. It is amazing and irrefutable.

Now think about one of the struggling organizations you know—the one that doesn't seem quite able to get it together. It feels as if there are constant crises—some small, some large—all distractions from getting the work done. Leaders may stay the same or change. It doesn't seem to matter. For some reason, this organization can't get anywhere close to humming. In fact, you may know one or two organizations that don't exist any more because everyone became exhausted from years of ineffectiveness.

If you scratch a little deeper in these two organizations and explore their leader history—who led and how the transitions were planned for and managed—you'll find an interesting pattern. Sometimes from the inception and always over time, weak organizations struggled with leader change and became weaker as a result of it and strong organizations successfully managed leader change and became stronger.

As you read this book, you will see that your organization can adopt the strategies that strong organizations use—either intuitively or intentionally—to make smooth leadership transitions and nurture strong leaders at every level of the organization. You will see that these organizations became strong and stayed strong because they invested in critical infrastructure: leader recruitment, development, and succession.

The rest of this chapter offers:

- A deeper look at the unique leadership advantages of the nonprofit sector and both the barriers and reasons to make a commitment to investing in leader transitions and leader development

- An introduction to the practices and tools that make becoming a *leaderful* organization possible

- Some practical suggestions on how to decide where to start and how best to use this book based on your circumstances and goals as a leader

The Nonprofit Leadership Advantage

Let's begin by appreciating the unique advantages that involvement in the good works of the nonprofit sector offers. Some may seem self-evident, others less obvious. Appreciating these strengths informs our attention to building leaderful organizations.

Passion and Meaningful Work

Most if not all surveys of nonprofit leaders that ask about the motivation of leaders, staff, or volunteers find the commitment to the cause to be the driving force. The groundbreaking CompassPoint Nonprofit Services 2001 Leadership Lost study reported that 39 percent of the responding executives took their current job because it was a "mission I believe in, and chance to have an impact."[2] This response combined with opportunity for professional growth accounted for 70 percent of executives (p. 12). A 2003 study by the Illinois Arts Alliance Succession Arts Leadership for the 21st Century reported that three-quarters of respondents are very satisfied with their job and "mission and the organization's artistic product were major sources of satisfaction." Anecdotal information on conversations with thousands of private sector career changers report a desire for more "meaningful work."[3]

Size and Economic Impact

The nonprofit sector employs 9.4 million paid workers in the United States, according to the 2006 report *Employment in America's Charities: A Profile,* by Lester M. Salamon and S. Wojciech Sokolowski and the Johns Hopkins Center for Civil Society Studies.[4] When the 4.7 million full-time equivalent volunteer workers are added, the nonprofit workforce swells to 14 million workers and 10.5 percent of the nation's workforce. The report goes on: "Put somewhat differently, the paid workers of charitable nonprofit organizations outnumber those of the utility, wholesale trade, and construction industries; and the paid and volunteer workers together outdistance the combined employment of all three of these major industries taken together." This sizable workforce naturally attracts significant wage payments. Nonprofit paid workers thus received $321.6 billion in wages in 2004, more than the wages paid by the utilities ($50.1 billion), construction ($276 billion), and wholesale trade ($283.7 billion) industries, and almost as much as the finance and insurance industry ($355.8 billion)."[5]

Creativity and Innovation

The *Harvard Business Review* (December 2008) reported on GE's decision to develop and offer a four-day seminar, "Leadership, Innovation and Growth," to its top managers. Twenty-five hundred managers from 260 teams attended this seminar over a two-year period. While large corporations have money to pour in to such "extras," leading nonprofits foster creativity and innovation *out of necessity.* Limited resources and in-your-face needs demand extreme flexibility. Private sector leaders who transition to nonprofits are surprised at the opportunities to innovate and develop creative solutions to vital community needs.

Inclusiveness and Diversity

The nonprofit workforce mirrors America in its diversity and inclusiveness. There are rich traditions of ethnic-based organizations among our indigenous population and every immigrant group who calls America home. There are organizations for and led by people with disabilities. We organize by our age and gender. America's unique nonprofit sector has given voice to most conceivable causes and their leaders. The racial diversity of the leadership of our sector is mixed. Smaller and ethnic-specific organizations have a significant number of people of color in top leadership positions and on boards. However, there is significant room for progress in terms of the racial diversity of the top leadership of larger nonprofits and their boards.

Career Mobility and Opportunities to Lead

There are countless examples of volunteers who rise from staff to the executive of a nonprofit doing work they care about. Over a third of the close to six thousand young people who responded to the *Ready to Lead? Next Generation Leaders Speak Out* survey and report in 2008 indicated a desire to become a nonprofit executive director.[6] Look at the career trajectory of America's top leaders, including the President and First Lady, and you'll find nonprofit employment.

Readiness to Lead

The *Ready to Lead?* survey of six thousand next-generation leaders (under age forty) revealed other findings that indicate the long-term strength of the sector. The pipeline consists of highly skilled and educated individuals, 39 percent of whom have received a postgraduate degree and 92 percent of whom have a college degree.[7] A higher percentage of respondents who definitely aspire to become executive directors are people of color, and people interested in social change view the nonprofit sector as a desirable place to work and to seek employment.[8]

These and other assets of our sector provide our resiliency and capacity for amazing good. After a few years of underappreciating the leaders of our sector and their accomplishments, more recent comparisons of for-profit and nonprofit leadership reveal the depth and sophistication required to lead the nonprofit sector. It is this enormous base of talent and possibility to which we offer expanded choices for managing leader transitions well and fully unleashing current and future talent.

Our Leadership Challenges

Leading in the nonprofit sector is not easy. A number of challenges confront most leaders in the sector. Some are obvious, others more subtle, and some we might even put under what Jim Collins in *Good to Great* might describe as facing our "ugly truths."[9]

Three studies authored by CompassPoint Nonprofit Services with different partners sum up the leader challenges the nonprofit sector faces.

The first, which was completed in 1999, *Leadership Lost: A Study of Executive Director Tenure and Experience,* revealed that only 25 percent of the surveyed executives would consider another executive director job.[10] This study shed the first light on the vulnerability the sector faces by underinvesting in its executives and their transitions.

A 2006 follow-up study, *Daring to Lead,* added more depth to the earlier study.[11] This survey involved two thousand executive directors in eight cities. The main headline here was that 75 percent of the executives planned to leave their position in the next five years and 9 percent were already in the process. Related findings that add fuel to the attention to building a leaderful organization include the following:

- A third of the executives who preceded those surveyed lost their positions involuntarily.

- Seventy-one percent of the organizations had no succession plan.

- Executives believe they make significant financial sacrifices to lead nonprofits.

- Bench strength, diversity, and competitive compensation are critical factors to finding future leaders (Major findings summary, *Daring to Lead,* p. 3).

The 2008 *Ready to Lead?* report offers additional insights into the sector's leadership challenges, including:

The long hours and compromised personal lives associated with executive leadership are significant deterrents to pursuing top positions.

Nonprofit salaries and actual or perceived insufficient lifelong earning potential are barriers to executive leadership. Sixty-nine percent of respondents feel underpaid in their current positions and sixty-four percent reported that they have financial concerns about committing to a career in the nonprofit sector.

Lack of mentorship and support from incumbent executives in helping to pave a career path are serious frustrations for many next generation leaders.

Inherent nonprofit structural limitations and obscure avenues to career advancement are obstacles to leadership opportunities inside organizations.

The prevailing executive director job description is unappealing to many next generation leaders.[12]

The Bridgespan Group 2006 study of nonprofit sector leadership shortage reported an estimated gap of eighty-four thousand leaders for the nonprofit sector. A 2009 follow-up study reported this gap growing despite the 2008–09 recession.[13]

These studies, earlier project activities by The Annie E. Casey Foundation and NeighborWorks America,[14] and the TransitionGuides experience in working with over four hundred nonprofit organizations point to the following leadership challenges.

There are some ugly truths behind these challenges—the "elephants in the room" that need to be named. Here are some candidates for your consideration; it is likely you may suggest others that are equally or more compelling.

Nonprofits Too Often Treat People as Disposable Commodities

We use our commitment to mission to avoid looking at what investment of time and resources we are making to our current leaders and staff. When a leader or staff person leaves, we find someone to replace that person. In too many cases that is our leader and staff development plan. In some cases, zeal for mission becomes a barrier to needed investment in people and infrastructure.

We Collude with Funders and Government Agencies to Create Fantasies About What It Costs to Run an Effective Organization and Provide Services That Change Lives and the World

The pressure from some funders and boards to keep administrative costs minimal undermines the capacity of the sector. A similar impact occurs when government contracts pay for services at rates that don't support livable wages or investment in the development of staff and managers. Executives and boards who live on the edge with the next funder needed to make the budget balance are at significant risk when the executive, the funder, or the economy shifts. Sustainability is not possible because the underlying economic assumptions are not real. The lack of investment in infrastructure or support for leaders makes difficult jobs impossible. Some funders prefer to fund a few hero organizations well and act as if the other organizations don't exist or are happily underperforming.

We Prefer Hero Leaders to Ordinary Leaders

The upside of our attraction to the hero leader is the inspiration and modeling they provide. President Barack Obama and Mother Teresa are two prominent examples. In every community, there are locally and often nationally recognized "go to" individuals who are the strong backbone for change and action there. Unfortunately there is a shadow side to our fascination with hero leaders. While perhaps hard to admit, we are equally fascinated by scapegoating hero leaders when they fall. In addition to the pendulum swings of opinion about hero leaders, this fascination takes the rest of us off the leadership hook. Many don't aspire to be hero leaders. Our models of the requirements to be successful as a leader get exaggerated and become unattainable. *The Ready to Lead?* finding cited previously pointed to the lack of interest in executive positions in the nonprofit sector as currently structured because the people doing them didn't seem to have a life. The jobs were unattractive and appeared not doable on any terms that the participants found acceptable.

We Romanticize the Private Sector and Its Leaders

An increasing number of for-profit leaders are engaging with nonprofits and offering advice on how to improve the nonprofit sector. For some this naïvely means nonprofits should become more like for-profits. For those who scratch below the surface, there is a growing respect and recognition that leading a successful nonprofit is at least equal to and in many ways more difficult than leading a for-profit company.

Our Top Leadership Lacks Diversity and We Are Doing Little to Fix That

The *Daring to Lead* study of nearly two thousand executives found that 82 percent of the executives were white.[15] The sample for this survey was eight major cities in the United States. Perhaps more telling is the absence of leaders of color in most meetings of the major nonprofits and foundations in most communities. A 2007 study by the Urban Institute reports that nationally 10.5 percent of nonprofit board members are nonwhite.[16] While there is no guarantee, it makes sense that boards that are more racially diverse will have more success in hiring leaders of color. Without acknowledging white privilege and its impact on communities of color, we struggle to move forward.

We Don't Have Enough Leaders in Development

Many younger leaders and managers have a similar disbelief about the alleged upcoming shortage of talent. Like people of color who are incredulous when white leaders say they can't find candidates of color, young leaders believe ample talent exists. The issue is making room for the next generation, supporting their values and way of making mission commitment work, and investing in their development and preparation. Many argue we don't have a leader shortage; we have a clogged pipeline that needs a good scrubbing.

Most, perhaps none, of these practices are intentional. But we are challenged to turn around a system that has grown up over many years and carries with it some ugly truths from the past. What follows offers a way forward, which if practiced over time would confront our challenges and ugly truths.

The Leaderful Organization

What is a *leaderful organization?* My first awareness of the term came from the article "We the Leaders: In Order to Form a Leaderful Organization" in the December 2005 issue of *Journal of Leadership & Organizational Studies.*[17] A colleague and TransitionGuides senior consultant Karen Gaskin Jones began using the term in our succession planning workshops. Over time it became a placeholder for a vision of organizations that make a consistent commitment to leader development and preparing for and managing leader transitions. For our purposes, a *leaderful organization* is a nonprofit that consistently pays attention to and invests in leader transitions and leader development. These organizations live out their belief that there is a direct link between the effectiveness of their leaders and their impact in the world.

A large West Coast nonprofit has the mission to empower leaders and communities in the United States and other countries around the world to improve the quality of life. Concern about leadership has been central to their fifty-year history. In 2006, their CEO and board decided to review their informal practices and make a commitment of time and resources to leader development and succession planning a central component of their new strategic plan. Among their actions were adoption of emergency backup plans for top managers, development of an emerging leaders program with a national leadership development training organization, completion of a bench strength review, and a commitment by all senior managers to attend a university-based seminar to create a shared experience and language. These actions helped a leaderful organization expand its capacity.

An East Coast community development organization executive was frustrated by the constant challenge of fund-raising. He enrolled in a year-long executive leadership training program to see what he was missing. Through that process he realized he needed to shift his attention from the details of projects to hiring and empowering a team who could develop more affordable housing projects each year. This conclusion and the support he received from the training resulted in a personal commitment to learning about leading and managing and investing in the development of his managers and staff. Fifteen years later, after successfully building the organization and its capacity, and three years in advance of his retirement he began to work with the board on a plan for his transition. The transition occurred, was successful, and the new executive is continuing the established habit of investing in leader development and leader transitions.

A Midwest health clinic served new immigrants. Over time consumers of the clinic began to work for the clinic in entry-level jobs. The executive and board decided that the best way to build the organization was to use a dual strategy of hiring the most experienced and skilled managers they could afford who were committed to mentoring and developing their staff and managers. For over eight years this conscious commitment resulted in over 60 percent of the management team consisting of recent immigrants who first came to the clinic for services.

Each of these organizations faces the same challenges and opportunities that all nonprofits face. They stand out in their fields and the sector because of their ongoing and growing commitment to leader development and leader transitions. They are building leaderful organizations.

No organization ever arrives and sits still in leader development. The radical changes in the economic and funding environment in recent years demonstrate the need for leaders who are nimble and able to be strategic and make hard decisions. The organizations above and most organizations will struggle from time to time to find the time and resources to do everything they want to do to advance a leader development culture. They may pull back and go through rough times. Yet the investment made in leader development and attention to powerful leader transitions give these organizations a resiliency and strength to make it through tough times and to thrive in good times.

Let's look briefly at the two cornerstones of building a leaderful organization: attention to leader transitions and leader development.

The Leader Transition Opportunity

Changes in leaders are happening all the time and with more frequency. Leadership transition is perpetual, ubiquitous, and unavoidable. *Leaderful* organizations face this reality boldly and pragmatically. Thus, they get better results than organizations that are haphazard about or inattentive to leadership. To be *leaderful* requires preparing for leadership transitions and managing them well.

Leader transitions are like a string of pearls on a necklace and the links that hold them together. If one link is weak, the necklace is threatened. If several get weak or one breaks entirely, the beauty and integrity of the whole necklace is destroyed.

If you look at "great" organizations in any sector, they consistently are well led. None are perfect; there may be a bumpy or even failed transition along the way. Hiring is more art than science, so not getting the right fit between a hire and the needs and opportunities of the position is to be expected. Leaderful organizations pay attention to their leadership string and what holds it together. They catch mistakes that threaten their capacity and invest the time and resources to increase the odds of sustained excellent leaders.

There are two practices that advance a leaderful organization during and before leader transition: 1) *succession planning* (which is of three types—emergency, departure-defined, and ongoing leader development/talent management); and 2) *executive transition management* (which includes the three phases: prepare, pivot, and thrive, as well as attention to organizational capacity, direction, priorities, required leader competencies, a proactive search, and successful entry and connection of the new executive).

William Bridges, a leading author and consultant to major corporations and organizations on the topic of organizational change and transition, highlights the difference between *change* and *transition.* Change is the event. A new executive begins in January. That is the change. The transition process for the new executive and the organization began long before she arrived and will continue for months, and in some cases years. The transition, Bridges offers, is the emotional and psychological process that accompanies the change.[18]

Following Bridges's notion of transition, it makes sense that leaders who are passionately committed to a cause will struggle with handing off leader roles. Preparing for succession and managing transitions well are vital to long-term sustainability.

The Leader Development Opportunity

Attending to leader development is at once simple and complex. At its simplest, there is a decision to encourage managers and staff to develop and grow. Most people have a basic idea of their skills and abilities and what they enjoy doing. Executives and managers of leaderful organizations tap into this knowledge, encourage a clear articulation of potential areas of growth, and support this growth in whatever ways they can. This process gets repeated, and as managers and staff grow, they encourage the growth and development of others. Sometimes there is money to support courses or seminars, sometimes not. Sometimes there is a formal coaching or mentoring program, often not. *How* leader development is supported is less important than the commitment and culture that supports it.

Leader development becomes more complex as leaders work to make it part of the organization's practices. This usually leads to discussions of values and what it means to be a leader in the organization. From these discussions, competencies and attributes of leaders get defined, with requirements for different leadership positions.

How leaders are defined is tied to mission and strategic priorities. What competencies does this organization need to get maximum results? How much time and money will we invest in leader development and for whom?

Leader development is usually a messy evolutionary process. Each organization finds its own way.

How This Book Is Organized

The remainder of this book is organized around two topical areas and concludes with a set of appendixes that offer tools and samples. Each chapter includes case examples and stories. *All the stories are fictional.* They are composites of real-life experiences brought together in such a way as to be authentic and not specific to any individual or organization. All the names used in the stories and the organizations are also fictional.

At the end of each chapter is a set of reflection questions. These questions are organized for three audiences: 1) individual leaders, 2) organizations, and 3) supporters and stakeholders, including funders, membership associations, management support organizations, and other capacity builders and consultants.

Chapters Two, Three, and Four address what in my experience are the most important contextual issues that impact leader transitions and leader development. These three critical issues are as follows:

Chapter Two—Managing the Power of Emotions

Leader transitions are emotional processes for the departing leader and the organization. Leader development begins with attention to leader self-care and leader self-awareness. It is difficult to grow as a leader without facing some feelings you would prefer to avoid. Managing diverse staffs and boards of many backgrounds and points of view stretches the most evolved leader. This chapter frames the emotions most commonly in play and provides tools from multiple disciplines that other leaders have found quite useful.

Chapter Three—Founders and Founder Transitions

If strong emotions are in play in most leader transitions, then imagine the feelings of the founder of an organization. References to "my baby" and the birthing process are fairly common when discussing transitions with founders. These are the most complex transitions and most important to the long-term viability of the organization. This chapter goes beyond the popular and not so helpful "founder's syndrome" to the understanding of the unique gifts and challenges of founders and provides tools and a guide for founders, their boards, and their successors.

Chapter Four—Seeking Diversity Through Leader Development

All organizations are diverse. Some are more diverse than others. While there are many important dimensions to diversity, this chapter looks in depth at racial/ethnic and age diversity. As America becomes increasingly racially and ethnically diverse and the workforce is comprised of multiple generations, leaders must have skills in building racial/ethnic and age-diverse organizations. Developing leaderful organizations that are effective in working with people of different races, ethnic backgrounds, and ages requires a commitment to action by leaders. This chapter makes the case and offers a path and tools for achieving this goal.

The next four chapters introduce proven practices that advance a leader development culture. These practices are executive transition management and succession planning. Three types of succession planning are provided that offer choices to meet the current needs of each organization.

Chapter Five—Executive Transition Management

The patterns of executive transitions define the strength and sustainability of an organization. Humming organizations get stronger each time they hire a new executive; struggling organizations get weaker each time they make a poor hiring decision or fail to attend to the transition issues that are key to the new executive having a chance at succeeding. Executive transition management combines strategic thinking, organizational development, and executive search to maximize the transformational opportunity that executive transition offers. This chapter describes how it works and the process for implementation.

Chapter Six—Getting Started on Succession Planning

There are many approaches to definitions of succession planning. Here succession planning broadly refers to the planning and actions that ensure there is effective leadership over multiple transitions in an organization. Experience in introducing succession planning to nonprofits of all sizes and types suggests that attention to emergency backup planning for the executive (and in larger organizations senior managers) and development of a board-adopted succession policy is the best place to start. This chapter introduces the reader to succession planning and how to put the "succession basics"—an emergency backup plan and succession policy—in place.

Chapter Seven—Departure-Defined Succession Planning

When an executive plans to depart in one to four years, a unique opportunity exists to build organizational capacity. This opportunity usually occurs when the executive plans to retire or move to a different field or kind of position. Departure-defined succession planning supports executives and boards in using the planned departure to build leadership and look at organizational strengths and areas for growth. This chapter details when this makes sense, how to do it well, and the amazing benefits and opportunities it offers.

Chapter Eight—Leader Development and Talent Management

Leading is a team sport. No leader can do everything that needs to be done. Thinking about how to build the best possible leader team and involve all staff as leaders is the goal of leader development and talent management. This chapter looks at leader development from both the individual and organizational perspective with action steps and tools that are proven. Talent management is a for-profit practice with broad applicability when adapted to the nonprofit culture. This chapter introduces talent management and how to apply it in nonprofits of any size.

Chapter Nine—Many Paths to a Leaderful Organization

Finally, we need to tie all this information together in a way that helps you envision the leaderful organization. Chapter Nine helps you see the many paths and what individuals, organizations, and supportive stakeholders can do to sustain attention to leader development and leader transitions.

Appendixes

The Appendixes (also available online) offer additional examples of tools and resources around major topic areas. Appendix E offers several inventories that support a leader reflecting on key areas of personal and organizational leader development and developing action plans to advance important personal or organizational goals.

How to Use This Book

There are a variety of ways to approach this book. Some readers may be inclined to follow the book in the order of the chapters. That works. Other readers may want to begin with areas of pressing interest. That works just as well.

Regardless of your preference, most readers will want to begin by reading the chapters on emotions (Chapter Two) and race and age diversity (Chapter Four). These issues are relevant to every leader; failure to attend to them creates the highest potential for derailing leader development and transitions.

If your organization has not done work on succession planning, reading the succession basics (Chapter Six) will be among the more helpful places to start.

Here are the audiences for whom this book is intended:

- Seasoned executives and founders
- Board leaders

- New executives

- Potential executives and managers

- Funders

- Technical assistance providers and other supportive stakeholders

The following section offers alternative paths for each of the audiences. Please tailor your path to meet your needs and interests.

For Seasoned Executives and Founders

If you have no imminent plans (within the next year or less) to depart from your executive position, then there are four chapters you won't want to miss. I suggest you begin with the founder chapter whether you're a founder or not. As you read, see what applies and what doesn't. How clear are you about when you might consider leaving and what you might want to do? Next you will want to read Chapter Two to make sure you are paying attention to the emotions and self-care. This may seem obvious. It is a huge challenge for most long-tenured executives and founders. You have a lot of skin in the game. You don't want to undermine or weaken your contribution by ignoring the emotions of transition.

If you plan to leave your position in the next one to four years, you will want to go to departure-defined succession planning (Chapter Seven) next. This will give you some ideas on what you and the organization can do to ensure sustainability and a positive leadership transition when it occurs. If you are not sure when you might leave and are of an age where retirement is on your mind, read this chapter. You also may find the leader self-assessment inventories in Appendix E (also available online) useful for your personal and organizational leader development or transition planning.

If you don't have an emergency backup plan and the board has not adopted a succession policy, you'll want to read Chapter Six and pick from that low-hanging fruit.

Once you've addressed the issues related to transition and succession to the extent needed, you'll want to head to Chapter Eight to look at how to advance leader development and talent management. This can be one of your greatest legacy gifts to the organization. Read it carefully with an eye to what commitments you are willing to make, when, and why.

In short, you are the primary audience for this book and eventually you will want to read and study the whole book.

For Board Leaders

If your executive is long-tenured or a founder, you will want to start with the chapter on founders (Chapter Three). (Even if your executive isn't the founder, long-term executives have many of the same characteristics as founders, and it will help you understand your executive better.) Since you won't avoid the emotions of transition and day-to-day leadership, Chapter Two is strongly encouraged.

If your executive is planning to leave in the next year, the chapter on executive transition management (Chapter Five) will provide a detailed road map and lessons about the key issues and steps to ensure a successful transition.

If your executive is planning to retire or leave in the next one to four years or this is a possibility, you will want to read Chapter Seven about departure-defined succession planning.

If your executive isn't leaving and you don't have an emergency backup plan or a succession policy, Chapter Six will guide you in a simple process to put these in place. Once those are in place, if you haven't read and addressed the issues, you can turn to work on increasing diversity and inclusiveness (Chapter Four) and advancing your leader development and talent management (Chapter Eight). You also may find the leader self-assessment inventories in Appendix E (also available online) useful to your personal and organizational leader development or transition planning.

For New Executives, Potential Executives, and Managers

New executives, potential executives, and managers should head to leader development and talent management for ideas on how to develop as a leader and advance a leader development culture. Start with the section on individual leader development. If you have not completed a leader self-assessment tool, you will want to do that (see Chapter Eight for possible tools). Ideally you can do this self-assessment with a trusted mentor or coach.

This process will result in personal decisions about how to further your growth as a leader. Your action plan ought to include reading, participating in peer learning, and seeking out a leader development program that will advance both your skills and networks. In addition, pay attention to Chapter Four for the importance of attending to diversity as part of your personal development.

If you are not sure you are in the right position or organization, ideas in Chapter Eight will help you assess where your talents might best be used. This chapter will also provide ideas on actions you and your peers can take to increase attention to leader development in the organization.

If an executive or other major leader transition is imminent, head to Chapter Five, which covers executive transition management. This process will ensure that the staff voice is heard during the transition and that the organization is stronger after the leadership change. You can also adapt the principles to transitions of key staff members or board leaders.

For Funders

Funders individually and collectively have significant influence over organizational behavior, often way beyond their financial contribution. Funders who are students of capacity building will want to skim through the entire book and go more deeply into areas of interest. Funders who don't currently support leader development or capacity building might want to study the first and last chapters to see if the case is persuasive. (If it isn't, contact the author at TransitionGuides and let us know why not.) If it is, read on to determine where you might want to consider and commit to increasing your leadership and funding.

Regardless of whether you support capacity building among grantees, you will want to read the chapter on executive transition management to learn about why some of your important grantees flounder or die during leader transition and what can be done to reduce that risk.

If you or your foundation or both are concerned about the lack of racial and age diversity on boards and among executives and senior managers, then you will want to read Chapter Four carefully. If this hasn't been an issue or concern, you may want to read Chapter Four and ask why it isn't a concern. It should be.

If you manage a leadership or capacity-building portfolio, you will want to build on your knowledge and strengths. If you are up-to-date on executive transition management, head to succession planning. If in succession planning you have a lot of knowledge of the basics, then spend your time on departure-defined succession planning (Chapter Seven) and leader development and talent management (Chapter Eight). Talent management may be a new term to you. It has great power to accelerate results. You'll want to become familiar with how this for-profit practice is used by leading nonprofits.

For Capacity-Building Providers and Other Supportive Stakeholders

For capacity-building providers, membership association leaders, and other stakeholders who are engaged in some fashion in supporting the development and growth of nonprofits, follow your nose to the chapters that will best serve you.

If the organizations you serve have a number of baby-boom generation executives and managers, you will want to read the founder chapter (Chapter Three) and executive transition management chapter (Chapter Five). As consultants or technical assistance providers, we are prone to dismissing or underestimating the power of emotions and the need for attention to our own self-care. Chapter Two is an important read for that reason.

As leaders, we also have a responsibility to advance more diverse and inclusive organizations because it leads to better results. Chapter Four provides some ideas and practices to consider. Ultimately it is the consistent attention to leader development and talent management that will advance the work of the sector. Chapter Eight provides you and those with whom you work with practical tools and processes.

Conclusion: Join the Campaign

Each chapter and the book conclude with reflection questions and a framework for developing a personal and organizational action plan. Our hope is that you will pick out at least one question that is useful to you and answer it. This process will connect the material to your situation and perhaps result in a commitment to action or an important decision.

Larry Hirschorn of the Center for Applied Research suggests that social change happens best when there is a *pull* for change.[19] The hope of this book is that it will fuel the pull for more intentional attention to leader transitions and leader development. Experience shows both the power of such attention and the challenge of keeping funder and leader commitment to it. Through your commitments and actions, the pull for better led and more effective organizations will grow. Thanks for reading on and considering joining the campaign!

REFLECTION QUESTIONS

The questions are organized around three points of view:

1. *The individual leader*—questions to consider in your role as a leader and ones you can act on personally regardless of organizational support

2. *The organization*—questions to consider relative to organizations in which you are an executive, board leader, or potential leader. These actions require organizational support and commitment.

3. *Supporting stakeholders*—questions relevant to funders, association leaders, and staff, consultants, and others who in some fashion are engaged in work with nonprofit organizations

For the Individual Leader

1. What are your strengths as a leader? What leader roles and activities make your spirit soar?

2. Where are you on the continuum of investing/not investing in your personal development as a leader?

3. In what way might you grow as a leader and increase your capacity to advance the mission of organizations to which you are committed?

For Executives and Board Leaders of an Organization

1. What do you most value about an organization to which you are committed and its work?

2. What role does effective leadership play in making real the work you value?

3. To what extent does the organization invest time or money in preparing for leader transitions and leader development?

4. Which of the ugly truths or leadership challenges above are most important for this organization to face?

For Funders, Capacity-Building Providers, Association Staff, and Other Supporting Stakeholders

1. What do you value about the organizations you support or to which you provide services?

2. How does leadership or its absence influence what you value in these organizations?

3. How does your organization invest in leader transitions and leader development for your organization?

4. What ugly truths or barriers are most important for your organization to face in order to better support or serve the organizations to which you are committed?

2

Managing the Power of Emotions

EMOTIONS ARE UNAVOIDABLE in organizational life. The health and success of organizations are directly influenced both by how emotions are attended to and how they are avoided. All of us are complex humans with a range of emotions and ways of reacting to our feelings.

Emotions are intensified in times of change. This is especially true when executives leave their positions—not just for the executive, but for most others in the organization and those attached to it. And the fact is, the one constant about nonprofit organizations (or any organization) is that they must adapt continually to internal and external factors; that is, they face change every day.

During any change—whether an executive departure, a merger, a budget overhaul, or something else—emotions become intensified. People get edgy and fearful. Morale and productivity may plummet. People behave in unusual and sometimes embarrassing ways. The board may become angry, fragmented, or resentful.

Here are some classic and perhaps extreme examples of emotions influencing leaders and organizations:

Jim Smith led a public policy advocacy organization. He was the second executive and built the organization from a four-person operation to become a nationally recognized leader in its field, with operations of $4 million.

Jim's strength was advocacy. During the eight-year Bush administration, Jim became increasingly frustrated and angry about the lack of progress on the issues he cared about. During the same period, both his parents died and his wife developed a major health problem. Jim's anger spread to staff meetings and interactions with funders and the board. After much encouragement by the board chair and other friends for Jim to get the help he needed, which he rejected, the board asked Jim to retire or be fired. In this case, we see a good executive whose mounting frustrations and difficulties adapting to a changed external environment led to ineffectiveness and eventual exit.

Zelma Jones founded a health organization that focused on health issues for African-Americans. In the first ten years, she and her staff were successful in engaging foundations and pharmaceutical companies in supporting research on health care disparities for African-Americans. Most of the funders were white; Zelma and most of her board and staff were African-American. Over time the board became split between leaders who were grateful for the support for their work and other leaders who felt the response to the obvious inequities was grossly inadequate. Zelma was a conflict avoider and wanted everyone to get along. She spent endless time on the phone and meeting with the board members trying to build consensus and reduce the tension. As the economy worsened, funders reduced their support and the board disagreement intensified. Zelma developed migraine headaches and was unable to work one or two days a week for many weeks. After months of feeling poorly, Zelma resigned. The board was unable to agree on a successor and appointed an interim executive as a placeholder. Without Zelma's efforts at reconciliation, division in the board worsened, funding declined further, and eventually the organization ceased operations. Here, we see a case where the executive had served as the emotional buffer zone for a troubled board. This unfair position eventually wore her down, and the board could not reshape itself in time to rescue the organization.

A leading organization in New York City went out of business in 2002. The reported reason was a lack of financial support for the work of the organization. That was certainly the presenting issue. However, underneath the obvious was a long trail of unattended emotions by the founder executive and board. The founder had a deep commitment to social change. While financially well off, he insisted on low salaries for himself and the staff so all money could go to the mission. Staff grumbled for years, but salaries stayed low. The founder developed a terminal illness and refused to accept he was dying. He continued to try to work. His anger leaked out into dealing with the board and staff. Funders began to worry about the future of the agency. The board was frozen and didn't know what to do. There were countless private phone calls about what to do but no leadership to take action. The founder died. The board appointed a staff interim and hired a new executive who left after three months. The board turned back to the staff interim who demanded a salary increase to take the position. The board agreed. The rest of the staff revolted. The years of anger and frustration about salaries and a host of other issues had degraded the organization. Program quality declined. Funders withdrew. The organization eventually closed down.

Why this agency no longer exists has to do with a complex set of issues related to market to be served, services, funding options for the services, leadership, strategy, and execution. Yet underneath all those important factors is the impact of emotions and how leaders did or did not address them. Consider for a minute an alternative story for this agency. Might the organization still exist if:

- Staff and board acknowledged their anger and frustration and confronted the founder about salary issues and the limits of paying "missionary wages"?

- The founder was able to see that his caring so much for the organization was threatening his own and the organization's health? What if he asked for help and resigned when he got ill or took a sabbatical?

- The board found a way to both support the dying executive and pay attention to what the organization and staff needed?

While the ending is dramatic for this agency (and for the other examples above), the story of unattended emotions and their subtle and obvious effects on organizational health and effectiveness are much more prevalent.

Like other stories in this book, these stories are fictional. They represent compilations of stories learned during my experience as an executive transitions consultant. While the details may not be precise, the outcomes are.

How leaders—executives, boards, staff, and funders—manage their feelings and self-care has a profound impact on the health of the sector. Of course, this isn't unique to the nonprofit sector. What *is* unique to the nonprofit sector is our missionary history and the sometimes misplaced emphasis on selflessness and caring that can lead to the destruction of personal health and an inability to lead effectively. The results when carried to an extreme are death or disability for the leader and decline or death for the organization.

Much is written about the mind-body connection, a subject beyond this book. However, while we will focus largely on the emotions that are common for leaders during transition or succession planning, we will address briefly the connection to physical well-being and the "spirit" of the leader. We use "spirit" here to mean the values and belief system of the leader and the collective values and beliefs of the organization. Emotions, physical well-being, and our values and beliefs are connected. When one dimension is under stress or struggling, it spreads to the whole person.

Leaders who lose their internal capacity for self-care eventually burn out and do harm to themselves and their organization. This risk is intensified during transition.

The act of leading is intellectual, personal, and emotional. Leaders who attend to and manage their emotions and self-care are more likely to have a successful transition and build organizations that are leaderful and sustainable than leaders who struggle to manage feelings and care for themselves. No leader is perfect; we are all ordinary human beings with different talents, genes, and life experiences. The goal of what follows is to heighten awareness of the importance of emotions and self-care and to offer options for managing the emotions and self-care of leadership transition.

If you are skeptical, you might want to skip to the Reflection Questions section at the end of the chapter and do your own self-study of how you handle emotions and self-care. The next section describes the emotions that are most common in leadership transitions and provides examples of how they show up. This is followed by three approaches to managing emotions and self-care: emotional intelligence, Twelve Step or recovery wisdom, and appreciative inquiry. The chapter ends with some final words on self-care and organizational leadership and reflective questions.

Transitions and Emotions

Imagine yourself as an eavesdropper at the coffee shop or bar of a conference of leaders who, over the past five years, had been involved in one or more leadership transitions. Here's what you might hear:

From CEOs

- "I can't believe they don't want me to be on the search committee. Who knows this agency better than me?"

- "I don't know how much longer I can do this. If I can get the budget balanced and a $500,000 reserve, I'll retire. I'll be seventy-five in April."

- "I have groomed my successor for five years. I can't for the life of me understand why the board wants to do a national search and waste all that time and money."

- "Did you hear about what happened to Jane? With no warning, the board fired her."

- "My new board chair doesn't get it. She wants to meet with me weekly and for me to do a written report for her weekly and the board monthly. What happened to the trust and family culture that we've fostered for twelve years?"

- "I wish the founder would get out of the way. His office is right next to mine, and the staff love to talk to him and compare him to me. I'll never get any staff loyalty as long as he is around."

- "I don't want to kiss up to one more funder. I told the board either they raise the money or I am out of here."

From Board Leaders

- "I don't know how to tell my executive director the board is not satisfied with her performance. Every time I bring up even the smallest concern she gets defensive."

- "We love our executive. He takes care of everything and we just show up every three months. I'm worried though about what might happen if he weren't there."

- Our executive thinks it's the board's job to do all the fund-raising. He submits three grant applications a year, and we do all the rest. I work on fund-raising every weekend, and I am tired of it. Something has to change—and it may be *him*."

- "I was the first African-American on this board. Everyone is polite, but nothing I say seems to be heard. Now we're getting ready to hire a new executive, and the candidate pool looks just like the rest of the board. I've been pushing for a broader search, but I might as well be pushing a boulder uphill. I don't know how to move this organization into the new century."

Transitions are messy because there are so many feelings in play. If you are a seasoned nonprofit leader, you have no doubt been in several, if not many, conversations about difficult or failed transitions. These are not unique to nonprofits; you may have suffered through one already.

William Bridges, a leading author on the topic of change, explains that transition is the emotional and psychological process that accompanies change. It begins before the change and continues for months, sometimes years, beyond the change event.[1] The quality of our attention to this emotional process influences the effectiveness of the change.

Think about a habit you have attempted to change more than once. It might be what you eat, how often you exercise, or what time you retire for the day. If you are like most people, the process of changing this habit was not an overnight success. We can't will ourselves to change. We must first come to terms with what we are giving up and what we hope to gain by change. Whether a personal habit or an organizational change, this process triggers emotions that influence the outcome of the change process.

Bridges observes that there are typically three phases to a transition: an end, a neutral period, and a new beginning.[2] Poorly handled endings result in less successful and sometimes failed beginnings. The threat of the neutral zone—a time of discomfort and confusion as well as creativity—can cause leaders and organizations to avoid change or to rush through it in ways that contribute to future difficulties.

The most obvious manifestation of avoiding change and the discomfort of the neutral zone occurs when boards refuse to accept that a beloved leader is leaving after repeated notification or when a board accepts unacceptable performance to avoid the pain of ending and confusion of transition. An almost comical example of avoidance is the procrastinating board member, where the executive has given written notice of an intention to leave on a certain date, and the board member is charged by the board chair with collecting information about transition and consulting services. Not wanting to accept that this transition is happening, he "forgets" to make the calls until an hour before the board meeting. During that hour he frantically calls three consulting companies and says: "I have a board meeting in an hour and our executive is leaving. How can you help us?"

Avoidance, though, is a symptom of other emotions—usually fear of some sort, one of the most common emotions triggered by transition. Other common emotions during transition include excitement, sadness, frustration, anger, and peace. None of these are mutually exclusive; in fact, sometimes they are happening at the same time. Let's begin with excitement, fear, and their combination—anxiety.

Excitement, Fear, and Anxiety

Something new, unknown, or unexpected can bring a sense of excitement. We eagerly await a vacation or, as children, the end of school or our birthday or a family holiday. Similarly, the retiring executive or one going to a new position is eager for the change while having some anxiety about the unknown. Excitement produces energy, which can be used in various ways. Positively, it results in a clearer focus on what is important and a desire to take the actions required to get to the new beginning.

Excitement is fairly easy to understand: Something new is around the bend. It's as though a big new gift awaits us. We have a new shot in life. Variety will open a new window into ourselves. We will meet new people. We will face new risks, and for many of us—especially those executives who tend to be adventuresome—that is in itself exciting.

Though I do not wish to dwell on the negative, it is the painful emotions that require more explanation and usually require more psychological effort to manage. Sometimes excitement becomes agitation or anxiety; if combined with perfectionism, it can result in a breathtaking effort to get everything right and cleaned up before departure.

The combination of excitement and fear can contribute to a sense of anxiety. Psychologist Fritz Perls describes anxiety as "the gap between now and then."[3] Using that definition, most people experience some anxiety in big change—whether an ending or a beginning. Here are some of the forms of fear that we've observed fueling anxiety and sometimes excitement:

Financial Fears Raising operating and working capital is the lifeblood of nonprofits. Leaders and their connections influence success in fund-raising. Change in leaders often produces changes in fund-raising capacity. Boards, staff, and executives are afraid that the loss of a talented executive or of a well-connected board member or two can threaten the organization. This fear has many manifestations and impacts on transition. Boards ask executives not to leave or to stay involved out of fear of losing fund-raising capacity. Executives postpone leaving even when it is time because they want more financial security than is possible under their leadership. Large donors or influential board members use their connections or fund-raising prowess in ways that create dependency or hold the organization hostage. The latter occurs when a board member becomes the champion or patron for a staff person whose performance is unacceptable.

Reputation Fear or Fear of Failure Successful leaders, particularly executives who raise significant dollars from philanthropy and corporations, are often great salespeople. They are able to create a positive identity for the nonprofit and to effectively market its strengths and value to the funders and community. Many nonprofits are economically fragile. Even in the most successful of organizations, it is not surprising to find areas of underinvestment, most commonly infrastructure (people, technology, or systems) of some kind. The entrepreneurial executive often knows where some of the liabilities are and is blind to others. The transition process and neutral zone provide the freedom for others to begin to raise these concerns. This can result in the executive fearing that her image and the organization's may be tarnished.

Similarly board members and staff may have real concerns about their ability to succeed without the executive or a founding board member. For example, Alex Vasquez was the charismatic founder of a community health center. For over twenty-five years he had become the "go to" leader in his community on health and most issues. When he announced his retirement, his board feared the center would not survive without Alex. (It did; his successor has served successfully for eight years.)

Fear of failure can also be a trap for successful long-term executives who wonder if they can be as successful someplace else. One executive described it as the fear of "playing past the money." In the sports or performance worlds as in leadership, it is the tension between staying too long in one place and wondering if more success is possible.

Fear of Loss of Power, Control, or Status This is a cousin to reputation fear. Here the leader is aware of the fact that there are losses in leaving a leadership position. For the executive used to being in charge and with a high degree of control, the neutral zone experience of a board that is stepping up or even not involving the executive in key decisions can be quite disconcerting. For leaders with long tenures and for whom this leadership role has been a capstone or career high mark, they have a real and perceived concern about the loss of influence and ability to get things done that comes with giving up a powerful position. For internal candidates promoted to executive, they experience a big transition of role from colleague to boss or authority figure. Here the fear may be about the loss of status as equal and friend with former peers.

Sadness and Withdrawal As humans, we tend to develop habits and ways of adapting to situations. In observing people in transition, we have different ways of handling endings. Some leaders rush through a transition and treat it like a hundred-yard dash. Others avoid it at all costs and make the smallest of changes into a lifetime process. And most of us are someplace in between.

How we grieve and say good-bye to people and experiences that are ending varies tremendously. For example, one executive was accustomed to putting on a positive face at any sad event. She moved through her transition with apparent ease, and successfully handed off top leadership after founding and building an organization over thirty-five years. Her husband retired at about the same time, and together they moved out of state. But the positive face was just a face: all this change resulted in depression that required medical treatment sixty days after retiring.

Some executives handle the transition by grieving privately each time they do an important activity for the very last time—final board meetings, final ceremonial events, final review of a great subordinate. Still others begin to avoid spending time with colleagues and friends on the job because they are sad about the prospect of leaving and may even feel guilty about it.

Withdrawal can take many forms. Besides avoiding informal social contacts, leaders may detach themselves from management and key decisions in ways that are surprising or upsetting to the staff and board. A highly reliable executive may miss a grant application deadline. The executive who provided much of the energy for special events may disappear and have little or no involvement. Like an adult child grieving a parent, the leader may use withdrawal to take a much-needed personal "time-out."

Executives with histories that include issues such as depression or addictions should take extra care during these times.

Frustration and Anger Leaders are used to getting things done. Successful leaders develop processes and relationships that make it simpler to get important things done quickly and well. Frustration is one of the characteristics of the neutral zone during transition. That's because things are not what they used to be. The leader's ability to make things happen quickly is changing. This and a redefined role with the board or how the board is handling (or not handling) the departure planning can all lead to frustration and anger. The differences in how people handle change add to the frustration; the person who sprints through change is going to be frustrated by one who plods through cautiously—and vice versa.

So imagine the many possibilities for frustration during transition. Here are some classic possibilities:

- A board chair who is a slow changer refuses to accept that the executive is leaving and takes months to appoint a transition committee chair. The executive and other board members who want to get on with it are steaming but don't know what to do.

- An executive who is a sprinter through change decides she wants to move on. She talks with her deputy about becoming the executive, grooms her privately for six months, and announces to the board at a board meeting that she is leaving in thirty days and recommends that the deputy be appointed executive.

- A founding board member who became the agency executive has turned seventy-five. She wants to step down and go back to being board chair. She can't face the possibility of ending and sees death as her exit strategy from the organization.

Each of these examples will result in some form of frustration and covert or overt anger among staff, the board, and the executive. When these emotions are ignored, they contribute to further organizational instability and decrease the odds of a successful transition. Growing frustration often results in withdrawal and the premature and unnecessary departure from the organization of key staff and board leaders.

Joy and Peace Leaders who master the art of "preparing the way and letting go" discover there is a profound peace and joy that accompanies successful transition.[4] For these executives and board leaders, there is both a personal capacity to deal with the many feelings that accompany change and a willingness to accept, tolerate, and respect how others handle change.

This inner peace comes at unexpected moments when there is a success led by others on the team or when a board transition committee embraces its charge and provides positive leadership in the process of deciding on a future direction. Joy may come in the quiet reflections on the good work the organization is doing or at a touching farewell event.

Getting to joy and inner peace is not easy and can appear illusive if not impossible at moments during transition. There are practices and points of view that support leaders and organizations in building leaderful organizations by managing well-leader transitions. The next section offers practical tools from several sources that in different ways broaden the choices for how leaders respond to emotions and change.

Handling Individual and Group Emotional Responses

You are probably familiar with some, perhaps many, of the tools described in this section. The intent here is to offer a beginning menu and serve as a reminder that there are many resources and ways for leaders to practice self-care and to continue to learn and grow. These tools are not prescriptive and not all will make sense to every leader today. The reader is encouraged to read with curiosity, explore anything that seems useful, reconnect with what you know, and stay open for what the future may reveal for you.

Appreciative Inquiry

For many people, fear is the predominant emotion that can get in the way of positive relationships and effective and creative work. It shows up in many forms as illustrated above. Ultimately, the response boils down to the fear that "I will lose something I have or not get something I want." As fear increases, the ability to see the positive diminishes and everything negative looms larger than life. For those inclined to obsession, the negative thoughts become endless.

A powerful antidote to fear and to advancing positive relationships and work is appreciative inquiry. Developed in the 1980s by David Cooperrider and Suresh Srivastva, this approach argues that organizations will find more success in team building and profitable returns if they focus on their positive attributes rather than missteps and failures.[5] Through a series of meetings revolving around collaborative brainstorming and personal inquiries about triumphs and victories, the trajectory of the individual and group mentality will shift toward the positive. It is a process of realization of potential by focusing on positive attributes, positive experiences, and positive results (work-related, for group and individual). Rather than attempting to fix failures or shortfalls, emphasis on past and present victories is ideal.

At its simplest, appreciative inquiry is a powerful way to start any meeting, particularly a challenging and potentially emotional one. As a transition committee of a board convenes with an executive who has just given notice of her intention to leave, the chair might begin by suggesting: "Let's take a minute and reflect on XYZ organization and what we appreciate about its work." Or to focus more directly on the executive: "Let's take a moment and reflect on what our organization has accomplished over the past five years under Alfredo's leadership."

Used more systematically to support planning and communications among groups, appreciative inquiry involves a method of moving from positive appreciation of what *is* (discovery) through exploration of what *might be* (aspirations or dreams) to brainstorming what *should be* (design) to developing plans and commitments *to act* (destiny).[6] This approach moves groups beyond weighing positives and negatives and getting stuck on negatives to focusing singularly on the positive and the desired aspirations and how to get there.

The benefit for leaders and organizations in transition is that time, energy, and resources are focused on positives and possibilities, thereby moving the organization squarely in the direction of their desired future. One housing organization used a traditional SWOT (Strengths, Weaknesses, Opportunities, and Threats) approach to assessing their organization during an executive transition. Given the anxiety about the transition, the conversation focused almost exclusively on the weaknesses and what was not working. Meetings dragged on and the board became quite discouraged about the organization's future. A similar organization used the appreciative inquiry approach and focused on what the board and staff appreciated about the organization and their aspirations for the future. This resulted in a highlighting of organizational assets to communicate to potential candidates along with a short list of goals to advance the vision that was commonly held. The latter process led to a more successful transition and first year for the new executive.

EMOTIONS IN A GROUP

Increased awareness of the emotional dimension of leading is beneficial in a number of ways. It reduces the likelihood of a project being derailed by unspoken concerns that are influencing behavior. Such awareness broadens the choices a leader has in difficult and awkward situations. In other cases, paying attention to our own and others' feelings can result in more fulfilling professional relationships.

Like any possible strength or asset, if overused, awareness of and attention to emotions can become a liability for a leader. For instance, a work team that spends too much time talking about feelings and process can become ineffectual at getting the work done. The other risk of group emoting is that some individuals may share what others consider to be inappropriate and perhaps a violation of their emotional safety. In some cases, this can lead to people feeling exposed or vulnerable (if they realize, upon reflection, that they've said too much). In other cases, people exposed to "too much information" can be upset by witnessing someone else's exposure. The important thing to remember is that staff meetings are not group therapy. It's a leader's responsibility to intervene when too much personal information is being shared and to help set the group norm about appropriate sharing of emotions.

Emotional Intelligence

Inappropriate expression of anger in a workplace is an example of emotions out of control. A frustrated boss who regularly blows up and berates employees has a difficult time building leadership and retaining staff. Staff live in fear of the next explosion and stay out of his way as much as possible.

Daniel Goleman, in his classic book *Emotional Intelligence: Why It Can Matter More Than IQ,* launched a generation of research and writing about the importance of managing emotions.[7] Emotional intelligence (EI), broadly defined, is the ability to recognize and translate emotive signals and to respond to them in an appropriate manner. For example, a frown on someone's face in the middle of a conversation may represent their feelings of disagreement, dismay, or misunderstanding. An emotionally intelligent person would see the frown, interpret the frown, and respond by reiterating their statements, asking if there is a need for clarification, or simply acknowledging a difference of opinion between the two parties. Depending on the emotional intelligence, the person may find the most ideal way to react in order to promote his or her goals or to forward the interests of the group.

Salovey and Mayer (1997) created a *four-branch model*[8] for more accurately defining emotional intelligence:

1. *Perceiving emotion*—This involves "initial, most basic" recognition of emotions being present. The authors focus on both self-awareness of basic emotions such as happiness, sadness, anger, and fear, which are nearly "universally recognizable in human beings," as well as the ability to observe both nonverbal and verbal clues in others. Nonverbal communication includes

facial expressions and gestures; for verbal communications, the vocal tone is as important as the words. The authors emphasize that perception of basic emotions is integral to early development of emotional intelligence.[9]

2. *Using emotions to facilitate thought*—Individuals will begin to recognize that emotions can lead to cognitive functions, leading the authors to believe that "emotions prioritize thinking."[10] With age and maturation, emotions begin to direct "a person's attention to important changes." "For example, a child worries about his homework while watching TV."[11] This worry should indicate to the child that he should turn the TV off and attend to his homework in order to keep in good spirits. Another aspect of emotions facilitating thought is the vital ability to anticipate emotional and thus cognitive responses to future external stimuli. The authors explain that there is a "processing arena in which emotions may be generated, felt, manipulated, and examined so as to be better understood."[12] This could allow someone in any number of situations to decide how to proceed. An executive director, for example, could contemplate the wide array of emotions he may feel at the time of his future departure, and could take actions presently to manage or better assure a positive response.

3. *Understanding emotions*—Once a leader can recognize and think about emotions, she can explore what information the emotions are conveying. As this skill deepens, the leader is able to mentally weigh options in responding to emotions and over time to have a larger or wider range of possible actions as she learns from and applies evidence gathered and learned in past emotional experiences.

4. *Managing emotions*—Over time and with practice, a leader is less prone to a conditioned response to certain behavior or emotions and learns how to regulate voluntary emotional responses in order to "manage one's own and others' personal and social goals."[13] After an angry encounter, a person could withdraw from the negatively charged situation and harness their emotions to their benefit. "The emotional insight and energy provided by such experiences may be applied to the reasoning process, and may both motivate it and provide a means by which to, for example, elicit others' anger in opposition to the injustice."[14] Optimally, besides avoiding inappropriate responses, people can take advantage of their feelings, negative and positive, to produce a beneficial end.

Emotional intelligence is helpful to both individual leaders and groups (board, staff, and committees). The founder or long-time executive who is considering leaving the organization has a lot of feelings about this decision. Without self-awareness about the feelings and a way to process and manage them, they can become overwhelming. The emotionally intelligent executive is aware of his sense of loss, grief, and sadness; allows time for it; and finds healthy outlets to manage it. Similarly, board leaders may have many mixed feelings when a beloved executive says he is leaving. Anger and feelings of abandonment are not uncommon. Acknowledging feelings through the four-step process above and the cultivation of emotional intelligence by leaders reduces the risk that emotions will derail the organization.

Stages of Grief

An ending or loss is a death of sorts. So one clue to what emotions are in play during transition is to look at the stages of the grieving and dying process articulated by Elisabeth Kübler-Ross. She observed that caregivers who avoided or failed to understand the feelings associated with dying were less able to connect or be helpful. She contributed to our emotional intelligence about dying by offering five stages to the grieving process. These are not linear steps, but they are often present in the process of accepting a loss.[15]

Admittedly, leadership transitions are not as final as death and most may not be as dramatic. Yet eventually, most people and organizations face a transition that hits hard. It may not feel like death, but it hurts and feels like death's cousin. We invite you to suspend judgment and explore the utility of these ideas to your personal and organizational handling of transitions.

The stages described by Kübler-Ross include:

- *Denial and isolation*—refusal to accept reality and the possibility or likelihood of death or loss

- *Anger*—as the reality becomes undeniable, rebellion and outrage at the possibility

- *Bargaining*—a step toward acceptance, an attempt to temper or adjust the reality to be less final or certain

- *Depression*—deep internal sadness when the reality is unavoidable and the full weight of the loss on the horizon is clear

- *Acceptance*—a state of peace and tranquility with the reality that may come for short periods or be an ongoing state[16]

For leaders who have worked together for a long time, endings can be quite emotional and traumatic. Those who have sacrificed time and treasure to build an organization experience this process in some fashion when one or more beloved founders move on. Organizations struggling to survive experience this process as the prospect of laying off staff or closing the doors becomes real.

Recognition that this process is at work allows for appreciation and compassion for leaders and staff who are in different places with regard to loss. Without becoming armchair therapists, leaders can become more sensitive to how feelings are at play when a big change is taking place. Acknowledging these feelings and providing a supportive environment helps reduce the risk that emotions associated with transition will derail an organization or damage a leader who has served long and generously.

Physical Exercise

Unaddressed emotions can lead to stress and resentments. Other techniques described herein provide leaders with a range of options for identifying, articulating, and managing emotions. Physical exercise provides an outlet to get tension and stress out of the body and to free energy for positive uses. Walking, running, swimming, tennis, team sports, aerobics—all provide useful outlets that renew the body, mind, and spirit. Those who have a habit of regular exercise may tend to sacrifice this time when work is demanding. Transitions are demanding. Exercise is particularly helpful during times of change or stress, so continue with any exercise regime.

Spiritual or Religious Practices

Deciding whether to have spiritual or religious practices is a personal decision. For those who have decided in the affirmative, these practices offer a number of beliefs that provide nourishment and focus for leaders during change (and at other times). Among a few of the many possible tools or aids are:

Beliefs that guide action—Simple directives based on your faith and religious practices can provide a moral compass and rudder during challenging moments as a leader. Examples from different faith traditions include: "Do unto others as you would have them do unto you," or "Love your neighbor as yourself."

Prayer—Different faiths practice prayer in different ways. One of the benefits is that it frees the mind from self-absorption and the illusion that the individual can and should figure out and solve all problems. Prayer may involve a surrender to something bigger than oneself, which helps alleviate the burden of transition and deepens the sense that one is not in the struggle alone.

Meditation—For some, meditation is a spiritual practice of mindfulness or becoming "centered." For others, it is a quieting of the mind to listen to an internal guide or wisdom. For yet others, meditation is a path to integration of what feels like a fragmented self.

During times of stress, it is natural for leaders to feel pulled in many directions, to have many and at times conflicting feelings, and to be overwhelmed. Connecting with any of these practices provides an antidote and an internal state of quietude to listen and become less frazzled. The Quakers, who embrace quietness as a powerful tool, have a saying: "The way will open."

Twelve Step Wisdom

Since the founding of Alcoholics Anonymous, addicts of many types have turned to the practice of the Twelve Steps, developed by Alcoholics Anonymous for relief from both physical addiction and to achieve emotional sobriety. The Twelve Steps help addicts understand, resolve, or live in acceptance of emotional situations, and hence lessen the opportunity that emotions will contribute to relapse.[17]

Much is written about the application of these steps for persons who *are not* addicted. In fact, many Twelve Step practices are sound grounds for maintaining good mental health.[18] Here, we will explore some of the underlying principles and tools that support emotional sobriety, and which can be used to cope with the emotions surrounding transition. They include:

Surrender—While leaders have and can develop much influence and power, every leader faces daily situations that are out of her control. This tends to increase as a leader approaches transition. Leaders who lose sight of this reality risk a slow deterioration of influence or even self-destruction when ego, charm, power, and self-will are insufficient to achieve the desired result. The wisdom of the Twelve Steps is to give up, to surrender the results. The leader does the best she can and then lets go of the outcome.

Live in the day—Renowned self-help writer Dale Carnegie encouraged "living in day-tight compartments."[19] Those practicing the Twelve Steps call it living "one day at a time." While leaders need to make plans for the future, the only day to live well is to live well *today*. When worry, doubt, and projection about the future dominate the day, a leader's energy is diverted and his results are reduced.

Let it begin with me—Families of alcoholics use the same Twelve Step approach to address how alcoholism in a family member or friend impacts the individual and the family. It is normal and understandable for family members to look to the alcoholic as the source of all their problems. Instead the principle of "let it begin with me" is embraced as a central principle for living with alcoholism in a relative or friend. This simple slogan moves a person from victimhood to choices and is central to Twelve Step wisdom.[20] Leaders and staff can use this slogan to move through challenging issues.

Detachment—This also comes from Al-Anon, and describes how a spouse or child of an alcoholic learns to handle the frustration, fear, and anger that come with the unpredictable and at times disruptive behavior of the alcoholic. Detachment is a two-step process of first separating the behavior from the person. We can look for good in people who disappoint us if we choose, and we can still address the behavior. The second step is to be realistic about what change may or may not happen. If a person consistently disappoints or doesn't carry through on commitments, detachment allows us to let go of the expectation, to remain calm, and to move on. The application for leaders is to detach during the many times when other leaders disappoint or frustrate us by not performing as agreed or as expected. Unchecked, this concern becomes resentment, then strained relations, and eventually harm to the people involved and the organization.

Addressing time or money issues—Another Twelve Step program assists people who are challenged by debt or the misuse of time. Members come to see that part of the problem is a vagueness about time and money. There is a lack of reality that leads to what some call "time-debting"—giving away time a person doesn't have, just as debtors have made commitments beyond their financial capability. During transition, this may show up as the executive tries to add the work of transition to an already overwhelming daily schedule. In other circumstances, the previous executive's years of just barely raising enough money create a burden for the new executive and board who lose the previous executive's relationships and magic that kept the budget balanced. Attention to his beliefs and choices about time and money may help an executive or leader struggling with being overwhelmed or fearful of imminent or future financial failure.

Boundary setting—Leading has been described as finding one's voice. For some the process of feeling secure as a person and believing in our capacity to contribute (that is, finding one's voice) involves getting more clear about boundaries. Melody Beattie, a leading writer on codependence, says boundaries are like fences.[21] Depending on the situation, each person can decide to be more open or to raise the fence and be more detached. Another way to think about boundaries is in the arena of friendship. Some casual acquaintances you might invite into your hallway or foyer. Others you might invite into the family or living room for a chat. Still others you might invite into the kitchen for a deeper conversation over coffee. Leaders who struggle with boundary issues usually act in one of two extremes. At one extreme, the leader has no boundaries and sees everybody's problem as his problem. This manifests itself in getting involved where not needed or wanted, interrupting when someone else is speaking, or needing to control every situation. At the other extreme, a leader is withdrawn and isolated and makes no contribution. Learning about boundaries and how to adapt behavior appropriately expands a leader's capacity to relate to others successfully.

Resiliency Rituals

A leader's day can be intense and involve rapid transitions from one meeting or event to another. Brian Fraser, executive coach, transition consultant, and author, in his Resiliency Corner article for the TransitionGuides eNewsletter, March 2009, observes: "Leadership transitions create stress and strain. Resiliency is of great benefit in identifying dangers early and handling them with calm, curiosity and appreciation. Such resiliency does not happen automatically. It must be learned and practiced."[22]

Fraser cites research by Al Seibert (2005) of Holocaust victims to define resiliency as "coping well with high levels of disruptive change and sustaining good health and energy under constant pressure."[23] Most nonprofit executives and leaders understand that type of pressure and stress. Fraser turns to Jim Loehr and his colleagues at the Human Performance Institute to define ritual as "a consciously acquired habitual pattern of thinking and acting linked to a core value that enhances engagement and mission success."[24] Fraser goes on to suggest three types of rituals for nonprofit executives:

a. Rituals of calming that begin with physical health and attention to diet, exercise, and breathing

b. Rituals of curiosity that encourage the use of open-ended questions to explore issues rather than contention, criticism, and complaining

c. Rituals of appreciation that encourage attention to focus on positive future possibilities and current assets and strengths[25]

(Learn more about how nonprofit executives are applying resiliency rituals at www.transitionguides.com/newsltr/Full%20Articles/LG%20March%202009%20Transition_Resiliency.pdf.)

Leadership Programs

Many leadership programs today address how our thoughts and feelings influence our actions as leaders. The Center for Creative Leadership offers a weeklong leadership program that offers participating leaders a mirror into their whole selves and how the leader is influenced by mind and emotions. Landmark Education (www.landmarkeducation.com) offers transformational courses in the areas of leadership, self-expression, communications, and personal productivity that participants report make a profound, lasting difference in the way they live their lives. Some MBA programs and leadership programs offered by communities or community colleges may also offer opportunities for increasing self-awareness and the capacity to manage emotions that every leader faces during transition.

Conclusion: Emotional Awareness Opens Options

Sociologists distinguish between private and public places. A waiter's behavior in the kitchen picking up an order (a private place) may be quite different from his behavior in the dining room with customers. Similarly, in the world of managing feelings, there is personal and often private work and there is the public life of the leader. This chapter encourages leaders to pay attention to the power of emotions and to connect their head and heart in leading. This begins with self-awareness—what feelings are and how they are present in the everyday experiences of living and leading. Without such self-awareness, the leader is vulnerable to unnecessary derailments and strained relationships. With growing self-awareness comes expanded choices. Consideration of any of the tools described in this chapter—and testing them out—broadens the choices and responses of a leader preparing for and involved in transition. Without such broadening, the leader may become the victim of conditioned responses, some learned early in life and totally inappropriate to the situation.

All of the techniques and processes described here are important to leaders, whether they are preparing for transition or whether they are still fully engaged in the organization. However, their practice and use becomes critical as the time for transition approaches, and they are essential during transition. These techniques will ease some of the discomfort associated with transition. But more important, they will help the leader and the organization manage the transition to its most mutually beneficial conclusion.

When a leader expands her awareness about emotional reactions to pending transition, she opens up more choices—for herself, for other leaders, for her staff, and for the organization. By attending to these matters of head and heart, she can harness new energy that strengthens the organization even as she prepares to leave. Ultimately, the mission and the community benefit—and her legacy will be one of grace and strength in change.

REFLECTION QUESTIONS

For the Individual Leader

1. What emotions have surrounded the past major life transitions you have faced? Consider graduation from college, marriage, divorce or the ending of a relationship, the loss of a loved one, leaving a job, or the loss of a dream.

2. Fear comes in many flavors. Can you list the types of fear you feel? Which fears seem grounded and realistic, and which ones are based on unlikely scenarios? Which cause you the most stress?

3. What habits of self-care have worked best for you? Are there habits you want to reactivate or new activities you want to consider to better care for your body, mind, or spirit?

For Executive Directors and Board Leaders of an Organization

1. How has your board responded in the past to major changes at the organization? What sort of emotional reactions did you observe? How did the board handle its reactions?

2. How has your staff responded in the past to major changes? What sorts of reactions did you observe? How did the staff handle reactions?

3. What traditions or actions has your organization used to support board and staff during a change? What is appreciated and ought to be

used more often or more consistently? What new actions might you consider?

4. Think about yourself, your staff, volunteers, board members, clients, funders, and other constituents. Relative to a potential or imminent executive or key leader transition, consider the following:

    - What is each losing?

    - What is each gaining?

    - In what ways will each express emotion?

    - What different practices might help each deal with the uncertainty of change?

    - What in our shared past makes us uniquely able to thrive in the coming circumstances?

    - Who do you think will want to rush through change? Who will want to deny it? Who will respond pragmatically?

    - In what ways will each feel most respected and attended to during this change?

    - What would a positive transition look like from each group's perspective? A negative transition?

For Funders, Capacity-Building Providers, Association Staff, and Other Supporting Stakeholders

1. How do you personally model attention to emotions and self-care in your work?

2. How might your organization offer support or resources to grantees, clients, or members that encourage attention to emotions during change and leader self-care?

3. What, if any, information in this chapter might you share with colleagues in your organization or grantees, clients, or members?

3

Founders and Founder Transitions

FOUNDERS OF NONPROFIT ORGANIZATIONS are some of the most beloved and misunderstood leaders in the world. They are beloved because their passion for doing well or righting some wrong is so apparent and compelling. They are misunderstood because of the very nature of their role and the unique relationships and leadership opportunities that come with it.

Think about what drove the size of the independent sector from 739,000 nonprofits in 1977 to 1.19 million by 1997. Over 450,000 founders or groups of founders decided they had a better idea and were sufficiently committed to form an organization. There were so many motivated nonprofit founders that "between 1987 and 1997 the number of charitable organizations in the country increased at an annual rate of 5.1 percent."[1] This increase was "more than double the rate experienced by the business sector."[2] As a result, more children read or get immunized, people affected by HIV/AIDS benefit from services that didn't exist for them previously (food, health, and social networks), and neighbors are renovating abandoned properties and rebuilding commercial strips. Global warming is under discussion and strategies to address it are under way. Our arts and leisure activities and park systems are broader and more accessible than at any time in the life of our nation. Founders are beloved because they make a difference and make our communities and world better.

Carlos Sanchez founded an immigrant rights legal services organization when he was fifty. He was tired of the abusive and illegal treatment immigrants from his native country and others were experiencing. He worked as a paralegal and went to law school at night. After he graduated, he tried working for legal services for eighteen months and felt too constrained in serving immigrants. He borrowed fifty thousand dollars through a home equity loan on his home and started the organization. He invited successful business owners from his country and friends from law school to serve as the board. Together they raised the money and launched a successful organization. From the outset, Carlos planned to serve as executive and then hand the organization over to a successor. He invested part of his salary in a small business and served as an advisor with an eye toward working there when he left the legal services organization. He hired and groomed two senior managers, both of whom were capable of succeeding him. Over time one of the two decided she didn't want to be executive. The board hired the other as executive. Carlos transitioned to his business and is a regular donor and attends the annual gala.

Anne Chin founded an organization for girls to provide an alternative after-school program for urban girls. She had served as an executive for a local girl-serving organization and as a senior manager for the national organization with which it was affiliated. She was frustrated with the slowness of change and the lack of creativity in offering after-school experiences. Her point of view was that every girl was a leader and her job was to unleash that leadership potential. She built her staff team from two to twenty with that philosophy, hiring several girls who had been program participants. She was a founder who took delight in letting go and watching others lead on the staff, in the boardroom and in the program. The board has adopted a succession policy and is confident that there are dozens of leaders who can follow the founder when she chooses to move on.

Judith Francisco founded a cultural arts center. She loved everything about culture and was involved in the development of each of the center's four flagship programs. Unlike Anne, she believed some people had more leader potential than others. Her job was to find "good leaders" and work with them to carry out her vision and programs. Her approach resulted in a revolving door of managers who felt stifled and frustrated by Judith's need for control and to have her "hands in the clay." The turnover resulted in the programs being less effective. Funders reduced their grants. The board became concerned and gently asked Judith what was happening. Judith blamed the economy and changes in funder priorities. Three years later, a new board chair became convinced change was needed. She asked Judith for quarterly performance goals and a written report, both new to Judith. The board chair initiated a planning process and hired a consultant to collect the information needed for planning. As the concerns mounted, Judith first became angry and then withdrawn. At a tear-filled lunch with the board chair, she resigned effective immediately.

To better understand why one founder succeeds and others struggle and often leave frustrated and feeling abused, let's look at what literature and experience tell us about founders, founder transitions, and leader development.

For purposes of this discussion, a *founder* is an executive or volunteer leader who takes the lead in creating or birthing an organization from an idea. Often there is more than one person involved. But usually from the outset or as the organization evolves, one person emerges as the "founder executive" who makes the most substantial commitment to the cause and is or becomes the chief staff leader. Our focus here is on that person, who plays a key role in shaping the organization and its culture and whose departure, therefore, has major repercussions.

There are also many executives who because of long tenure or their role in transforming, turning around, or otherwise rebuilding an organization take on over time many of the characteristics associated with founders. What follows is relevant to both founders and leaders with founder-like characteristics and to board leaders, funders, staff, and the consultants who work with them.

Before deciding if this section is relevant to you, consider the following:

- As a result of the growth of the sector cited above, many organizations have founder executives. In addition to founders serving today, many organizations are still dealing with founder departures years after the founder departed.

- Founder transitions are the most complex and challenging, with the highest risk of failure or of the successor being short-term.

- There is continued birth of new organizations and merging of other founder-led organizations because of size or economic realities.
- One-third of executives leave involuntarily, creating opportunities for executives to lead turnarounds.[3] When an executive leads a turnaround, she often takes on founder characteristics.
- Because the ending with a founder is often mishandled, the founder transition can continue to influence and often limit the board and staff for years and through multiple executives.
- Founders are among the 33 percent of executives asked to leave involuntarily. When this happens it is often ugly and traumatic for the organization.[4]
- Understanding the unique role of founders informs the discussion of why more nonprofit organizations are not led (or founded by) leaders of color. Founding (and staying in power) takes access to resources, often associated with white privilege.

Founders are usually beloved for their passion and vision and the good they do. They are misunderstood because of the complexity of their role and the challenges of successfully transitioning their leadership. These competing values have resulted in the unfortunate and pejorative term *founder syndrome*. We find this term distracting and not helpful.

What follows offers the reader a deeper appreciation for the role of the founder and specific actions that founders, board leaders, staff, funders, and successors can take to move us away from the perception of *founder syndrome* to a more balanced and thoughtful sense of respect, support, and partnership with founders.

What follows is organized into four sections:

1. Understanding the founder's unique characteristics, roles, and challenges
2. How founders can build leaderful organizations
3. Preparing the organization for founder succession
4. Following the founder

Understanding the Founder

From the first idea, money raised, and board member recruited, the founder's life and leadership role grows and becomes more complex and challenging. As a result, founders and the legacies of their coming and going affect many more organizations and people than is readily obvious. As we will describe in more detail, it is not just the founder's life that becomes more challenging with time: the board and staff roles also grow more complex.

When endings are incomplete or don't happen, we accumulate unfinished endings like a growing tail of a dinosaur. They pile up and over time create so much additional weight or "baggage" that new beginnings are difficult if not impossible. Just as we sometimes have "unfinished business" in our personal life, an organization can build a long tail of incomplete or avoided endings that weigh it down. Board, staff, and funders may not know specifically what is blocking progress or fostering frustration. For too many organizations, unresolved issues from the founder era are part of a long, heavy tail dragging behind the organization.

For this reason, even if you are not a founder or are not dealing with a founder, the odds are you are part of an organization where the founder's beliefs, values, and practices still have an impact—for better or for worse. Let's look at a few examples.

One founder built a system of health advocacy organizations around the country. He believed salaries should be kept low, so every dollar raised went largely to the mission. He died in his office and the organization struggled through two short-term successors before hiring an executive who served effectively for six years. She had grown up in the organization and accepted a below-market salary. When she left, the board stretched and hired an executive at a salary nearly double. Staff salaries were not increased. Staff eventually revolted, and the executive quit because of the uproar with the board and staff. One year later, the organization was out of business.

Another founder loved ideas and the excitement of new programs. He had a very broad vision for reducing poverty through comprehensive services, and so he kept adding more and more new programs. For the first six years, funders, board, and staff were excited about what the organization was doing and accomplishing. In the seventh year, growth required hiring a deputy director. After a few months the deputy began to ask questions about the growth and future viability of the vision. And there was good evidence of mission drift: some programs just seemed like "neat ideas" that had only the slightest real connection to the initial vision. Frustrated by overwork and by a sense of diffusion, staff began to leave, and new hires did not last long. A few newer board members recognized and shared the deputy director's concern. They volunteered for the program committee and began using their report at the board meetings to challenge the executive director and his approach. The rest of the board, loyal to the founder, dismissed the concerns. Eventually, the deputy left under pressure from the founder and the discouraged program committee went back to routine reporting. Staff turnover remained high and the organization's support from funders declined because of the growing perception of mission drift.

As noted above, we have a term to describe the part of the founder legacy that is misunderstood and challenging. Some call it the *founder syndrome*. Like many diseases or undesired conditions, we don't always know exactly what it is. We do know that founders, boards, staff, and funders fear it.

McLaughlin and Backlund (2008) give power to the term by including it in the title of their book *Moving Beyond Founder's Syndrome to Nonprofit Success.*[5] They acknowledge "founder syndrome" as a pejorative term and define it as ". . . the imbalance of power in a nonprofit organization in favor of the founding executive that occurs because of the unique advantages of assembling the board and staff of the organization."[6] While part of the title, the authors avoid the term because ". . . it carries too many negative connotations, as though the circumstances surrounding the creation and early management of a nonprofit organization are little more than a clinical disorder."[7]

As a sector, we have work to do to better understand the founder's unique role and the accompanying challenges for board, staff, and funders. The benefits of improving our understanding are as follows:

- More of the good done by founder-led organizations is sustained.

- The board and organization better understand the predictable challenges and transitions that accompany the founding and development of an organization.

- The successor is less likely to become an unintentional interim director (that is, the collateral damage of a failed transition).
- The founder gains better knowledge of the role and recognition for bold and courageous leadership and is more likely to continue to advance the organization's cause after departure.

Let's summarize what we know about founders, their role, and their challenges. McLaughlin and Backlund (2008) make the following points in defining founders:

Founders Have a Vision and Passion for a Cause

Board leaders from for-profit companies often wonder in amazement at the energy and dedication with which founders pursue their ideas. Why would anyone work that hard for that compensation and the continuous uncertainty and headaches? The authors explain: "Most (founders) have a true vision, a highly personal, gut-level motivation to do something for others."[8]

Founders Are *Employees*, Not Owners

Unlike for-profit entrepreneurs who start businesses, founders do not own the organization or reap financial benefits when they move on. This can be a tension point for the founder as they consider how to maintain control over something they birthed. It can be particularly challenging for founders who put up personal finances to start the organization or live on a very modest salary during the start-up. There is no down-the-road payback for this investment.

Founders Have Both a Visionary Idea and the Capacity to Implement It

Most executives take over an organization whose purpose is established and with which there are some shared beliefs about the direction and goals and systems or operational behaviors that support these beliefs. Founders and the first-generation board and staff *create* these beliefs and systems. Turnaround executives who come in when an organization has lost direction and is floundering are often "founder-like" executives and perceived that way by the board and staff when the turnaround is successful.

Nonprofit founders share many similarities to founders of for-profit companies, including entrepreneurial characteristics. Sue Stevens has conducted research on nonprofit founders of arts organizations. In her study, she found many comparisons to entrepreneurs of for-profit companies. She cites a study of the transitions of founding CEOs of a sample of Fortune 1000 companies. That study and her work found that where the founder focused on what was best for the organization, the transition succeeded.[9]

Because of their unique role in recruiting board members and birthing the organization, the founder often has extraordinary power and control over the organization. Most founding board members are recruited by the founder. In our experience helping boards prepare for a founder transition, we often hear board members describe themselves as "advisors" to the founder. Block and Rosenberg (2002) confirm this impression in their findings that boards of founder-led organizations met less frequently and the founders were more likely to develop their board's meeting agenda. Unlike subsequent executives who build social and political capital and the trust of the board over time, the founder has this trust and capital instantaneously.[10]

Block and Rosenberg's 2002 study of the founder's relation to his board confirm these commonly held perceptions. They observe that it takes ". . . a demonstrable long-term mistake (of major significance) or a series of mistakes" for the founder to begin to lose the confidence of the board.[11] Founders often recruit friends as board members. In some cases the founder's board perceives itself as advisory only or becomes a rubber-stamp board. Founders often have strong relationships that produce the organization's funding. This combination (recruiting the board and raising the money) makes accountability and oversight a challenge. Even in the face of major errors or actions that threaten the future of the organization, many founders survive with minimal repercussions.

This inclination to unusual authority and limited accountability intensifies the risk that the organization will outgrow the founder's strengths and skills. Without a high degree of self-awareness and a source of honest feedback, it is possible for founders and the organization to get stuck. This occurs when the organization loses touch with the changing needs to achieve mission or is so focused on mission that the focus on administrative infrastructure and management is lost.

This is among the founder's bigger risks. Persistence can turn into obsessive actions that are unresponsive to the organization's changing competitive environment. A broad and compelling vision can be diffused into too many ideas and an unfocused organization. The obvious shift to a need to build systems and an institution can befuddle some founders. Where founders lose the implicit trust and support of the board, it is usually because too many board members see too big a gap between where the organization ought to be headed and where the founder wants to lead.

The author's experience with dozens of founders and their transitions from the executive role suggest the following additional challenges for the founder and the board (see Tom Adams's *Founder Transitions: Creating Good Endings and New Beginnings* listed in the Resources section) including the following:

The Organization and the Founder's Identity Become One. The Founder Is the Organization and Vice Versa

As a society we are drawn to heroes and scapegoats. When succeeding, founders make great heroes. They take on a big issue or problem and make some progress. It is natural that the identity of the organization and founder get enmeshed. The challenge is to ensure that this is a temporary event and that, for the health of the founder and the organization, their unique and separate identities get reestablished early in the organization's life.

Founders Are Often Ambivalent and Conflicted About When to Leave Their Executive Position and What, If Any, Ongoing Role to Have in the Organization

Founders start organizations because they care passionately about an issue or cause. They found an organization to make progress on that issue. Some founders become ambivalent about departing from their organizations because they can't imagine how else to work on the issue. Other founders fear that the organization will collapse without their leadership. And others like the status and power that comes with leading the organization. For others, their entire life *is* the work and the organization; such founders can't imagine a different and equally satisfying future. And of course, most founders combine some or all of these motivations. As a result, many founders want to stay involved after leaving the executive position or to say yes to the board who encourages an ongoing role.[12]

From these reflections we can draw the following conclusions:

1. We need and rely on founders and their vision and passion. Their role is essential to the growth and vitality of the nonprofit sector.

2. There are predictable and normal reasons that result in founders having unique power. This power is derived from the very act of building the relationships to found an organization.

3. The founder needs a high degree of self-knowledge and understanding of organization development and life-cycle dynamics to avoid some predictable sticking points or traps.

4. The founder's personality and background, as with all leaders, adds to the complexity of planning for founder transitions. Because of the founder's unusual power, the founder's personality may become a bigger factor.

5. Calling these normal conditions that accompany the founding of an organization a "syndrome" does *not* advance understanding of the unique role and challenges that accompany founding an organization.

6. There are specific actions that founders, their boards, and successors can take to reduce the risk of trauma and loss of mission capacity during the founder era and the transition from it.

What follows offers guidance on these actions aimed at celebrating and making the most of the founder era and thoughtfully transitioning to the post-founder period.

How Founders Can Build Leaderful Organizations

It is possible to prepare for and successfully move from the founder executive to a successor. Some forward-thinking founders begin preparing for the founder transition early in the organization's life. Other founders serve for fifteen or twenty years and use the last three to five years to prepare the organization. Both approaches work. As the sector makes more normal the handling of founder transitions, the benefits of early attention to succession planning is becoming more apparent.

Redington and Vickers in their short booklet *Following the Leader: A Guide for Planning Founding Director Transition* (2001) provide a number of practical suggestions for founders and their boards. Their central idea is that for a founder to succeed, it is important at some point to shift from the *leadership of building and creating an organization* to the *leadership of preparing the way* and *the leadership of letting go.* Their approach on the one hand acknowledges the unique and powerful role founders play in organizations, and on the other hand, the importance of being intentional in planning for a handoff.[13] Founders by definition are involved in the early life-cycle phases of an organization. As the organization moves into a more institutional phase and systems become more formal, the founder's role shifts.

Whether the founder is preparing the organization for her departure or preparing the organization to successfully move to another phase of the life cycle, the need to practice the leadership of letting go and preparing the way becomes essential. Founders who continue to lead the organization as if in a perpetual start-up organized around his or her energy and vision run a high risk of getting stuck and becoming irrelevant or hard to support. Board leaders and funders blindly follow passion and commitment to mission for a while. Eventually they want to invest in an organization that will continue to do good work beyond the founder period.

The following are examples of letting go and preparing the way in action.

Examples of the Leadership of Letting Go

As noted above, founder boards are often "friends of the founder." The board often serves more as an informal advisor to the founder than a governing entity. When a founder begins to move to a "real board" that has more independence from the founder's vision and methods, several things happen. First, the vision becomes a shared vision shaped by the founder and the board. Second, decisions are made by the board and the founder is no longer unilaterally in control. Over time, as the board steps up, responsibility for fund-raising, direction, priority setting, and the overall health of the organization shifts to a shared responsibility of the founder and board. Sometimes this happens gradually over time; in other cases it happens in a short period of transition where the board faces the decision to continue the organization or to disband as the founder moves on.

For example, the founder of a disability rights organization shifted to a more formal governing board in her third year of operation and built an organization that has continued to grow and thrive after she retired. In addition to attention to board development and sharing the creation of the strategic plan, she encouraged each of her three managers to expand their leadership roles. With each annual performance, she developed goals related to working with the board, funders, and the community. She also encouraged each manager to play an active role in their state and national associations. As a result, the organization was seen by stakeholders and funders as an organization with a broad and talented leader team. This reputation and commitment to letting go and preparing the way contributed to a positive succession when the founder moved on.

In situations where the founder holds on to too much responsibility and control, organizational identity stays tied to the founder and its capacity often diminishes.

For example, one founder of a national organization unconsciously revealed his identity confusion. All the offices had the person's name to the right of the door. To the right of the founder's door was the organization's name. When his board began to question the vision and direction, he fought back and tried to outsmart the board. He was eventually dismissed by the board from the organization he founded.

Examples of Preparing the Way

Most founders believe in a cause with every fiber of their body. Working on the cause is a calling and can be an "until death do us part" commitment. This zeal makes thinking about preparing the organization for life without the founder difficult.

While all founders have passion, many see the merits of building an organization that lasts beyond what they can contribute. Sometimes easily, sometimes out of frustration and pain, founders come to question if their talents and skills are what the organization needs to move to the next milestone. While oversimplified, the successful entrepreneur who hands day-to-day operations over to an operations manager or COO "gets it" that to continue to grow, other skills are needed.

Joe Johnson founded three different organizations. In each case he took an idea, shaped it into a proposal for an organization with a group of interested stakeholders and funders, and served as the first executive. He led each for between four and six years, then worked with his board to plan for succession and left. In one case he knew his successor and served as an informal, invisible advisor for a year or so after departure. In the second case, he limited his post-departure involvement to an annual contribution. In the third situation, he groomed an internal successor, served as codirector with his successor for one year, and then departed. He has lunch with his successor a couple times a year and has no ongoing role.

Before committing to letting go or preparing the way, the founder needs an honest self-assessment and a process for deciding what she wants. This is often not an easy question to answer. Consultative sessions (akin to focus groups) held by The Annie E. Casey Foundation with founder executives revealed much ambivalence about how long to lead, what would trigger a decision to move on, and how to go about making this decision. Workshops attended by over three hundred founder and long-term executives further reinforced the importance of encouraging and supporting founders in whatever personal process helps the founder clarify personal goals and commitment to leading the organization.[14]

The absence of this clarity often results in mixed messages from the founder to staff and board about future leadership. This ambivalence in some instances undermines the credibility of efforts to "prepare the way."

Preparing the Organization for Founder Succession

When preparing for transition, founders and their organizations have a number of factors to consider. These include how long the founder has been with the organization, whether he is nearing the point of "overstaying" or holding the organization back, how "beloved" the organization is to him (and how beloved he is to staff and board), and how to time the announcement and actuality of departure.

As the founder begins to convert her departure from vision to reality, she needs to begin modifying management—delegating more authority and gradually reducing her prominence. She may take on special new initiatives that will pave the way for the transition and help ensure the organization's stability after she leaves—a final fund-raising push, for example.

Finally, once the successor is selected, the founder and successor need to set up guidelines for contact. In some cases, the founder may choose or need to be involved in orienting and briefing the new executive director. And the founder may play a new role in the organization after departure—though here, great care is needed. In some rare cases, the former executive director has stepped into a new role as a staff member. But while it is seductive to stay on the board or stay involved in some other way, there is a big risk that such involvement will unintentionally undermine the successor. At a minimum, it helps for the founder to "disappear" for six to twelve months to give the successor time to take charge. If the founder continues to play a role, it's best if that role is completely at the pleasure of the new director.

LEADERSHIP IN A TOUGH ECONOMY

The 2008–09 recession is causing some founders and long-term executives to reevaluate their readiness to retire. In some cases, this may result in creative approaches to phased retirement for the executive or new roles in the organization to meet personal economic needs. While there are exceptions to the principle that a founder needs to fully move on to make room for the successor, caution is needed in exploring this possibility. The ultimate test of creative leadership changes is simple: "Does it serve the mission of the organization well?" The second most important question is, "Does this arrangement support the full empowerment of the new executive?" Leaders with egos in check, great communication skills, an effective and involved board, a shared vision, and commitment to the organization and their roles can make this work.[15] A facilitated process that ensures that all points of view are examined increases the odds for success.

There are a set of actions that if taken by founders and boards of founder-led organizations will reduce the trauma of founder transition and better prepare the organization. Based on work with over a hundred founder-led organizations, these strategies include:

Executive Coaching

Ellen Wu founded a West Coast organization to improve housing in neighborhoods serving Asian immigrants. Over ten years, the organization grew to be the leading provider of housing in six communities and three states. Ellen was thrilled with the progress and exhausted. She worked with an executive coach to better manage her workload first. This led to a planned sabbatical and then coaching on how and when to leave the organization she founded. She successfully transitioned four years after beginning the coaching.

Board Development Followed by Strategic Planning

Founder John Smith knew his board was indeed "his" board. He recruited them all; they were loyal to him and his vision. They tried to do whatever he asked because they believed in him and the mission. Working with a board governance committee, John talked about his intention of retiring at age sixty-five and the importance of having a strong board. Working with three board members, they identified five people who, if on the board, would bring leadership and independence. A year after joining, one of the new members became board chair. She and one other board member recruited three additional new members. With this new leadership, the board launched and completed a strategic planning process. When John retired three years later, the board was ready with its own sense of direction and ownership of the mission.

Management Team Development

Jane Coyle preferred to manage through one-on-one meetings with key managers. The work got done and the organization thrived. Over time Jane became frustrated that managers didn't take more initiative. She reached out to an organizational development consultant she knew. With the consultant's coaching and involvement, Jane shifted to weekly management team meetings with rotating leadership of the meeting among the managers. After about six months she took a four-week vacation and had no contact with the office. When she returned from vacation, she found her managers taking more initiative and responsibility. Over time she built on this progress and developed planning, budgeting, and performance management systems that further strengthened the leadership team. Done well, and often with some outside consulting assistance for the founder and the team, this commitment speeds up the leader development culture and the founder's efforts to prepare the way.

Executive Sabbatical

Leslie Mayer founded an organization serving homeless persons. When she turned sixty, she decided she'd like to leave the organization in five years at age sixty-five. After looking at what was written on founder succession planning, she decided the best thing for her to do was to take a six-month sabbatical. She worked with the board and leadership team to ensure the organization was financially healthy enough to sustain her absence for that period. She negotiated with the board an agreement that she would be paid at 50 percent of her salary during the sabbatical and that other employees would have a choice after ten years of service between a two-month sabbatical at full pay or a four-month sabbatical at half pay. (Leslie's was six months because she was using up her vacation time.) Before taking the sabbatical, the organization completed the succession basics and a sustainability audit. This provided a plan for what needed to be done before the sabbatical as well as some priorities during the time. Leslie retained a coach to help her plan for the sabbatical. The board asked their strategic planning consultant to assist in facilitating three meetings of board and staff to prepare for the sabbatical and two meetings after the sabbatical to guide Leslie's reentry and to ensure there was a plan for taking advantage of the expanded leadership capacity after Leslie returned.

Emergency Backup and Succession Basics

Maurice Jones wanted to begin succession planning for the organization where he had been second executive after the first executive was fired by the founding board after six months. He had served for twelve years and, while he had no plan to leave, wanted to get ready for succession. He approached the board chair and suggested he work on emergency backup plans for him and his four senior managers and that the board set up a sustainability planning committee to work with him and to develop a succession policy. (See Chapter Six on succession basics.) The process of looking at key functions for his position and the managers was eye-opening. Maurice was first backup for all the managers. Recognizing this wouldn't work long term, Maurice and the board and management team worked together to develop a plan for strategic hiring to build more capacity and cross-training for senior managers and their direct reports.

Sustainability Review and Audit

Susan Ortega was board chair of an organization with a long-time founder executive. After completing the succession basics, Susan and the executive talked with the consultant about possible next steps. Together they decided to do an organizational review that focused on sustainability of the organization. The three of them (board chair, executive, and consultant) agreed to lead the process. The first step was to recruit two managers and a staff member and three other board members to serve on an ad hoc sustainability committee. Next were discussions with the managers, staff, and board about important areas to be reviewed. Having completed the succession basics and a focus on leadership, the committee decided to focus on finances, fundraising, and the organizational system. Through a survey and small group discussions, they developed a report and set of recommendations to improve sustainability. Whether tied to planning for a founder departure or as part of annual planning, this review and, as needed, a deeper audit of the key systems and infrastructure provide the founder, managers, and board with a road map for preparing the organization. (See Appendix C—also available online—for an example of a sustainability audit report.)

Departure-Defined Succession Planning

Jim Smith's story above is a great example of a founder and board who practiced departure-defined succession. Jim worked with the board chair to shift to a governing board, and then worked with the new board and board chair to create the organization's first strategic plan. As part of that plan, they defined the succession basics and included leader development and succession planning as a strategic priority. Four years later, Jim retired and a new executive took over who has now served for eight years and doubled the impact of the organization. (See Chapter Seven for more details.)

Leader Development and Talent Management

Alfredo Gonzalez led a large national and international nonprofit. He had founded it with two other leaders who were no longer involved. There were three board members who worked for large for-profit companies. Each of them was required to do a bench strength analysis and report to the CEO each year. This report detailed for themselves and each of their managers who could take over the position immediately, in one to three years, or in four to five years and what training and assignments would best support each person's development. Alfredo was intrigued by this idea. He interviewed each of the board members and the HR person in their company responsible for overseeing the process. He formed a small board committee with these three members and the board vice chair. They discussed how to introduce such a system. Alfredo agreed to take this on and to use the committee as a sounding board as needed. Over a three-year period, Alfredo and his managers defined what leadership meant for this organization, the core competencies required for all positions and those specific to each position, and put in place a simpler bench strength review and talent development system adapted to their nonprofit environment and organizational culture. (See Chapter Eight for more details.)

Executive Transition Management

The complexities of founder transitions demand attention to more than just the search for a successor. The stories above offer plenty of evidence of why an approach to founder transition that focuses on both the transition and the search is imperative. (See Chapter Five for more details.) A community-based human services organization board worried when Selma Jarvis, a founder of twenty-five years, announced her plan to retire in a year. Selma knew the board needed to lead the transition and search. Through a local management support organization, she learned about executive transition management services and arranged a meeting for the board chair with the director there. This introduction resulted in the support organization being retained to assist the board and staff with the transition. Selma was able to step back and be on call as an advisor and to support the board in planning and carrying out the search. Through the use of a consultant facilitator, Selma and the board chair communicated regularly throughout the process. Selma felt respected; the board chair had an outside resource to reduce the demands on her. The result was a positive ending for Selma and the hiring of a new executive who has sustained and advanced the organization's impact.

Interim Executive

Janet Moi founded an organization whose mission was to support Asian immigrants in finding homes and first jobs. After ten years of leadership, she wanted to do something else. After completing a sustainability audit and raising operating support for the following two years, the board and Janet agreed the organization would benefit from an interim executive for a six- to twelve-month period while they recruited a successor. Janet was ready for change and didn't want to stay another year. Several board members were involved with churches that required interim pastors when a long-serving pastor left. These board members learned there were trained interim executives for nonprofits in their community and convinced the board that having an interim would help the board and staff get ready to work with a new executive. Because everyone liked working with Janet, there was concern over whether anyone could succeed. Some board members were hesitant about the idea because they thought it might weaken fund-raising or be hard for the staff to go through change twice. By raising the operating funds for two years through a special campaign and talking with the managers and staff about the benefits of an interim staff, the board and staff agreed to hire an interim. The interim served for ten months, prepared the board and staff for working with someone different, kept operations going well, and assisted in the entry and orientation of the new executive. (For more on interim executives, see Appendix A—also available online—and Chapter Five.)

Following the Founder

Being a successor to a founder is an acknowledged high-risk leader position. Anecdotal data abounds with stories of executives following a founder (or other beloved executive) who failed or had a short tenure. We call these executives "unintentional interims." There are multiple factors that contribute to this happening. If the organization hasn't completed its ending work with the departing executive, it is hard for the successor to lead. In other cases, the financial condition of the organization is much worse than the board knew about and the new executive feels betrayed and leaves. In still others, the board or staff are in disarray and the new executive lacks the experience or skills to address the issues.

Successors collude with the founder syndrome when they naively accept an executive position without doing their own due diligence. Many unintentional interims recognize in hindsight that there were signals of potential difficulties when they were being interviewed. Enthusiasm for the opportunity or awe for the organization and the reputation of the founder often cause potential successors to ignore their own warning signals. For founders to successfully transition, the founder, the organization and its board, and the successor need to prepare well. Here are some steps someone considering following a founder ought to consider taking:

Pay Attention to Who Does What in the Interview and Selection Process

If the founder is active in the selection process other than in a courtesy meeting with the candidates, beware. This typically means the board is still very dependent on him and may not be ready to step up and work with a new executive. In other cases, if the board appears disorganized or one leader dominates the process, pay attention to what this says about board leadership and the support you will or will not have.

Ask to See the Bylaws and Board List, the Financials, and the Strategic Plan

Sometimes there are peculiar agreements in founder-led bylaws. A review of the board list indicates whether the board has grown past friends of the founder and what corporations or funders are connected. If a review of the audit and the current financials makes you nervous, ask to look at current accounts payable and receivable. More than one successor to a founder has discovered little or no money in the bank and more debt than she was told. Dig deep until you are satisfied. Similarly if there is no or an out-of-date strategic plan, ask what that means and about openness to relooking at direction and goals.

Talk to Executives and Staff of Peer Organizations

Sometimes an executive's reputation is accurate and real. Other times founder executives are well loved by funders and feared or despised by staff or other organizations. It is hard to get an accurate picture of the strengths and limitations of a founder. It is worth a few phone calls to round out your picture of the position you will inherit and what will be required of you.

Meet with the Staff Before Accepting the Position

This is among the most important steps. In a facilitated transition, the consultant will make sure this happens. (If there is no executive transition management consultant in a founder transition, you might ask why and if there is openness to outside help during your entry.) If there is no consultant, you have a right to and need to meet with the senior managers in a large organization and with key staff in a smaller organization. This gives you a sense of their openness, an idea of what their hopes and fears are, and an opportunity to do an initial assessment of what help is available.

Build Your Support System Before Accepting the Position

If you accept this position, you have a tough, rewarding, and at times quite challenging job ahead. It is unpredictable where the challenges will come; they will turn up. Planning ahead to make sure your personal support network is in place is key to your success. You may be fortunate and get great support from the board and staff. Regardless, broaden your support network to include another executive, a supportive nonprofit board member friend, and perhaps a coach.

Conclusion: Founder Transition Success

Eventually *every* founder will move on. Success for everyone—the founder, the organization, and the successor—is thoughtful attention to preparing the organization and to a process of letting go tailored to the founder and her organization. These actions, coupled with smart due diligence by a potential successor, will contribute to successful founder transitions and the elimination of the "founder syndrome."

Because of the unique roles of founders, failure to pay careful attention to a founder transition significantly increases the odds of short tenure for the new executive. Short tenures at best limit growth and cause a short downturn in effectiveness. At worst, short tenures of executives can lead to a loss of funding. Loss of funding can lead to another short-tenured executive. This downward cycle ultimately can result in the failure of the organization.

Paying attention to leader transitions is an essential step in becoming a more leaderful organization. Paying attention to *founder* transitions is an essential step in avoiding months and perhaps years of underperformance. It is impossible to advance leader development when the top leadership position is in chaos. It is in everyone's interest to pay attention to and get help to manage a founder transition.

REFLECTION QUESTIONS

For the Individual Leader

1. Are you a founder or an executive whose experience is like a founder's due to tenure, turnaround or transformational work you've done, or other leadership role? What are your greatest hopes and fears for the organization you have founded? What might you do to advance your hopes and reduce your fears?

2. Have you been a part of or know about a founder executive transition? What happened? What are the lessons for you and any organization with which you are involved?

3. If you are involved in a founder-led organization, one that was founder-led, or one that is about to or recently experienced a founder

transition, what are the top three ideas you want to pay attention to from this chapter?

For Executives and Board Leaders of an Organization

1. If you are involved with a founder-led organization:

   a. Has the founder begun "preparing the way" and "letting go"? If yes, how is it going? If not, is it time? What are the next steps?

   b. Of the suggested strategies to prepare for founder transitions, which ones have you completed or are in the process of completing? Are there others you might begin?

2. If you are facing a founder transition:

   a. What are the biggest risks your organization faces during transition? What can you do to reduce their threat?

   b. What help do you and the founder need to successfully complete the transition?

   c. Have you thoughtfully considered how to ensure a good ending with the founder? Are the board and staff ready to work with a new executive and willing to let go of past expectations based on the founder era? If not, what steps are needed to ensure a good ending and a great beginning with a successor?

For Funders, Capacity Building Providers, Association Staff, and Other Supporting Stakeholders

1. Does your organization pay attention to the unique challenges of founders and founder transitions? What are your beliefs about the "founder syndrome"? What has been your experience with founders and their transitions?

2. Are there actions you might consider to increase support for founders and founder transitions based on what you have experienced and read here? Please be as specific as possible.

3. Can you imagine how fewer failed or troubled founder transitions will benefit the cause you care about?

4

Seeking Diversity Through Leader Development

BUILDING A LEADERFUL ORGANIZATION demands attention to diversity and inclusiveness. Without consistent and thoughtful exploration of the many dimensions of differences and their importance to mission results, leaders and organizations underutilize their collective power for good. Though people often think of racial differences when the term *diversity* is raised, the concept encompasses many types of differences (and has myriad interpretations). Diversity can relate to value differences, religious affiliation, gender orientation, ability or disability, and much more. Though the types of diversity are, well, *diverse*, the principles for approaching the issue are similar. In this chapter, with due respect for the amazing number of differences organizations need to learn to embrace, we focus on two prominent manifestations of diversity: racial and ethnic differences[1] and generational differences. This chapter explores how attention to diversity can increase organizational capacity and effectiveness, particularly as your organization capitalizes on transitions in its leadership. Let's look at some examples.

The largest mental health organization in a community in the Midwest was the go-to organization for a wide range of service needs. Government and the community relied on this agency to serve children, adults, and families with a wide range of intellectual and physical disabilities. Founded by leaders of various faiths and congregations thirty years ago, the organization had a committed and entrepreneurial executive and a dedicated staff. The organization's growth had been fueled in part by its low salaries, which kept costs low. The government felt it got great services a lot more efficiently (and cheaply) than it could have delivered them. Over the past ten years, the racial composition of the community had changed from 80 percent white to 80 percent nonwhite, with rapidly growing Hispanic and Asian populations and a stable and significant African-American population. The white executive and the mostly white board recognized the need to increase the racial diversity of the staff and board. However, every effort to diversify the board or senior staff failed. After the third attempt, the executive stopped trying. Four years later, the county council shifted to predominantly people of color, reflecting the changed community demographics. A new and more diverse government team was hired. Not surprisingly, the agency began to be viewed as out of touch with the community—because it *was*. Gradually, the agency's role and size diminished. The executive retired, frustrated by the agency's inability to change and to compete successfully for government contracts.

An immigrant-serving organization in the West had been founded by a young Mexican immigrant out of her concern for how immigrants from her country were treated. She had led the organization for twenty-five years. Her passion for serving her community led to success in attracting others to the board and in raising money for staff, an office building, and services including housing, language education, and after-school programs. As the organization grew, the once primarily Latino community welcomed an influx of East Africans and Southeast Asians, and the staff were also younger—in many cases a generation younger than the founder. She struggled to balance her role as inspirational leader, community liaison, and executive. With encouragement from the board, she hired a director of operations. He was considerably younger than the executive and pushed for more autonomy. He felt the executive was too controlling and did not trust staff enough. And, in fact, the staff really liked him. They appreciated his trust in them, the way he seemed in touch with their interests, and the way he combined a serious concern for the interests of the diverse community with a less dogmatic political-philosophical view of the issues. The executive was frustrated by what she saw as lax discipline, slippage in the quality of the services, and a dangerously naïve political outlook. After a year, she abruptly terminated him. Other young people on the staff, loyal to the director of operations, demanded a meeting with the board to protest the firing. The executive asked the board not to meet with staff and undermine her authority. The board compromised: a small staff delegation met with the chair and vice chair. The executive felt betrayed and humiliated and resigned. The board rehired—as director—the former director of operations, who was more skilled in leading and managing a racially and generationally diverse staff. After a rocky year, the organization continued to grow in its impact on the community.

A human services organization in the Northeast was led by a white woman. As her community became more racially diverse, she recognized the agency would need to change. She sought out a friend whose agency had successfully gone from a predominantly white board and staff to a more racially and ethnically diverse one and had experienced significant growth in its role in the community as a result. Her friend suggested she attend a workshop offered by a national human rights organization. The topic was white privilege and the role of whites in expanding inclusiveness. At that workshop she explored her own beliefs and broadened her understanding of the complexity of the challenge. She came away with a commitment, knowledge that she needed help, and some beginning steps to engage the board. She retained a diversity consultant as a coach to guide her in beginning her conversations with the board. The board first formed a small ad hoc group charged with working with the executive and consultant on shaping a plan to increase the effectiveness of the organization through broadening inclusiveness, particularly of people of color. This work group (over time and with some struggle and debate) became the leaders and champions of a three-year process that resulted in a 35 percent increase in people of color on the board. It also led to a 40 percent increase in people of color in manager positions over five years. This agency grew and doubled its services in that five-year period.

No matter where you live and work, you have experienced how differences challenge a group or community. That may not be the way you typically think about the situation; however, at its root most relationship issues come down to differences. If you have served as a nonprofit leader for long, you have perhaps been in many rooms crowded with other nonprofit leaders like yourself. At the risk of overgeneralizing and perhaps offending, here is what you see:

- If the group is national nonprofit executives of large agencies, it is largely graying white men and some white women.

- If the group is midsize and smaller national organizations and in areas where women have advanced in leadership, the group is largely middle-aged women, mostly white, with a few women of color.

- If the group is foundation executives, it is largely white men and women, again with a trend to the gray.

- If the group is executives of local nonprofits, 85 percent are white and over half are women.

- If the group is deputy and associate directors of local nonprofits, there are more leaders of color (20 to 30 percent perhaps, 35 percent if human services oriented) and mostly women. You will find greater age diversity, though over half are fifty or older.

You can fill in what is missing. The point is if you are a leader of color, you are fairly lonely for peers in most executive gatherings. If you are a woman of color, you are even lonelier in circles of larger organizations. If you are a young executive, under thirty-five, you are rare. If you are a young leader of color, you are endangered.

Why does diversity matter? After all, some will argue, America has settled its race challenge by electing President Obama. That's an important step, but we've barely begun! Communication across boundaries of race, ethnic origin, and age remain major challenges for most if not all communities and leaders. We wish it were easier and there were a magic pill like an election to change all the dynamics. If an election would do it, would not the advances in race relations be more profound in communities and states that have elected nonwhite mayors (Baltimore, New York, Atlantic, Chicago) or governors (Virginia, Louisiana)?

Politics aside, there is a compelling case related to group effectiveness and results achievement that is tied directly to the presence or absence of diversity. University of Michigan researcher Scott E. Page in his book *The*

Difference (2007) provides the science that supports the fact that diversity in groups leads to more creativity and positive results than homogeneity. Page asserts that "collective ability equals individual ability plus diversity" and "diversity trumps ability" are "mathematical truths, not feel-good mantras." Page points out that his research is focused on cognitive differences, not identity differences. He explains: "Diversity, as characterized in this book, means differences in how people see, categorize, understand, and go about improving the world. . . . In fact, identity diversity and cognitive diversity often go hand in hand. Two people belonging to different identity groups, or with different life experiences, also tend to acquire diverse cognitive tools." Page is quick to point out that diversity does not always result in better outcomes. The nature of the work and the teamwork skills of those involved influence outcomes. However, if a group is not diverse, there is less likelihood of the benefit that diversity offers.[2]

For example, a large human services organization moved from an all-white management team of women in their forties and fifties to a racially diverse team led by an African-American man over a two-year period. As the new leadership team talked with clients and assessed services, they concluded that the traditional hours of operation of 8:30 to 4:30 five days a week did not work well for clients. They had a 30 percent missed appointment rating, resulting in less revenue than was projected. It became clear that the agency's previous management team had failed to understand the difference in ability to take time off between middle-class individuals and low-wage working families. By shifting to evening hours three evenings a week and to Saturday hours twice a month, the missed appointment rating declined to five percent, key indicators of family health improved, and overall revenue increased by 22 percent.

Another lens that adds credibility to attention to racial diversity has been the documented disparities in access to education and health services based on race. Until the past ten years, leaders from the dominant white culture have given little sustained attention to racial disparities. As the diversity of the population has grown, attention to disparities by race and ethnicity has increased. Research by The Annie E. Casey Foundation as part of its Race Matters Initiative documents major disparities based on race and consistent high correlations between race and poverty. Nonwhites, in this case African-Americans, Latinos, and Native Americans, are more likely to be in low-income brackets. Using health care disparities as one example, the Race Matters research found that if you are Latino, African-American, or Native American, it is much more likely that you are covered by inadequate insurance or are completely uninsured. Thirty-five percent of all Hispanics are uninsured, followed closely by American Indians at thirty-three percent. By comparison, thirteen percent of whites are uninsured. More racially diverse leadership can bring new insights to these disparities and, as suggested above, new creativity to strategies for positive change.[3] (See www.aecf.org/KnowledgeCenter/PublicationsSeries/RaceMatters.aspx for the Race Matters On-Line Toolkit.)

Diversity and Inclusiveness

Before going further, let's make sure we are using words in the same way and explore why this chapter focuses on race and age.

Diversity here refers to differences. Human beings are different in many ways. Science is regularly shedding new light on differences in areas as broad as personality types, level of activity, physical ability, intelligence, capacity to envision, and many other traits. In organizations that have diversity programs, the term often more narrowly refers to gender, race and ethnicity, age, sexual orientation, and physical ability. Racial diversity and racial and ethnic diversity are used interchangeably to mean diversity related to race, ethnicity, or both race and ethnicity.

Inclusiveness is a broader term that refers to a process of intentionally developing a workplace, group, or community that is open, welcoming, and respectful of individuals and groups of all types of differences. Inclusive organizations proactively strive to recruit and engage people of diverse backgrounds in the creation of a vibrant and vital team.

The Denver Foundation launched its Expanding Nonprofit Inclusiveness Initiative (ENII) in the fall of 2002. The Web site for this project (www.nonprofitinclusiveness.org) is a terrific resource for organizations exploring diversity and inclusiveness. Early in their research, the Initiative leaders defined attributes shared by inclusive organizations: "They (inclusive organizations) are learning-centered organizations that value the perspectives and contributions of all people, and they incorporate the needs, assets, and perspectives of communities of color into the design and implementation of universal and inclusive programs. Furthermore, inclusive organizations recruit and retain diverse staff and volunteers to reflect the racial and ethnic composition of the communities they serve."[4] Efforts to improve success in attracting and retaining a race- and age-diverse staff and leadership most often advance the inclusiveness of an organization.

Another broad term used in discussing diversity is *cultural competency.* Attempting to define culture and the related term *cultural competency* can be difficult. Patricia St. Onge, the lead author of *Embracing Cultural Competency: A Roadmap for Nonprofit Capacity Builders*, states: "In my experience, cultural competency is a way of being in the room. This means bringing my whole self to the encounter and seeing everyone else in their complexity."[5] This deep look at diversity in groups and organizations cautions against the perspective that hiring racially diverse people directly addresses differences in access to power and influence.

Without hiring or recruiting people of color and other people of different backgrounds and ages, organizations do not change. However, change does not happen without resistance. Patricia St. Onge and the coauthors point out in *Embracing Cultural Competency* that organizations may be surprised when there is conflict as a workplace or community group becomes more racially and age diverse.[6] Scott Page from the University of Michigan similarly observes that having a diverse team takes time to work through different points of view and find the positive creative solutions. Leaders used to homogenous groups—white or of color—sometimes are impatient with the effort required to successfully involve leaders from different experiences.[7]

The authors of *Embracing Cultural Competency* point out another way organizations limit the power of racial diversity. The authors observe that some organizations avoid the challenge of working through how people from different races or cultures work together by recruiting leaders of color who are "bicultural." These normal group conflicts are sometimes avoided by organizations and communities who " . . . hire or elect people of color who are fully bi-cultural and comfortable navigating the dominant culture. This requires far less of a community or organization in terms of its own introspection. The perception is that there is very little need to address the systems of oppression if enough of the faces in the front of the room look like the communities who are being oppressed. We need to move to the point where the communities and organizations are themselves bi- or multi-cultural."[8]

As noted above and in a persuasive article by Heather Berthoud and Bob Greene, "A Multi-Faceted Look at Diversity: Why Outreach Is Not Enough," there is a normal tendency in organizations to focus on *recruitment* to increase diversity among board leaders or volunteers. Their article offers a more comprehensive look that focuses on continuous learning at the individual and organizational level and attention to organizational culture, self-awareness, external relations, and interaction.[9]

While a broader lens of inclusiveness and cultural competency are helpful, even necessary, for long-term change in organizations, their complexity goes beyond the focus of this book. Given demographic change in America related to age and race, and the challenges that many nonprofits face in achieving and sustaining diversity, it is not possible to address leader development and leader transition without attention to race and age diversity. This focus in no way suggests that other disparities—those related to gender, sexual orientation, ability, economic class, and other issues—do not persist as pernicious, difficult problems for the nonprofit sector. Those disparities and the resulting discrimination continue.

The focus in this chapter on age and race and ethnicity is intended to highlight two of many dimensions of diversity and inclusiveness that need attention and to offer strategies that are relevant in leader development and leader transitions. These strategies and the discussion below have relevance and are applicable to broader change goals for diversity and inclusiveness in organizations and the sector.

Building Racial and Ethnic Diversity in Leadership

Racial and ethnic identity in America remains controversial. It makes sense that discussions about something as personal as our identity would have strong feelings attached. Given our history of inequity based on race, class, and national origin, it would make even more sense that there are differences of opinion and ways of framing the race question. Our purpose here is not to engage that debate; rather, the point is to acknowledge that leaders in America do not lead in a "color blind" world and that race matters. Peggy McIntosh, a leading feminist and anti-racism researcher, wrote her own personal reflections on the topic called "White Privilege: Unpacking the Invisible Knapsack." Her point was that as she grew in awareness of the privileges she enjoyed as a white woman, she realized why attention to differences is important in fostering communication and change. In her now classic article, she identifies a list of fifty ways in which white privilege influences her daily life.[10]

That reality is the point of this discussion. As humans we all have baggage to unpack and lessons to learn about ourselves and others. To lead effectively requires leading and following people of different racial and ethnic backgrounds. What follows elaborates on ways to move in that direction as a leader and organization through attention to leader transitions and leader development.

Racial Diversity Improves Effectiveness

Given the wide range of experiences in America around relationships among people of different racial and ethnic backgrounds, it is not surprising that the unanimous case for how attention to racial diversity in leadership increases organizational effectiveness hasn't been made. For those looking for the science, it is beginning to be there, but if you choose to be skeptical, you can be. What follows are some of the most persuasive arguments for attention to racial diversity to increase effectiveness.

Racial and Ethnic Diversity Is Increasing at a Rapid Rate. Healthy Communities Require Racially Diverse Leaders in More Than Token Numbers and Roles A funder affinity group, Grantmakers in Health, in a monograph called *Seeing the Future with 20/20 Vision* (March 2009) observes: "For many, diversity is this nation's demographic headline. It is projected that minorities—defined by the U.S. Census Bureau as everyone except non-Hispanic single race whites—will make up the majority of the U.S.

population in 2042."[11] The monograph cites a 2008 Census Bureau report which predicts that:

- By 2050, 54 percent of the U.S. population will be people of color.

- The non-Hispanic single-race population will decrease from 66 percent of the total population in 2008 to 46 percent in 2050.

- The Hispanic population will nearly triple from 46.7 million to 132.8 million (15 percent of the population to 30 percent) from 2008 to 2050.[12]

Given these changes in the U.S. population, attention to diversity seems a no-brainer. As is obvious and often pointed out in discussions about embracing diversity, changing the race of leadership does not automatically equal better results such as a healthier community. However, evidence shows that when leadership is more diverse, there are new perspectives, different conversations, and new approaches to increasing community health and resiliency. As the historic domination of nonprofit leadership by white men and women changes, new solutions to challenges will emerge.

As one example, at the local community level, organizations led by Asians and Latinos in Washington, D.C., are being supported by nearby suburban governments to expand services to their jurisdictions and open offices there. Why? In 1990, the county population was less than a quarter people of color.[13] Almost twenty years later, the proportion of people of color has grown significantly. As a result, new services are now available in the county for immigrants and people of diverse racial and ethnic backgrounds.

Addressing Significant Racial Disparities in Health Care, Education, Economic Opportunity, Housing, and Other Fields Requires Racially Diverse Leadership to Increase Impact There are demonstrable disparities in experiences of health care, education, and economic opportunity among whites and people of color. If the nonprofit organizations that address these disparities and the philanthropic sector that makes decisions about how charitable dollars are invested continue to be 90 percent or more white, the sector is limiting its capacity to understand and serve the populations it purports to help.

For example, the American Hospital Association (AHA) has developed a program to increase the racial diversity of boards of hospitals. In cooperation with state association members, the AHA is offering a daylong workshop for leaders of color interested in serving on hospital boards to become oriented to the industry and to meet CEOs of hospitals in a social networking environment. This is one step in better connecting hospitals to their communities and looking more deeply at health care disparities.

Racially Diverse Consumers Have Increasing Opportunities to Influence Community Services in Health, Education, and Purchasing Customer satisfaction is a key indicator of organizational effectiveness. New federal requirements for quality studies to improve outcomes in health care will influence how hospitals and health care deliverers operate and are paid. Ability to connect with and serve their community will influence growth and results.

Examples: As the Hmong population grew in Minnesota, foundations and government invested in interpreters to ensure quality health care. In New York City, whose population includes many races and ethnic groups, it is common for human services organizations to have the capacity to serve clients in ten or more languages.

Organizations with Racially Diverse Leaders Offer More Opportunity for Staff Retention and for the Development of Future Nonwhite Staff Leaders Changing from a mostly white-led organization at the board and executive level is difficult and does not happen overnight. Sometimes an organization recruits a few leaders of color, but due to a lack of support, they depart after only a year or two. Such turnover has multiple costs, including time and money for recruitment, loss of leadership perspective and momentum, and the loss of credibility with other leaders of color who question whether there is a real commitment to diversity. In comparison, organizations that make a sustained commitment to the goal of diversity find ways to increase employee satisfaction and retention among nonwhite employees and to mentor and develop a growing talent pool of future and more diverse leaders. Without intentional and long-term commitment, employees and leaders may not trust the organization and may doubt that the organization provides real career opportunities for people of color.

For example, an international nonprofit working in the areas of health, workforce, and leadership used a two-step process to expand attention to diversity and mentoring of leaders of color. First it established a diversity initiative that sought input from all staff; collected data on race, ethnicity, gender, compensation, and position in the organization for all staff and managers; and began a series of education and awareness efforts. Once this was in place, this organization used a succession planning process to expand professional development, mentoring, and action learning with a dual goal of increasing leadership capacity and bench strength and increasing the number of leaders of color in a management position. Each manager was required to set goals annually for developing talent and coaching managers with potential for advancement. These actions, taken over four years, increased the number of managers of color by 20 percent while the organization's budget grew by 30 percent. Leaders of color reported that mentoring and coaching by managers—managers of color and white managers—contributed significantly to their advancement.

Economic and Racial Disparities Have an Impact on Everyone in a Community Racially diverse leadership increases odds that persistent poverty and the challenge of two Americas—one privileged and one poor—will receive serious attention. This is critical for nonprofits that address these issues.

For example, Associated Black Charities in Baltimore has launched an innovative project called More in the Middle. This effort seeks to address economic, educational, and health disparities among African-Americans in Baltimore in a number of ways, one of which is to intentionally work to expand leadership by African-Americans in major nonprofit organizations. Leaders of this effort see a multiplier effect as possible every time a leader of color moves to an executive position. Hiring decisions, purchasing decisions, mentoring of next line managers, and role modeling all result from increased access to executive positions by leaders of color. Associated Black Charities is developing social networks of African-American leaders as available talent when CEO transitions occur. Leaders there believe that increased African-American executive leadership will eventually reduce economic and racial disparities in Baltimore.[14]

Why Increasing Diversity Is So Hard

There is a mix of interest, concern, frustration, and apathy among both leaders of color and white leaders about the importance of the topic of racial diversity. This mix is influenced by age, race, and prior life experience. Some of the experiences that lead to different views include:

- Leaders of color who have adapted to a predominantly white culture and biases and see little value in being honest about how they perceive race relations in an organization

- Younger generations who have grown up in a more racially diverse school system and have more diverse social networks, and therefore don't see a need to focus on race or diversity

- Whites who believe race is not a factor and that America has made great progress in equal opportunity—what's the fuss?

- Whites who feel there is too much attention to increasing opportunities for people of color and that advancement is harder for whites, as evidenced in college admission debates and reverse discrimination suits

- Whites (or leaders of color) who have tried unsuccessfully to increase racial diversity on a board or staff, had some short-term success, but have seen that success eroded by either the early departure of the person of color or their becoming inactive and ineffective

These experiences and attitudes make it easy to be apathetic about racially diverse leadership, to have low expectations, and to withhold commitment to change. This becomes a self-fulfilling prophecy that plays itself out in many organizations and communities regularly.

The difficulty of increasing racial and ethnic diversity among nonprofit leaders is therefore complex. Simple or quick solutions tend to be one-dimensional, have limited long-term results, and often fuel frustration and misunderstanding. Among the drivers of the complexity are the following:

Communication About Race Is Challenging Our first African-American U.S. Attorney General, Eric Holder, shortly after his appointment in February 2009, observed: "Though this nation has proudly thought of itself as an ethnic melting pot in things racial, we have always been, and we, I believe, continue to be, in too many ways, essentially a nation of cowards. Though race-related issues continue to occupy a significant portion of our political discussion, and though there remain many unresolved racial issues in this nation, we, average Americans, simply do not talk enough with each other about things racial. This is truly sad. Given all that we as a nation went through during the civil rights struggle, it is hard for me to accept that the result of those efforts was to create an America that is more prosperous, more positively race-conscious, and yet is voluntarily socially segregated."[15]

Past hurts and misunderstandings cause leaders of color and whites to avoid bringing up race in mixed company. Some contributing factors are:

1. Differing perceptions abound on whether there is a need for change—and if so the causes—as noted earlier.

2. Too much focus is on recruitment and not enough on preparing the organization, making room for differences, and supporting retention and growth opportunities for leaders of color. The focus on recruitment assumes that finding the right person is the answer and puts the responsibility for a successful entry on the leader of color. Lack of appreciation or openness to differences and the normal tendency in groups for newcomers to feel that they don't belong leads to short tenures and more frustration by both leaders of color and white leaders.

3. Leaders who have not examined their own beliefs and are unwilling to learn in order to work with people from a different background often unintentionally undermine efforts for change. A trust relationship is required for honest communication. If that doesn't exist, it is easy for real communication not to happen and for leaders to stay locked in their current beliefs, whatever they are. This change, like most change, starts with individual leaders doing their own work and taking risks, which leads to change in organizations, systems, and the sector.

4. Historic inequities in opportunities between whites and people of color show up in disparities in the proportions of African-American and Latino populations completing high school and

college and the extraordinary number of young people of color who have been incarcerated. This limits the size of the talent pool and increases the competition among people of color with college degrees. According to data provided by the Associated Black Charities and TransitionGuides, a mere 2 percent of the Latino population and 14.9 percent of the African-American population in the Baltimore-Towson and surrounding metropolitan areas have a bachelor's degree or higher.[16]

Nonprofit organizations face additional complexities when trying to increase diversity. These include:

1. *Recruitment difficulties.* Nonprofits usually offer lower salaries, inferior benefits, and significantly less investment in professional and career advancement than the private or public sectors. In addition, many people of color are unaware of the leadership and economic opportunities in the nonprofit sector.

2. *Limited nonprofit access to leaders of color.* Nonprofits lack social networks across race. In addition, most nonprofit leadership recruitment efforts cannot afford a search firm, further limiting access to potential leaders of color. Where search firms are used, there is a concern that the search firm may not use approaches to recruitment that result in racial or ethnic diversity in the pool. In some instances, search firms are perceived to be making a token effort to "color the pool" and not working to bring forth candidates of color with a high probability of selection.

3. *The reliance of the nonprofit sector on charitable dollars raised from wealthy individuals, foundations, and corporations, largely led and controlled by whites.* This increases the advantage for white leaders in the critical role of lead fund-raiser.

This complexity and the range of opinions about whether and how to enact change results in stasis—or at least in the *perception* of stasis when one observes gatherings of top leaders of larger nonprofit organizations. (The lack of investment in consistent data reflects the larger ambivalence about whether this is a real issue or one worth investing in.)

To build leaderful organizations that attract and retain a racially and age-diverse leadership requires action at the individual, organizational, and systemic levels. What follows are strategies that offer a map for leaders, organizations, and the sector to advance our understanding of the link between diverse leadership and effective organizations. The strategies focus on leader transitions and leader development, cornerstones of any change effort.

Strategies for Leader Development and Transition Planning

Given the challenges described above, and the limited impact of isolated and unstrategic efforts to recruit more diverse leaders, three interconnected areas are recommended for consideration. They are 1) education and support that advance change, 2) organizational planning, and 3) leader transitions and succession planning.

Education and Support That Advance Change The first challenge is how to have a conversation that has integrity and is safe for people with many points of view and feelings on this topic. Organizations benefit from the support of a facilitator experienced in planning and executing dialogue and awareness education. Diversity consultants and facilitators with organizational development experience come with their perspectives and occasionally blinders on this topic. In selecting a facilitator, due diligence requires obtaining references from leaders and organizations who have made progress as a result of assistance from that facilitator. Many nonprofits look to board members or human resources consultants for this assistance. (Some questions to explore in choosing a facilitator or guide are found in Appendix B—also available online.)

The conversation requires a champion. Ideally the executive or CEO is fully supportive *and* a champion. For example, the CEO of a large community development nonprofit had increased interest in her succession plan. She was the second executive and had served as CEO for over two decades. Rather than focus on her successor, she encouraged the board to look at succession more broadly. She connected this interest to the organization's diversity and inclusiveness initiative, which had begun four years earlier. She asked her HR department to identify a consultant who could lead the board and senior management team in a series of facilitated conversations about the connections between diversity and inclusiveness, talent management and succession planning.

The CEO and senior managers of another organization decided to follow a private sector approach. This involved organizing a diversity and inclusion council to serve as a sounding board and guiding group for the effort. The council planned and carried out (with human resources staff and consultants) education and awareness opportunities. It also designed an employee recruitment incentive program that included efforts to increase and retain a racially diverse staff.

Once the conversation has begun, many organizations turn to data collection to better understand both facts and perceptions. Sometimes the CEO and senior managers are interested and open to some degree or another, but not champions. Effective data collection that looks at quantitative facts about race and ethnicity, gender, age, and tenure of employees along with employee satisfaction surveys and facilitated focus groups can lead to a major organizational or personal "aha!" This learning process increases commitment to learning and change by top executives and the board.

Champions come in many forms and lead in a variety of ways. In successful efforts from the author's observation, they have three characteristics:

1. Champions do their individual work within a view of historical patterns. They examine their own beliefs, values, biases, and blind spots. They invite and get help to learn how they can advance their understanding and be effective in practicing their beliefs. White champions often come to appreciate the benefits of white privilege in new ways and its relevance to efforts to expand access to leadership among leaders of color. Leaders of color explore differences of opinion within their own racial or ethnic group and among people of different racial and ethnic groups and those who are multiethnic, as well as seeing increased opportunities for collaborating with white leaders for change. They find ways formally and informally to connect with other leaders interested in diversity and leadership.

2. Champions respect other points of view and seek to find common ground without sacrificing their principles, identity, or integrity.

They expect that not everyone will agree or see these issues as important. Some may question their motives and wonder why this is important to them. They persist and seek to continue to learn and broaden the group of those involved.

3. Champions take the long-term view and do not expect magic or quick solutions to complex issues. Champions focus on the solutions while not sugarcoating historic differences when it is relevant and important to consider and address them.

Organizational Planning   Some organizations do major strategic planning every three to five years and update their plan annually. With the rate of change in the environment increasing annually, organizations are less inclined toward the heroic yearlong process and more toward simpler approaches like that pioneered by David La Piana and others.[17] Regardless of the planning process, in some way most organizations develop annual goals and a statement of desired results. This planning offers an opportunity to infuse in these discussions a focus on how race, age, class, and other diversity factors are influencing both the work of the organization and the desired results. The questions below can all be included in the planning process as a way to expand the organization's approach to diversity, especially among its leaders.

- Who is our primary customer? How is the profile of our primary customer changing or how has it changed? What are the implications for our services and staffing?

- What is expected of the board? What connections and competencies are needed on the board to achieve our mission and vision?

- What is required among the staff and board to be culturally competent?

- Does the organization have written emergency backup plans and a succession policy to guide planned and unplanned transitions?

- How diverse and inclusive are the board, staff, and senior management? How might more diverse and inclusive leadership advance results?

- What are the ages and tenures of key board and staff leaders? How prepared is the organization for the succession of key leaders?

For example, one association of grant-makers realized that the board and executive had never discussed the succession of its first and long-serving executive. The board decided to make leadership succession an explicit part of its strategic planning. Their consultant helped them develop an emergency backup plan, a succession policy, and a strategic plan that included a focus on leader diversity, recruitment, and development.

A community health center in the Midwest had set up a community services task force. Its work was to plan and make recommendations on changes needed to better serve the Latino population in the service area, which had grown by 300 percent in five years. This process looked at the skills and competencies required of the board, managers, and staff to adapt to a significant shift in customer population. When the executive announced her departure to lead a clinic in a nearby large urban center, the board made it a priority that the next executive have proven experience in implementing a change to serve a new population and the cultural competency to work effectively with the growing Latino population.

Leader Transitions and Succession Planning Leader transitions and succession planning are among the most powerful opportunities for leaders and organizations to look at and advance diverse, inclusive leadership. Ideally, attention to leader transitions and succession planning is part of the strategic and annual planning of the organization (described above). In some situations, the planned or unplanned departure of a key leader brings transition planning to top priority. What follows looks at both circumstances and possible approaches that help improve diversity during an executive transition and during succession planning.

Executive Transition Diversity Strategies. The impending departure of an executive is a powerful change opportunity for the organization. As noted in other chapters, leveraging this change requires planning and taking time to seize multiple opportunities. Here are concrete ways that boards can advance attention to racial diversity at times of executive transition:

1. *Have the diversity conversation.* As noted above, given the wide range of beliefs and experiences around racial diversity, there are many reasons not to raise the issue. In most leader transitions, setting aside the conversation is a mistake and a missed opportunity. If the board is leading the

search without outside assistance, candidates will reflect who the board knows and the selection process will favor people who look and think like those doing the hiring. So, ask yourselves if this hire is an opportunity to advance your commitment to being an inclusive and diverse board, executive team, and staff. If there is no policy or commitment to that goal, now is a great time to consider it. The community served, the mission of the organization, and the experiences of the current leaders will shape this conversation. Regardless of the immediate outcome, for the reasons above, it is an important conversation to start.

2. *Broaden the conversation to a focus on mission and results and not on appearances or oversimplification.* Leaders of color and white leaders share a frustration with conversations that focus on diversity for diversity's sake. The point is to be clear about the *mission* case for attention to racial diversity for this organization. That conversation will inform the approach to preparing the organization for a new executive, building a leader development culture, and increasing readiness for recruiting and hiring an executive.

3. *Decide how this transition can advance long-term inclusiveness and diversity goals (and avoid attempts at quick fixes or superficial change).* Adding one or two leaders of color to a board or hiring a leader of color as an executive or senior manager does not change an organization. If people who are different are expected to think and act like everyone else, then where is the value and creativity of diversity? Putting specific hiring goals in a broader context of long-term change significantly increases the odds of both a successful hire and retention.

4. *Based on goals, look at the composition of the transition and search committee and how to advance inclusiveness.* The selection of members for the transition and search committee is an important development opportunity. Serving on this committee requires leaders to learn more deeply about the organization and to take a stand about both the strategic direction and the future leadership. Leaders who take that stand are invested and committed to the organization. For this reason this committee is a great place to prepare future board officers and leaders. Similarly, if the organization is building on an established commitment to racial inclusiveness and diversity, recruiting leaders of color to have a voice in hiring the next executive is a powerful

strategy. It increases the inclusiveness of board leadership and advances the search by increasing access to networks that are more diverse racially and ethnically, provided the organization has a true commitment to the value of increasing diversity.

5. *Collect demographic data while planning the search.* Effective executive searches follow a short discovery phase (the "prepare" phase) where the fundamentals of mission, vision, strategy, and goals are reexamined. Often this includes a fresh look at future customers and a leadership that relates to these customers. Thus data collection for leadership transition provides an opportunity for a broader look at aspirations and the information needed to be effective. And because of the changing nature of our population across the country, most data will indicate increasingly diverse customers who will be better served by an organization that is culturally competent.

6. *Use the search to broaden social networks.* Successful searches have a marketing plan aimed at reaching and recruiting into the pool candidates who meet a defined profile. Frequently boards are anxious and in a hurry to fill the position. This undermines and limits the organization's ability to develop a strong and diverse finalist pool. Making a decision not to hire until there is a finalist pool that meets all the desired requirements is the first step. The second is to invest the time and money needed to broaden social networks and aggressively seek leaders who fit the profile. Whether it is the board and volunteers doing the networking, a consultant, or a search firm, if their networks are broad and diverse, the pool will be broad and diverse. If their networks are limited or not enough time is invested, the results will suffer. Take care not to fall into the trap of having a diverse pool in which candidates of color are not given full consideration—but instead are pulled in to make a white hire seem valid. This pattern is usually unconscious.

7. *Select a leader who can advance your goals.* Successful boards weigh the short- and long-term needs of the organization and the community served and select the finalist who best fits the present and future leadership needs. Sixty to seventy percent of nonprofit executives hired have not been executives before. While the hiring of an executive is an opportunity to advance inclusiveness, it ought not to be done in a way that sets a leader of color up for limited success or for failure. The organization is best served by an intentional

decision to take the long view on inclusiveness and hire an executive who can succeed in advancing the mission *including* its diversity goals. Sometimes that choice is an experienced leader of color. Other times it is a white leader with a track record in building a racially and ethnically and age-diverse team who can advance the inclusiveness culture.

8. *Help the new leader succeed.* The way relationships begin is often the way they end. Boards and staff who are thoughtful about how to welcome a new executive and make that person part of their community are investing in a good beginning. Attention to the culture of the organization and how it includes and makes space at the decision table for new members is part of this positive transition. People have different ways of thinking, expressing, feeling, and communicating. A new executive who comes from a different background, race, or culture has the challenge of being authentic and connecting with a group of people who have a way of doing things that may be different. Exit interviews indicate that executives leave prematurely when goals, roles, and communication expectations aren't clear. The more diversity there is, the more important it is to develop shared agreements about goals, roles, and communication.

Succession Planning. Succession planning also provides leaders with an opportunity to advance attention to inclusiveness and diversity.

Emergency back-up planning provides a concrete list of who will step up for key managers and positions in the case of an unplanned absence. A quick test of how an organization is doing on diversity is to look at the profile of that list. Are all the identified backups similar to the person they are replacing—that is, the same age, race, gender? How much diversity is there and for what positions? This superficial look at diversity is best followed by a deeper look at the mission of the organization and the competencies needed to achieve it. Are these competencies shifting because of the need for new strategies, new approaches to communication and networking, or shifts in the clients to be served? This analysis provides a foundation from which a leader development plan emerges that adds real value to the work of the organization.

A large human services agency in the West had struggled for years with why there was racial diversity in its entry-level management positions but very little in middle and top management. The process of completing the emergency backup plan for the senior and middle managers made clear a new set of competencies needed for the organization to stay relevant and grow. Over the next four years, by focusing on these competencies every time there was a promotion or new hire, the racial diversity of the middle management team grew by 40 percent and on the senior team by 25 percent. The executive observed: "Up until we did that analysis, we always wanted to have a more diverse management team. But each time we made a promotion, we seemed to end up with people like ourselves. Getting clear on competencies helped us train, recruit, and identify people who offered the skills we needed."

Departure-defined succession planning makes the most of the final one to four years before an executive retires or moves out of the top leadership role. Particularly when the time horizon is eighteen months or more, the executive and board have a unique leader development opportunity. Most departure-defined processes by definition involve seasoned leaders who have contributed to the shaping of the vision and building of the organization. Sometimes this is over four to five years; other times, over decades. Either way there is often a sense of respect and shared creativity between the executive and the board. Successful organizations pay attention to the executive-board relationship and how that shared power is harnessed for maximum good. Even if the executive-board relation has become a little frayed over the years, departure-defined succession offers an opportunity for a fresh look at leadership for the organization's future.

The process might begin with the emergency backup work described above. This offers the executive an opportunity to be proactive and to model for the board fresh thinking about competencies and leader development. Where the board is nervous about losing a beloved leader, the process might begin with a dual focus: emergency backup planning for the staff and a board self-assessment. Since the board will hire the next executive, it is important to make sure the board is ready for that responsibility. A quick look at who is on the board and the competencies required now and to manage an executive transition informs board development and recruitment. Boards that approach diversity as a simple formula make little progress. Leaders want to serve because of the competencies and connections they bring, regardless of racial or ethnic origin. At the same time, leaders of color are looking for an open and inclusive spirit on the board. If the board seems content to have one or two leaders of color who have little to no voice, these leaders won't stay long. As noted by Berthoud and Greene (2001), achieving diversity that adds to impact requires attention to more than recruitment.

Departure-defined succession planning also provides an opportunity for an organization to examine how it is doing in attracting and retaining diverse staff and board leaders. The extended time period before departure allows the organization to progress toward its diversity and inclusiveness goals before seeking a new executive.

A community development group in the Southwest knew its executive would retire in four years. Despite an occasional effort for change, the board and staff were 90 percent white and the community served was 65 percent Hispanic. There was a desire to be more inclusive, but it had never been a serious focus or priority. The executive and board chair attended a diversity workshop and committed to work together for change. Together they built support on the board and senior management team to hire a diversity consultant to help shape an action plan. Beginning with conversations aimed at appreciating differences in background, early life experiences, and opportunities, the consultant first broadened awareness among all the leaders. Next the board and staff began an organized process of networking with the Hispanic or Latino community and inviting leaders of the Hispanic community to share their stories and provide input on how the organization could better serve that community. This was not a smooth or flawless process. Mistrust and fear were present in many of the conversations. Yet with outside help and a commitment to a goal, the leaders persisted. Over the four years before the executive retired, the board increased its Hispanic representation by 40 percent. New funding became available and two senior managers retired. As a result the senior management team was 50 percent Hispanic when the executive retired. The board chair observed: "We were able to attract new funding because the community saw us taking concrete steps to involve leaders who could help us better serve our community. We are a more effective organization because we made the decision to get serious about racial diversity and its connection to our mission."

Leader development and talent management is the aspect of succession planning that makes attention to leader development, inclusiveness, and diversity an organizational habit. Once the succession basics are in place, the executive and board have a first understanding of backup potential for key positions. This first look at talent to meet current and future leadership needs can be deepened through:

- *Periodic (at least annual) conversations between managers and their staff.* This provides real-time feedback on the goals and aspirations of employees and clarification of whether a person imagined as a potential successor has the interest. This can be especially useful when trying to diversify the organization.

- *An annual update by the department or persons who handle human resources of the racial, ethnic, gender, and age profile of staff and management.* This should include a comparison to prior years and any available data for the mission area or sector.

- *Inclusion of leadership and staff diversity plans in the annual operating plan.* If the organization is concerned about these areas, they should be part of the periodic strategic plan update, and therefore part of the organization's leader development strategy.

One organization began with the succession basics for the CEO and four senior managers. This resulted in clarity about key areas where there was backup and areas of vulnerability. A few years earlier HR had begun an annual report on diversity and had engaged an outside consultant to assist with recommendations. This resulted in hiring a diversity director who had responsibilities both in training staff and in supporting the recruitment of diverse pools. The senior managers decided to engage managers and potential managers in a discussion of what leadership meant. Through focus groups, it was discovered that managers did not understand the promotional track and felt the only way to move up was to get the eye of the CEO. This feedback led to defining what leadership meant; the new definition was shared in a one-page summary with all staff, along with a set of leader competencies and four levels of progression from entry manager to senior manager. With this in place the organization created a next-generation manager program that included peer support, coaching, and a weeklong training program. Advancing racial diversity was a consideration in selection for this program. As a result, after three years the CEO was able to report progress in deepening bench strength and in the racial diversity of managers.

Such changes are possible in organizations of all sizes. In small and midsize organizations, the processes may involve all the staff instead of senior managers.

For example, in an organization with a staff of ten, the entire staff participated in collecting staff, board, client, and funder opinions on their services. They learned that two aspects of their program were most valued: flexible hours—being available to the community evenings and weekends—and the friendly and professional service from everyone on the staff. The staff team took this information and clarified the positive attributes needed to continue to meet and exceed these two standards. One team learned more about customer service and developed ideas on ways to sustain the friendly professional atmosphere and flexibility and to train new staff in this approach. A part of this exploration was how to make sure that cultural sensitivity was shown in how clients were greeted and served. The team paid attention to the language skills of the receptionist and counselors to ensure the ability to serve the growing number of Asian and Hispanic clients. A second work group of case workers looked at the services delivered and looked at what leading organizations in their field were doing to improve outcomes and quality of service. This review focused on organizations that served racially and ethnically diverse communities and how their services were adapted based on the needs and background, including racial and ethnic identity, of the clients. They recommended two changes they thought would strengthen the service and a plan for training all counselors and managers in these services. This process was so positively received by everyone that it is now part of their annual planning.

Action Steps

Attention to diversity can seem overwhelming and uncomfortable or even unnecessary. Finding a way to start the conversation requires a leader willing to take that risk. Here are some steps that help:

1. Begin with one-on-one conversations to better understand the facts and perceptions about race and its role in the organization. This may

involve clarifying past practices, attention to the profile of board and staff, perceptions of the connection of race to mission, and whether people of different races feel welcomed and heard.

2. Find an appropriate forum for a first conversation about facts and perceptions. This may be with the board chair or executive, a sympathetic chair of a board committee, or a senior staff person or HR director.

3. With guidance from a few allies, decide how to more formally raise the discussion with board and staff. Determine if outside help is needed to reach a productive outcome without raising unnecessary fears or concerns.

4. Focus the conversation on results and benefits to the organization and how attention to racial diversity is connected to mission effectiveness.

5. Explore with the board or staff (or a subset) possible areas of focus and places to start. Then pick one that seems right. This may be as simple as collecting more information internally or externally about leadership and approaches to increasing diversity or addressing a specific issue like having translators available at meetings to facilitate communication.

6. Persist, review, and celebrate progress regularly. Focus on incremental progress connected to mission and organizational goals. In the review process, identify insights or lessons learned and benefits, including unexpected ones.

Race for some is a taboo topic. For others it feels irrelevant, and yet others find it hopeless. It is a lot easier to write and talk about what isn't working than to work for systemic change. Small actions taken consistently can lead to major change that improves results for organizations and makes the world over time more fair, just, and inclusive.

Generational Diversity

There are always differences between generations. Most parents experience the differences profoundly during their children's teen and young adult years. What make today's generational differences unique are the size, complexity, and impact on work, life, and leadership. In his book *Generations,* Peter Brinckerhoff lays out, as shown in Table 4.1, the breadth of generations and

Table 4.1. Generational Differences

Source: Adapted from Brinckerhoff, P. *Generations: The Challenge of a Lifetime for Your Nonprofit.* Saint Paul, Minn.: Fieldstone Alliance, 2007, pp. 12–14.

Generation	Key Events	Key Traits
Greatest Generation *b. 1901–1924* *Population approx. 20 million*	The Great Depression The New Deal World War II (served in) "Came home to build the strongest economy in history"	Financial security Patriotism Belief in the power of institutions Respect for authority Selflessness Traditional Enjoy helping others Enjoy being part of large-scale, valuable change
Silent Generation *b. 1925–1945* *Population approx. 30 million*	World War II (adolescents on homefront) Family unity/social stability until: • Military draft (40 percent of men served) • The Cold War • The Vietnam War • Watergate	Loyalty Self-sacrifice Stoicism Faith in institutions Intense patriotism Value joint work ethic
Baby Boomers *b. 1946–1962* *Population approx. 80 million*	Wealthy nation The Cold War The Vietnam War Watergate • "First generation in nearly 200 years to rebel openly against [the U.S.] government"	Sense of entitlement Optimism Cynicism about institutions Competition Focused on career Endless youth Enjoy knowing "their value to the team, your need for them, their ability to improve your services" Enjoy public recognition

Generation X (Gen X) *b. 1963–1980* *Population approx.* *45 million*	Shadow of Boomers • "Boomers often held Gen Xers' careers back"; "filled up all the jobs and refused to retire" • Sought stability, but did not "translate into the idea of staying with one organization"	Independence Self-reliance Desire for stability Informality Fun Independent thinking Work-life balance Enjoy knowing "their value to the work of the organization"
Gen@, Gen Y, Millennials *b. 1981–2002* *Population approx.* *75 million*	Children of Boomers High-tech society/Internet Integrated schools racially and with "persons of all disabilities" Diversity in media, politics, and "business leadership positions" Multiracial social groups "Friends from multiracial homes"	Work-life balance Confidence Social commitment Complete comfort with technology Networking Realism Well-informed Superb time managers "Wired for collaboration and for working in groups" Enjoy/seek to find new perspectives and ideas

the distinct points of view each brings.[18] While there have always been generational differences, as we live longer and technology changes our world at a rapidly increasing pace, executives, boards, and those providing services are leading and serving a much broader set of generations. With these come distinct differences in ways of participation, communication, and work/family balance.

Of course, given the principle that there can be more variation within groups than across, these traits are not universal. Still, generational differences continue to shape workplaces and broader agendas of nonprofits and other sectors.

Frances Kunreuther, in her monograph for The Annie E. Casey Foundation, *Up Next*,[19] and her book with Helen Kim and Robby Rodriguez, *Working Across Generations*, debunks some of the stereotypes about differences in passion for change and commitment to social justice between the Baby Boom generation and Generation X.[20] Through a study of social change organizations in the Northeast and an organized set of listening sessions in nine U.S. cities, her research reveals what she describes as a "more nuanced story than found in the popular literature. We learned that younger directors and staff were dedicated and committed to social change. . . . We learned that younger leaders with a more contemporary frame of reference often felt invisible or undervalued by older leaders. We were moved by the conflict that young staff and directors felt as they struggled with how to stay in their organizations and make a full commitment to their families and friends."[21]

The *Ready to Lead?* study in 2008 confirms the desire of younger generation leaders to move up to senior management and executive positions and their frustration at the lack of opportunity.[22]

Communication challenges around age are similar to those around race. At the core of the communication breakdown around racial diversity is the frequently voiced white leader frustration at not finding leaders of color to hire or serve on a board and the incredulity among people of color with this contention. In the arena of age diversity, a lack of understanding and appreciation for different approaches and values in work can result in misunderstanding, mutual feelings of disrespect, and possibly wholesale dismissal between younger and older leaders.

Take the most commonly cited difference in work habits. Baby Boom leaders in the nonprofit arena are often driven people for whom work/family balance is not a huge priority. They grew up working long hours for a cause. Millennial and Generation X leaders have passion for the cause, but they are also committed to their friends and personal interests. When the Millennial walks out at 5 or 6 PM and the boomer stays until 8 consistently, resentment and disdain may grow. Leader development never starts, or gets interrupted, because trust and respect have been eroded.

Failure to learn about and address age diversity and the complexity of many generations in the workplace limits the power and impact of organizations and undermines efforts to build sustainable organizations with a "pipeline" or pool of future talent.

A number of challenges impede successfully engaging leaders from multiple generations in an organization:

- Overlooking the historical context and life experiences that influence each generation (see Table 4.1 and its approach to life, work, and mission).

- As Kunreuther, Kim, and Rodriguez point out, there is no one challenge or problem underneath the perceived generational tensions. With help from Patrick Corvington of The Annie E. Casey Foundation, they suggest five different factors relative to developing the next generation of leaders, including:

  - Baby Boom leaders' exodus

  - Lack of openings at the top of many organizations—no room for next generations

  - Top leadership positions are undoable and constructed for failure

  - Older leaders who are blind to younger generations' talents and lose great people because they don't offer real leadership opportunities

  - The organizational form that relies too much on hierarchical leadership when new organizational forms are needed[23]

- Board and staffs that don't "age down" (that is, recruit younger staff and board leaders), as Brinckerhoff describes it, are at risk of not serving their younger constituencies well or having the diversity of experiences in leadership needed to adapt to a rapidly changing world.[24] Decision making by aging white people may be very different from decision making by a group that is diverse in age and racial or ethnic background.

- Failure to keep up with technology changes undermines long-term effectiveness. Younger leaders add capacity and are great mentors to older leaders when engaged.

What follows illustrates how leader transitions and leader development offer opportunities to advance age diversity and organizational impact.

Generational Diversity Improves Effectiveness

A social change organization in the Northeast was founded by a white civil rights era leader. His passion for making the world more equitable was palpable. With allies and friends, he built a $5 million organization focused on research and advocacy, running it for more than twenty-five years. He was driven by the work and put little value in management and attention to staff. He expected everyone to be as passionate as he was and to work like him. Over time he developed a team of coleaders, all from the same generation with the same values and work ethic. There was no room at the top for new leaders or new ideas. There was a lot of talk about next generation and racial diversity, but interns and young staff cycled through the organization regularly. They stayed for at most three years and left feeling it was a great place to learn with no room for advancement. The executive became ill and was out for a year. His top team strained under the added responsibility. One of his key advocacy managers had a heart attack and never returned to work. When the executive returned, he was seventy-two and had less energy. He attempted to act as if everything was the same. Interns stopped seeing the organization as a great place to learn. Funders began to withdraw. Over the next three years this organization atrophied; it became a six-person, one-issue organization. When the executive could no longer work, the organization closed.

A community development organization was founded by four women in their fifties who were tired of vacant houses, slumlords, and drug dealers in their neighborhood. In the early years they were a unified powerful team and attracted funder support and a board committed to their work. Over time, for different reasons—one a family move, another a great career opportunity in government, and a third health issues—three of the four women left the organization. The remaining leader wanted to recreate the feeling and connection she had experienced with her three colleagues and friends. She hired younger women to work with her. The younger women circulated through and never stayed; the organization made greater demands on them than they felt were fair. The executive had a sudden health crisis. No one was prepared to step into her shoes—an especially troubling turn of events since the neighborhood itself had become populated by younger families who were demanding things to which the executive had turned a deaf ear.

Though the executive was able to return, the organization had taken a tough blow. The board took the message to heart and began talks with stakeholders and even former employees to learn how to adapt to the changed community. Currently they are seeking ways to reinvent the organization's culture, welcome younger staff, and develop a new leadership cadre.

Working in groups across generations make clear that age diversity is not a minor annoyance. When generational issues are not addressed, communication, access to talent, and communications with customers suffer. Think about the present reality and prospects ten years from now for organizations dominated by a board of aging Boomers, led by aging Boomers, hiring only people who look, think, and talk like them. Here are the risks that Brinckerhoff suggests these organizations face:

- Inability to communicate with younger donors, leaders, and potential clients who rely on social networks and online communication for what they value

- High turnover of younger and less expensive staff because of a feeling of not being respected and engaged in the way they'd expect from a mission-driven organization and frustration at what is perceived as a paternalistic or maternal management style that limits growth and opportunity

- Difficulty in managing well the "Boomers in" (retired Boomers looking to do well through second careers for volunteer work) and "Boomers out" (retiring Boomers) phenomenon that will grow in intensity after a slowdown from the 2008–2010 recession

- Failure to use technology that appropriately reaches the many generations being served

As with racial diversity, the incorporation of age diversity *by itself* doesn't make an organization more effective. However, organizations that are committed to learning and engaging all generations in leadership are more likely to adapt to changing needs and to effectively serve their mission.

Why It's So Hard

The decision to take action to increase age diversity seems like a no-brainer. Who wouldn't want an organization brimming with experienced Baby

Boom mentors and energetic, highly educated, and skilled Millennials and Generation X leaders? While it may seem obvious, achieving a humming, age-diverse organization is not easy. Many of the reasons are similar to the reasons that race diversity isn't happening more rapidly:

- It's often easier to stay in denial that there are age differences and stay with the people and ways of working with which we are comfortable.

- Change is difficult. There are losses associated with change, and older leaders at some level fear the loss and possibility of becoming irrelevant or unneeded. Perhaps more frequently than acknowledged, they are unused to—and reluctant about—sharing power, which may be seen as a loss.

- Communication and understanding another's point of view is challenging. Without specific actions to increase awareness and understanding of differences, misunderstandings and even disdain can develop.

- The current size of the older generations creates the impression that involving younger leaders can be avoided, at least for now.

- It takes time, commitment, and money to change. The bias in spending time and money is to programs, not to the people and people relationships needed to achieve mission and operate programs.

- Unlike the field of diversity, where there is a growing body of professional experience and guidance, there are fewer age diversity resources, especially specific to the nonprofit world.

The following section offers some opportunities and tools[25] to move past these challenges and become more leaderful by recruiting, developing, and retaining an age-diverse workforce and leadership.

Strategies for Transition Planning and Leader Development

Any effort at succession planning, leadership transition, or leader development ought to begin with a discussion of diversity and inclusiveness, addressing how generational and racial diversity influence mission results. Indeed, these two elements of personal overlap shape our organizational systems and life experiences.

Education and Awareness to Increase Generational Diversity As with race and ethnicity, finding a way to begin the conversation is important. Unlike racial issues, generational differences may be named in staff meetings or in one-on-one supervisory meetings. Often differences from an age perspective are dismissed by older leaders in a way that adds to the frustration of younger leaders. Education and awareness building that provides a broader context and a safe environment for exploring age differences is often an important first step. Brinckerhoff, in his work with organizations, encourages starting with the lighter moments. One way to do this is to lead a discussion that asks people to pick an object or event that represents their generation. This is usually a lively and nonthreatening conversation. This is followed by a second question that is a little more serious: name the single most memorable major event that influences how you think and behave. As you can imagine, the responses to this question are typically very different for various generations.

Another exercise that has been useful is to have a group create a historical timeline and then reflect on the differences and similarities in what was most useful. This exercise was used at a gathering that a foundation sponsored to advance the "next generation" leadership of color.

The Workforce Diversity and Inclusion Compact of the Nonprofit Workforce Coalition is an approach that focuses on racial or ethnic and generational diversity in combination. The Compact is a voluntary agreement that commits an organization and its leaders to being proactive and attentive to diversity.[26]

All these exercises or tools offer opportunities to deepen awareness and respect for the experiences of different generations.

Follow these exercises with a review of the findings about different generations, what they need from each other, and what this means in this organization now.

Without this attention to deeper understanding, it is hard to imagine older leaders taking a risk on promoting a young leader. It is also hard to imagine a younger leader being willing to be mentored by an older leader when there is a feeling of little respect or understanding.

Generational Diversity in Executive Transition Management The possibilities for positive executive transition are increased by prior attention to age diversity. Many hiring boards face a decision between a seasoned Boomer candidate and a younger applicant with great credentials, a good but abbreviated track record of success, and a strong desire to lead. Without an intentional discussion about age diversity, most boards hire people like themselves—middle-aged professionals who have worked their way up. There is no right or wrong to deciding which candidate to hire, but there *is* a risk that an organization will lose relevancy and become ineffective if it never hires anyone different from the current leaders.

One way to ensure breadth of perspective when hiring is to work for age (and racial) diversity *on the governing board.* Intergenerational boards are rare among nonprofits. The *Tropman Report*, a publication chronicling "strategic issues and management challenges" of the nonprofit sector in the Pittsburgh region, found the same lack of intergenerational boards common in the rest of the country. They reported that "the majority of board members (32 percent) and executive committee members (35 percent) are between age 50 and 59." Additionally, "eighty-seven percent of boards and 98 percent of executive committees do not have any board members under age 30." Furthermore, nationally "the average board member is 50 years old; more than 82 percent are older than 40."[27]

Brinckerhoff, in *Generations*, makes three straightforward suggestions for increasing age diversity on boards:

1. When the board nominating or governance committee is thinking about diversity and skill set needs of the board, add age and generational perspective to the mix.

2. Board recruitment is predictable, so plan ahead to expand generational diversity.

3. If you are breaking a generational barrier, recruit more than one member from that generation at a time.[28]

As you will learn in Chapter Five, there are three phases to executive transition management—Prepare, Pivot, and Thrive. There are opportunities to pay attention to age diversity in all three phases of the process.

During the Prepare phase—in which the organization readies itself for transition—ensure there is generational diversity on the transition and search committee, which may include nonboard members. Ask questions in the organizational assessment about how the organization is doing in serving, reaching, and involving different generations. Determine whether age diversity should be a strategic priority for the organization.

During the Pivot phase—in which the organization seeks its next director—have a conversation with the search committee, search and transition consultant, and board about any assumptions about age that are guiding the outreach and screening. Find out where the outreach for candidates is focused and why. Prepare the interviewing team so there is a shared appreciation of the value of generational (and racial) diversity and a blunt discussion about the natural tendency in hiring to look for someone like ourselves. Wait to begin interviewing until there is a finalist pool that is highly diverse. Finally, select and hire with an eye on both the present and future needs of the organization.

During the Thrive phase—in which the organization and new director adapt to each other—plan an orientation and welcome appropriate to the age of the new executive that involves all generations of staff, board, and stakeholders. In the goal setting with the new executive include a discussion of the findings of the organizational and board self-assessment and the board's point of view about next steps in advancing diversity and inclusiveness at the organization.

Succession Planning Emergency backup planning provides an obvious way to make a spot-check review of how your organization is doing in terms of age and other diversity. As you list emergency backup staff, look at the generational diversity of individuals who are ready to provide backup leadership. This exercise provides guidance for future recruitment and staff development. If the organization has decided age diversity is important and most of the leaders are from one generation, the work to be done is clear.

When preparing for departure-defined succession (in which the executive will leave in one to four years), attend to mentoring younger staff, addressing intergenerational communication or trust barriers, and expanding the mix of generations in the organization.

In *Working Across Generations*, leader Robby Rodriguez describes how one generation of activists founded an advocacy organization in 1980 and handed the organization off to him in 2005 at the age of twenty-eight. The circumstances were challenging: the founding director had recently died and his longtime codirector had moved out of state. As Rodriguez describes it, half the staff was under thirty and the entire board was over fifty. He summarizes the experience of taking charge this way: "The board, staff, and I were all extending ourselves by playing new roles in this new era. Still there were disagreements, suspicion and fears. Board members felt a heightened sense of responsibility to their oversight duties. I was learning I couldn't assume the same level of authority that (former executives) had. Staff members were getting used to a different leadership style, added responsibilities, and shifts in organizational culture. . . . But through new and shared experiences, we learned to trust each other and pulled through in a testament of our love for the organization and its work."[29]

Generational Diversity in Leader Development and Talent Management As detailed in Chapter Eight, leader development and talent management are strategies for intentionally investing in leader development. This approach is critical to success in attracting and retaining Generation X and Millennial Generation leaders and employees. The *Ready to Lead?* study, lessons from the Denver Inclusiveness Project, and focus groups by The Annie E. Casey Foundation all point to the lack of investment in professional development as a major deterrent to younger people making a commitment to nonprofit leadership positions.

This is a systemic issue that is not easy to solve. Nonprofit leaders take exception to the example of for-profit companies who invest a significant share of profits in developing their leaders and staff. Profits provide the resources for this investment. Mission-driven organizations with government, donor, or grant funding have fewer resources to devote. Yet without a commitment to grow these resources and invest in leader development, change won't occur.

The first step in using leader development and talent management to advance diversity is to make a financial and time commitment to leader development and talent management. This means adding money to the budget and setting aside time to pay attention to leader development and talent management. Here are some ways organizations have made the financial commitment:

- Setting a percent of the budget for training and development and protecting this commitment regardless of financial realities

- Finding a funder who will support training and development and including this as a priority in the annual funding request[30]

- Holding an event annually and dedicating a percent of the income to training and development

- Seeking public funds to pay for special programs that advance leader development

- Asking board members or major donors to set aside a percent of their gift for leader development

Using any of these approaches is possible when the mission-related reason for investing in leaders is clear. Here are examples of organizations that made commitments to increasing age diversity within their leader development efforts.

An education organization has monthly half-day learning sessions around key skills for leaders and staff and an intergenerational mentoring program. In addition to a supervisor who is expected to coach each employee around their professional development, each middle manager has a more experienced mentor. At each monthly team meeting, thirty minutes is set aside for mentors and mentees to meet and agree on their next action together in the coming month. In addition, each summer before school starts there is a three-day learning session for all managers and staff. This organization is considered a desirable place to work by young people of color in the community.

An environmental organization set aside funds for the executive and six senior managers to attend a three-day workshop offered by a major university on branding and marketing to multiple generations, a topic decided on by board and staff as a top priority for the organization. Two of the senior managers were from Generation X. During the workshop, the team observed the differences in perceptions among the generations on the team and talked about how their messaging was aimed singularly at the Baby Boom generation. This team-building and learning exercise resulted in an organization-wide project to increase awareness of generational diversity with specific goals for different generations. The organization experienced a 50 percent growth in income over the next two years as a result of changing its practices—which it had done due to its new understanding of generational needs and values.

A community development organization offered five trainings each year for its staff and those of its affiliate organizations. The training director decided these resources could serve more people better by holding a five-day leader institute twice a year. This experiment resulted in curricula that could go deeper and better address the learning differences of different organizations. As the number of Millennial and Generation X leaders increased at the five-day institute, informal networking time by generation was added and sessions addressed age diversity and cultural competency.

Organizations that commit to leader development usually begin to talk about talent management, even if not in those terms. Carol Pearson, executive vice president and provost at Pacifica Graduate Institute, has explored organizational culture using the concept of archetypes made popular by psychologist Carl Jung. Two of the archetypes capture the challenge for many nonprofit organizations in increasing leader development and talent management. The first she calls the Hero Culture. Such organizations count on a few hero leaders to do much of the heavy lifting. At another extreme is what she calls the Every Person Culture. In these organizations, all decisions are considered in terms of impact on everyone. Both these cultures have relevance to the development of talent in all generations at nonprofit organizations. Either, if used to the extreme, limits opportunities for younger leaders and organizational effectiveness over time.[31]

In the for-profit world, talent management conversations often focus on individuals considered to be "high potentials" or "high performers." As noted elsewhere, Lance Berger in his *Talent Management Handbook* refers to "super keepers" as leaders who achieve outstanding results and identify and develop other people who achieve outstanding results.[32] Discussions of super keepers and high performers may grate against the egalitarian culture of some nonprofits (the Every Person Culture). For others, commitment to the hero leader (consciously or unconsciously) makes it difficult to think about talent management—since an organization can have only a few "heroes."

Leader development is a one-by-one activity and requires commitment. That is what younger leaders expect and want. Here are some examples of how attention to talent management addresses age diversity:

- The executive of a midsize human services organization asked his five direct reports to analyze the talent pipeline in their departments. The executive then held a half-day leadership planning retreat with his direct reports to discuss the findings and decide on next actions. The organization hired a consultant to shape a leader development program and craft a three-year plan to increase management's age and race diversity.

- A large health care nonprofit CEO has the chief talent officer prepare a report annually on bench strength and backup for thirty key positions in the organization. This report details readiness to move up and provides a summary of the talent pool by gender, race, and age with goals for increasing diversity and inclusiveness. Once a month at the management team meeting, each of the eight senior managers reports on progress in bench strength and diversity goals. Monthly management roundtables include breakout discussions by race, age, and gender on how increasing cultural competency and diversity is affecting organizational results.

- The executive and a board leader with an HR background at a community-based housing organization with a staff of five decided to look at talent needs across staff, board, and volunteers. A work group from staff, board, and volunteers reviewed the strategic plan and forecasted five-year leadership needs, noting how race and age diversity might influence strategic plan results. The group met four times, invited input from a private HR director and a diversity consultant, inventoried its leaders (staff, board, and volunteers), and recommended a plan of action. The plan suggested outreach to younger people and the promotion of Latino leaders to better serve their community. After a couple of false starts where new people came and then left quickly, the organization found its rhythm and way in attracting and retaining diverse volunteers, board, and staff.

Action Steps

A great place to start is a generational self-assessment. If people resist the assessment, start instead with an education and awareness initiative. This initiative can include discussing how the organization includes people from different generations. Once the relevancy of the topic is established, Brinckerhoff offers two simple tables to assist with the generational self-assessment. Table 4.2 helps inventory involvement of different generations in the organization.[33]

Table 4.2. Board, Volunteers, Employees, and Community by Generation

Source: Adapted from Brinckerhoff, P. Generations: The Challenge of a Lifetime for Your Nonprofit. Saint Paul, Minn.: Fieldstone Alliance, 2007, pp. 52–54.

		Gen @ 1981– 2002	Gen X 1963– 1980	Boomers 1946– 1962	Silent 1925– 1945	Greatest 1901– 1924	Total (in %)
Board	#						
	%						100
Volunteers	#						
	%						100
Employees	#						
	%						100
Community	#						
	%						100

He suggests you look at the raw number and percents for each generation on the board, volunteers, employees, and community. For example, 80 percent of your board might be Boomers and 20 percent might be Gen Xers, with no Millennials, while your community may be 24 percent Silent Generation, 33 percent Boomers, 25 percent Gen Xers, and 18 percent Millennials (whom Brinckerhoff calls "Gen @"). After you study the numbers and percentages for the board, volunteers, employees, and the community you work in, you then perform a similar analysis on your clients and service recipients and on your donors.[34]

Once you've completed this analysis, you can discuss trends and how they will shape your organization, staff, employees, service recipients, and donors over the near future. If your organization is a service provider, Brinckerhoff provides a second tool on page 54: "Service Recipients by Generation."[35] This discussion will ultimately inform the conversation of generational diversity among board, staff, and volunteers—and affect your own leadership development plans.

After the generations inventory, organizational conversations help build awareness, trust, and new ways of working together.[36] Stephen R. Covey, in his book *The 8th Habit*, describes the power of individuals really listening to each other with a commitment to letting go of preconceived ways of resolving a difference through a new or third alternative.[37] There are a number of ways to have useful conversations, such as:

- Include intergenerational issues in planning and in reports to the board

- Encourage mentoring relationships between generations that go both ways—in which participants mutually learn and teach

- Review your customers and discuss how you might reach a broader range of age groups by changing your marketing and outreach

Though these actions may seem "adrift" from the goal of generationally diverse leader development, they are not. The reason is that the organization's culture needs to shift to welcome every generation's approach to work and problem solving. If you have not made these changes and you reach out to hire a leader from a generation that's not the norm for you, that leader may not be able to be effective regardless of your good intentions to diversify.

Every new hire is an opportunity to ensure that your finalist pool has age diversity and that you are open to hiring younger employees when their skills meet the requirements. Similarly, as your organization hires more young people, to retain them and make the most of their talent, the organization may need to add technical capacity and adapt to the technology expectations of this generation.

More generally, nonprofit systems and networks need to change to fully engage the next generation of leaders, as identified by Kunreuther and others. Two of these larger changes include the following:

Revisiting How the Executive Position in a Nonprofit Is Defined The issue here is that younger people look at what it takes for older executives to do their job, and they don't want to work that way. They see the demands as too all-consuming, leaving little possibility of a life outside of work. There are a number of suggested ways to make the top leadership positions more attractive, such as:

- Limiting or reducing the responsibilities so the job is more doable

- Splitting the job and pressures between two or more people through less hierarchical management structures, including codirectors

- Reducing the fund-raising pressure and demands through an overhaul of how organizations are funded to increase efficiency and reduce the inordinate amount of energy invested in fund-raising

Paying More Attention to Compensation and Financial Literacy Too many nonprofits pay unjust wages and do not prepare employees for long-term financial security. Nonprofits never enjoyed the luxury of defined benefit retirement programs like other industries. No longer are nonprofits led and operated by people of means with extra time. Nonprofits are among the largest employment sectors in most state and local economies. Attention to competitive compensation, to educating employees in personal and family financial management, and to increasing payment in retirement benefits will help attract and retain the more diverse leaders needed for the future.[38]

Conclusion: Meeting the Diversity Challenge

Bill Whiteside recruited and developed leaders for a next-generation training program for public administrators. He became the executive of a newly formed pilot effort called the Urban Reinvestment Task Force charged with increasing access to loans in low-income neighborhoods across America. This fledgling effort began in the early 1970s and eventually became known as the Neighborhood Reinvestment Corporation (since renamed NeighborWorks America). When Whiteside stepped down twenty years later, the organization had grown into a quasi-governmental organization with over one hundred affiliates across America and a huge budget. At each turning point in the organization's development, Whiteside was fond of reminding his staff: "It is far better to light a candle than curse the darkness."

Race and age diversity are undeniably front and center issues for the non-profit sector and for our nation and world. We live in an amazing and exciting time. Real change is happening, and the speed of change will grow exponentially over the next two decades. The numbers are irrefutable. Yet it is still difficult to light a candle or share its flame. It is all too easy to be discouraged or uninterested in how racial and generational diversity shape our impact.

While we have addressed racial and generational diversity separately here, they are clearly related. In fact, it is possible to combine the suggested action steps and increase attention to both. The important consideration in making progress that advances mission results is to go beyond the superficial level of identity, age, or appearance. To embrace diversity and its power for positive change means heading into a deeper understanding and acceptance of people with different experiences and views. At first this is challenging both to the individual leader and groups. Persistence, patience, and tolerance of misunderstandings speed up personal and organizational learning. Open conversations, humility, and compassion are essential.

Armed with these attributes, the organization will find that increased diversity leads to improved results.

REFLECTION QUESTIONS

Racial and Ethnic Diversity
For the Individual Leader

1. What point of view do you currently hold about the importance of racial and ethnic diversity in organizations and leadership and its connection to organizational effectiveness?

2. How has your perspective on diversity evolved or changed over your career as a leader? What has shaped or influenced your current point of view?

3. Have you read anything in this chapter about racial diversity that causes you to want to reflect more or explore any aspect of the topic? If so, what would you like to explore or learn more about?

For Executive Directors and Board Leaders of an Organization

1. How racially diverse is the board, management, and staff of your organization?

2. Do you think your organization ought to pay more attention to racial diversity?

3. If so, given what you know and have read, what action or learning do you suggest as a starting point?

For Funders, Capacity-Building Providers, Association Staff, and Other Supporting Stakeholders

1. What is your organization's perspective on racial diversity? Is there any reason to change this perspective, or is it working and appropriate?

2. Given what you have read, how might you be most supportive to organizations you are involved with when they are working to expand the racial diversity of leadership?

3. What systems or alliances do you belong to that you feel should increase attention to racial diversity?

Generational Diversity

For the Individual Leader

1. How are age or generational differences having an impact on you as a leader?

2. How important do you think attention to age and generational diversity is to your work over the next decade? Has your perspective on this topic changed? If so, how?

3. Have you read anything in this chapter about age diversity that causes you to want to reflect more or explore any aspect of the topic? If so, what would you like to explore or learn more about?

For Executive Directors and Board Leaders of an Organization

1. How diverse in terms of age and generations is the board, management, and staff of your organization?

2. Is generational diversity an area you think your organization ought to pay more attention to?

3. If so, given what you know and have read, what do you suggest as a starting point?

For Funders, Capacity-Building Providers, Association Staff, and Other Supporting Stakeholders

1. What is your organization's perspective on generational diversity? Is there any reason to change this perspective, or is it working and appropriate?

2. Given what you have read, how might you be most supportive to organizations you are involved with when they are actively working to expand the age diversity of leadership?

3. What systems or alliances do you belong to that you feel should increase attention to racial diversity?

5

Executive Transition Management

ORGANIZATIONS GET STRONGER, get weaker, or are unchanged after an executive transition. The executive is typically the conductor who understands the big picture and enough about the details to ensure success. Without the executive, smaller organizations risk the loss of key relationships and the knowledge of how everything works. In larger organizations, managers and staff anxiously look for signs of what will be the same and what is changing. Most organizations feel financially less secure at a time of executive transition and some become less secure following transition.

Given how much is at stake when executive transition occurs, it makes sense that a board would want to do everything possible to emerge from a transition stronger. Unfortunately that is not the case. Too often the rush to hire or a lack of appreciation by the board of the challenges that come from transition result in treating the executive transition like one more hiring process.

This approach misses the opportunity to take stock and strengthen and in some cases transform the organization. *Executive transition management* is an approach developed with field research supported by the W.K. Kellogg Foundation in the 1990s and refined by over a decade of practice. What follows describes how executive transition management can increase the odds of a stronger organization after an executive change and support major organizational transformation where needed.

Joan was an out-of-work social worker wondering what was next for her when her brother suggested she join him in volunteering with a new program feeding the hungry in New England. Joan accepted this invitation in 1976 and soon became the first executive director of the state's new Food Bank. She and a handful of volunteers worked out of a small vacant garage, gathering food and redistributing it to food pantries and directly to those needing food. By the 1990s, the Food Bank employed twenty-five employees and worked out of an abandoned four thousand square-foot warehouse. In 1996, this Food Bank fed five thousand people and made eight thousand pounds of food available.

Fast-forward ten years to 2005. The Food Bank had nearly completed a $15 million capital campaign and had built and moved into its new state-of-the-art twenty thousand square-foot warehouse and offices. That year the Food Bank provided twelve thousand pounds of food to nine thousand people through a network of thirty-seven food pantries. Joan was beginning to think about retirement. Her board was deeply concerned about the future of the organization without her. She was known throughout the state and nationally for her leadership and the work of the Food Bank. The governor and other elected officials, major food company CEOs, the media, thousands of volunteers and donors, and the board and staff thought about Joan when they thought about the Food Bank.

The Food Bank board chair and Joan learned about the executive transition management approach to transition. After checking it out, they enthusiastically embraced it. The board chair reflected: "Frankly, I was scared about the future of the Food Bank without Joan. Instinctively I knew we needed to do more than just hire a new executive. This process gave us language and a proven road map for a successful CEO transition."

Joan added: "I knew this was going to be hard. As I got into it and really embraced the process, I got excited about the possibilities for the Food Bank and the new opportunities for me. It was only after I left that the loss fully hit me."

In February 2006, Alicia became the new CEO of the Food Bank. She successfully built on the legacy Joan and her many colleagues had built. She strengthened the systems and helped the Food Bank focus on both feeding the hungry and eliminating hunger. There was no downturn in production or giving, despite a worsening economy.

This Food Bank is an example of two of the five classic types of executive transitions described by my business partner Don Tebbe in his book *Chief Executive Transitions: How to Hire and Support a Nonprofit CEO* (2008). The types are Sustained Success and Hard-to-Follow Executive. The other three types of transitions are:

- Underperforming Organization

- Turnaround

- First Hire (See the box "Transition Types" on the following page for an overview of the types, challenges, and possible results.)[1]

Executive transition is a powerful opportunity to advance the effectiveness of an organization. As the five transition types indicate, every transition is different. There is a unique history and culture that brings the organization to this particular transition. For each type of transition there is an often untapped opportunity for growth and added capacity when executive transition occurs.

The executive transition management (ETM) process is a capacity-building and leader development approach to executive transition. As you will learn in this chapter, it makes the most of the transition for the organization and its leaders, regardless of the circumstances. This is because during the ETM process, the organization does a thorough, 360-degree assessment of its capacities and its future. Done broadly, the process includes a careful look at internal staff development processes, including those that nurture future leaders at all levels. At its most powerful, the executive transition management approach transforms organizations. This happens when the outgoing executive and the board make a decision to look at the transition as one of the most important and powerful moments in the organization's life. This decision results in a willingness to ask the hard questions about the current and future work of the organization.

In an ideal world, the outgoing executive is a forward-thinking leader who knows how to be helpful and how to step aside in this process. This allows the board and staff to build on the best of the past and to freely think beyond the vision and worldview of the departing leader. Such attention to mission and strategy along with continued movement away from the hero or charismatic leader to the leaderful organization that counts on the whole team to contribute can result in exponential, transformative change.

In other situations, there is a strain between the board and outgoing executive. The challenge is to separate personalities from principles, focusing on where the organization needs to head and what needs to change. If the organization has a history of revolving executives, the opportunity is to understand why and what needs to change in order to successfully build a board-executive-staff partnership that will work over time. Taking the time to build this consensus instead of repeating actions that have consistently failed transforms leaders and organizations.

Sometimes the strain comes from disagreement about fund-raising expectations or the balance of authority between the board and executive. The "prepare" phase of transition gives everyone a voice and reveals both aspirations and concerns. All the leaders—board, staff, and stakeholders—have a chance to influence the transition and have input on direction, key issues, and the leadership competencies and team needed to move forward.

As the transition types indicate, sometimes the transformation is dramatic and at other times it is ensuring continued success. In either case the organization is stronger through planned and proactive attention to leadership change using the executive transition management approach.

TRANSITION TYPES

My colleague, Don Tebbe, has identified five classic types of transitions. These are detailed at length in his book *Chief Executive Transitions: How to Hire and Support a Nonprofit CEO* (2008). Here's a brief excerpt of his work.

Type 1—Sustained Success

- Organization is well led.
- Most or all components are performing well or at an exemplary level.
- Transition discussions are peppered with comments such as, "We can't afford to miss a beat."

Type 2—Underperforming Organization

- Organization may be performing poorly or it may have peaked and could start to decline without a change in strategy.

- Funders, board members, and key staff may be wondering if the organization is doing enough, and if its work and strategies have "gone stale" and need to be revitalized.

- Transition discussions usually include worried statements about the organization's business model or operating methods.

Type 3—Turnaround

- Organizational performance has reached a perilous state.

- External conditions may have deteriorated, causing a decline in support or a surge in demand for services that the organization cannot meet.

- Alternatively, mismanagement or a scandal involving the organization may have caused a crisis in confidence and morale.

Type 4—First Hire

- Organization is a start-up or is shifting from all-volunteer management to a hired executive.

Type 5—Hard-to-Follow Executive

- Organization is facing the departure of a founder, a highly entrepreneurial executive, or a long-tenured leader (seven or more years in the role).

- The looming departure presages major change as the organization's culture, performance expectations, relationships, and perhaps even its structure are a reflection of the departing leader's thinking and personality.[2]

Source: Tebbe, D. *Chief Executive Transitions: How to Hire and Support a Nonprofit CEO.* Washington, D.C.: BoardSource, 2008, pp. 12–13.

Let's look at the other types and a few examples of the power of intentional attention to executive transition:

Underperforming Organization—A local community development corporation was doing good work. Its small business loan program was helping immigrant entrepreneurs. Its home ownership program was assisting Latino families in buying their first homes. The organization was held back by frequent change in the executive director. Funding and productivity went up and down with the coming and going of executive directors. In the early 2000s, the board used the executive transition management (ETM) process and recruited a nationally known executive who relocated to the community. The first year went well as funding and program impact grew. An unexpected health problem caused the executive to have to shift to part-time and then step down. The Community Development Corporation turned back to its ETM process and hired an executive who has helped the organization increase the number of people served. In addition, the new executive has focused on how the community is improving as families gain more assets and neighborhoods become more attractive. In this case, we see how an underperforming organization built its capacity through an effective ETM process. It brought in a strong new director; when that director had to leave due to illness, it was able to repeat the process quickly and find another strong director who kept the organization on its upward trajectory.

Turnaround—One of the first organizations in the country to use the executive transition management approach was a housing organization. In 1992, local and national funders were frustrated and considering withdrawing funding support. This organization, whose mission was to create and advocate for affordable housing and neighborhood revitalization, experienced four executive directors in five years. As a result, there was very little benefit in the community and diminishing support. As the organization moved through its ETM process, the board with encouragement from its national organization decided that the best way to improve capacity was to find an interim executive with a specialty in organizational turnaround. They hired a "turnaround" interim executive and simultaneously engaged community leaders in defining the organization's future direction and needed leadership competences. After a national search, a new executive was hired one year later. This executive has dramatically increased the organization's budget and created a $15 million loan fund to assist low-income residents. Here, we see how an organization in tough straits capitalized on executive transition and catapulted itself into a superior future.

First Hire—Start-ups are challenging in any sector. They are particularly difficult for underresourced, passionately led nonprofits. When an organization hires its first executive director, everything changes. Volunteers who are used to doing everything find their roles changed. Expectations can wildly exceed the available resources. Tired volunteers can disappear. So, getting the right "first" executive can set an organization up for a great future, as in the following example of success. In the mid-1990s, a group of national leaders began meeting about the different types of risks facing the growing nonprofit sector. There was deep concern that failure to pay attention to basics such as liability insurance, legal issues related to tax status, or employment laws and regulations and a host of other sector issues was putting organizations and the sector in an unacceptable position. Out of this concern, a new national organization was born. Using the ETM approach, the pioneer leaders were able to plan their organization, hire their first executive, and successfully launch their services. Twelve years later, the organization is a national "go-to" organization for issues related to risk for the sector.

If you've been around the nonprofit sector for a few years, you know of failed transitions. This can often be the case in organizations where a hard-to-follow leader departs and the organization underperforms for years, sometimes decades.

Hiring is an art, not a science. It would be difficult to find a hiring manager who claimed total success with every hire she has made. For the individual hire, human resources practices are tools to reduce risk and increase the odds of success.

However, the hiring of a new (or first) nonprofit executive is not the same as hiring a typical manager or staff person. Hiring by a group of volunteers who have widely divergent opinions about what the key duties of the position are is a daunting challenge. It is not surprising that so many executive transitions fail or have limited success.

For-profit corporations seek to reduce their risk by paying very high fees to executive search firms to find the next CEO. These firms build in a guarantee to do the search over if the new CEO leaves in the first year—because one can't guarantee the success of a CEO. The most one can do is use a very effective, proven process. Few nonprofits have the resources to hire firms that offer similar guarantees.

Executive transition management does not guarantee success, if by success you mean that you hire the "right" executive the first time—someone who stays and leads well for a long time. What executive transition management does guarantee is that if an organization follows the process outlined below, the odds of a successful transition are significantly improved.[3]

And success *is* what we are after. So let's take a closer look at what success means in ETM.

What Makes Successful Transitions

Nonprofit organizations have missions that in some way advance the common good or quality of life of a community or group. Most simply, a successful transition is one where the organization advances its capacity to achieve that common good.

More specifically, one commonly used definition of executive transition success from the practice is: The organization hires an executive who meets the current and future leadership needs of the organization; in addition, its board and staff are well-prepared to work with the new executive.

Success requires attention to more than the executive search. Finding the right person is important. However, if the organization is not clear on its direction and priorities, and if it does not identify the key transition issues which will, if unattended, derail any leader, the chances of a successful search are remote.

Over the past two decades, the W.K. Kellogg Foundation and The Annie E. Casey Foundation have invested in the development and growth of the ETM approach. Both are results-oriented foundations with a commitment to evaluative learning. NeighborWorks America performed a five-year field study of one hundred executive transitions in the early to mid-1990s.

Their research revealed that most nonprofit transitions were nonroutine (71 percent), while 17 percent were routine, and 12 percent were start-up organizations. Routine transitions occurred when an executive left for a new position or retired and the new executive was hired without interruption to leadership or disruption to the work of the CEO. Nonroutine transitions either happened suddenly or had sufficient complexity to prevent a simple handoff from one leader to another.[4]

This finding supported the anecdotal awareness of how complex nonprofit executive transitions were. In each of the five classic types described above, there are challenges that demand attention to more than the search for success.

In 2000, CompassPoint Nonprofit Services did a retrospective study on a sample of its clients who had used their ETM approach, similar to the one described in this chapter. They found that the vast majority characterized their organization as "either healthier or much healthier since the new executive director was hired." Not only were the organizations reacting positively, but two-thirds of the new executive directors hired reported being "satisfied or very satisfied" with their new positions. This shows that the ETM process has been very beneficial for those that employed it. The organizations came out as a whole stronger, healthier, and more financially sound; *every* board respondent declared themselves as "optimistic" or "very optimistic about the futures of their agencies." One hundred percent satisfaction by the governing board is quite a testament to the power of the ETM process.[5]

As part of its learning about executive transition, The Annie E. Casey Foundation held separate consultative sessions with founder executive directors and board leaders or organizations with a founder executive director. This research highlighted that it was difficult for founders to decide when and how to leave. Moreover, it was equally challenging for their board leaders to balance respect for the founder's role and leadership with their own diligent oversight and guidance regarding the organization's direction and the founder's departure.

Using Don Tebbe's term of "Hard to Follow Executives," a study conducted by Managance Consulting with TransitionGuides indicated that over 30 percent of long-term executives and founders could be deemed as such. The experience of the collaborators and study authors, primarily Paige Hull Teegarden, Denice Rothman Hinden (both of Managance Consulting), and myself (TransitionGuides) "indicates organizations losing a long time executive or founder face particularly challenging issues during the transition."[6]

For over ten years, CompassPoint Nonprofit Services and TransitionGuides have been the leading providers and trainers of the ETM process for nonprofits. Between the two ETM providers, over 350 organizations have used the full ETM services. From the TransitionGuides and CompassPoint experience, approximately 85 percent of these organizations have hired an executive who has led the organization for three years or more. We do not have a study or a control group. However, as a proxy, the well-known *Daring to Lead* study indicates 33 percent of executives leave nonvoluntarily. If roughly 85 percent of ETM-hired executives are staying three years, we have some evidence that the ETM process is beating the odds at bringing on suitable executives.[7]

While the field is young and we lack clear-cut evaluative research, the commonsense case for investing in executive transition management is compelling. There is significant risk of failure in nonprofit leadership transition, and there is significant opportunity for the moment of leadership change to increase organizational capacity—even to transform the organization.

The rest of this chapter details the key decisions and introduces a step-by-step three-phase process (the ETM process). As the process steps are introduced, we will revisit our five types of transition and how the process adds value and improves outcomes for organizations. This chapter concludes with a summary of how the ETM approach advances leader development and the building of a leaderful organization.

Key Transition Decisions

Leaders of organizations facing a major leader transition have a lot of decisions to make. How these decisions get made will impact the success of the transition and the effectiveness of the organization. The biggest risk for organizations in transition is to ignore the basic facts about what is going on. These irrefutable facts will influence the transition whether attended to or not:[8]

- *Change* and *transition* are not synonyms! Change is the event and has a date certain. Transition is a process—an emotional and psychological process—that begins before the change and goes on long after it has occurred.

- There will be feelings associated with the transition. Ignoring the feelings can undermine the transition process.

- Getting to a positive beginning with a new leader requires attending as best as circumstances allow to a good ending with the departing leader and careful attention to the confusing and creative in-between time.

The big decisions that support attention to these influential facts can be organized into two types of decisions: 1) leadership decisions and actions, and 2) process decisions. Some are clearly one or the other; other decisions are a little bit of both. Let's examine these powerful decisions.

Leadership Decisions

Certain decisions about the positioning and roles of leaders in managing the transition process can have a profound impact on the outcomes of the transition. Later in this chapter, I describe processes that influence these decisions. Here we will focus on the decisions themselves.

Respecting and Connecting with the Departing Executive Executives leave for a variety of reasons: a new opportunity, retirement, time for a change, frustration with their current position, an unsatisfied board, or a dismissal. Regardless of the circumstance, it is the board's role to shape the ending (to the degree possible in the circumstances)—including an appropriate role for the departing executive in the transition process. This requires listening and getting behind the surface story to craft the best possible ending. It means crafting a plan for a positive ending as soon as possible. Announcing a search before this work is done is risky and often results in misunderstanding, feelings of disrespect by the executive, and a potentially abrupt or messy departure. Working out any financial decisions with the executive and planning an appropriate farewell and thanks are essential and often avoided or delayed critical steps. Messy endings do not speak well of the organization and can make it harder to attract great candidates.

Deciding Whether to Use an Interim Executive In some circumstances, the departing executive stays until the successor begins. In others, either because of the timing of the departure or the role of the departing executive (founder or hard-to-follow leader), an interim executive is needed. In certain situations, particularly where there is need for a repositioning, turnaround, or time for board and staff to let go of connections to a beloved founder, appointing an interim executive can greatly increase the transformative change that comes with transition. For this to happen, the organization must take care in defining the role and competencies of the interim and selecting an appropriate interim executive. Boards who take the shortcut of appointing a well-regarded staff member or board member without diligent consideration of the benefits of an external interim risk limiting or sabotaging the organization's future. There is no right or wrong decision; the important role of the board is to understand the possibilities and make a careful decision. (There are interim executives who are trained and specialize in this role in most communities and organized pools of interim executives in some communities and networks of nonprofits. The box "More on Interim Executives" and Appendix A have more information.)

MORE ON INTERIM EXECUTIVES

The nonprofit sector has adapted the interim pastor approach used in some religious faiths. In the church or religious congregation, the interim pastor is a bridge leader who assists the congregation in preparing to work successfully with a new pastor. The focus of the interim pastor's work is typically both interpersonal relationships with members and attention to organizational issues.

Interim executives carry out many different roles within a nonprofit organization, based on the need. In some instances, the interim is a caretaker leader to bridge the arrival of the next executive. For organizations with departing founders or long-tenured executives, the focus of the interim executive is on preparing the board and staff for a new leader and on organizational strengthening where needed. For organizations in crises or with a defined major issue, the interim is selected with skills in the areas that need attention before a new executive is hired.

Don Tebbe describes the potential roles of an interim executive in *Chief Executive Transitions* this way:

Contracting with an external interim executive who brings high-level skills and expertise to the organization can help the board tackle unique challenges related to the transition. In the right situation, the interim chief executive can potentially provide important benefits to the organization, such as:

- Conducting an organizational review or assessment that leads to greater clarity about strengths, weaknesses, challenges, and opportunities facing the organization and its new executive

- Helping the board clarify its vision and related present and future leadership needs for the organization

- Modeling appropriate executive behavior for the staff and board if the departing executive wasn't a particularly skilled or effective leader

- Helping the organization come to terms with its history, focusing attention on building on the organization's strengths while addressing weaknesses

- Providing the incoming executive with a skilled, knowledgeable mentor for the handoff process

Source: Tebbe, D. *Chief Executive Transitions: How to Hire and Support a Nonprofit CEO.* Washington, D.C.: BoardSource, 2008, p. 40.

Selecting a Transition and Search Committee Chair and Committee Members

Best practice is to focus on both the transition and search. As Don Tebbe wrote in *Chief Executive Transitions,* a successful search *does not* equal a successful transition. To increase the chances of success, the chair of the transition and search committee optimally has three key qualities:

- *Facilitation and communication skills.* The individual must patiently appreciate the process, its messiness, and uncertainties. She must listen completely and ensure sound decision making by the committee, and she must clearly communicate to the board, staff, and stakeholders. This committee is where unresolved or new questions about mission, strategy, and direction get aired and shaped for discussion with the board. Given the emotions of the process and its importance to the future, excellent facilitation skills are essential, including the capacity to build consensus among groups with diverging opinions, positions, and needs.

- *Deep knowledge of the mission, activities, and executive role.* Each transition is different. Understanding the past and future aspirations of the organization and how the role of the executive is evolving increases the likelihood of a successful hire.

- *Sufficient time and energy.* Leading a transition and search is intense. To many it feels like a part-time job. The committee chair can count on spending approximately six to eight hours a month for four to eight months on committee work plus two to three days on the interviewing and hiring process. Agreeing to the position without the available time is doing a great disservice to the organization. A bogged-down process frustrates the board, staff, and executive candidates and costs the organization time, money, and often access to great candidates.[9]

Once the chair is selected, attention to committee membership is equally important. Serving on the transition and search committee is one of the most powerful leader development opportunities there is in nonprofits. Committee members learn quickly about the organization's direction and goals, its strengths, and areas of growth, and they have an opportunity to shape the future via selection of the next executive. Serving on this committee is a great way to prepare to serve as board chair or to take on other important leadership roles in the future.

Involving the Board, Staff, and Stakeholders   Change brings uncertainty. Uncertainty can bring anxiety and fear. Each of us has our own way of dealing with uncertainty. Some ignore it. Others make it bigger and create drama or catastrophe in our minds or in our communication with others. Without involvement and consistent, clear communication, board, staff, and stakeholders become concerned and stories get created about what is going on. Besides the communication advantage, the appropriate involvement of board, staff, and stakeholders leads to better decisions about the future of the organization—any pivot it needs to make along with the transition—and the requirements of the next executive. It is the board chair and the board's responsibility to develop a transition plan that involves the full board, the staff, and the stakeholders in the process. Failure to involve a broad cross-section of the organization may result in hiring without clear priorities and expectations and without support from the rest of the board, staff, and key stakeholders. Furthermore, the new executive is often distracted by repairing relationships damaged during the poor transition process. Thus, an important consideration at the outset is how best to involve staff. For some organizations, a few staff are part of the transition committee, helping to ensure good staff communications and support. In other organizations, staff is involved at key points during the process. Similarly it is critical to be clear when the board will be involved and what authority is delegated to the transition and search committee.

Welcoming and Connecting with the New Executive Boards are sometimes weary by the time they have selected a new executive. Transition is time consuming and often ripe with energy-sapping emotions. If the organization has come through a difficult time, the board has the added stress of managing complex issues or a crisis. As a result, boards may be inclined either to pull back or abandon the new CEO. Or, if there has been a crisis, they may stay too involved and not fully empower the executive. These extremes undermine the success of the transition and result in slow and bumpy starts or a short tenure for the new executive. To avoid these extremes, the board should make sure there are some leaders responsible for welcoming and supporting the new executive. Small things like having a board leader welcome the new executive on her first day and introducing her to the staff make a lot of difference. Similarly, working with staff to develop a briefing notebook and a list of key relationships and offering to help with introductions also speeds up the relationship-building process.

Committing to an Organizational Review with Board, Staff, and Stakeholder Involvement Search firms typically interview some of the board, staff, and key stakeholders and use this information to develop a position or search profile. They focus on defining the competencies and attributes of the next leader given the challenges she will face. The transition approach has a critical difference: board and staff *shape* the priorities and direction and reach consensus on the required competencies. Here's another way to think of it: *executive search* is a human resources process, while *transition management* is an organizational development and human resources process. Thus good transition management includes time for an organizational review that builds on strategic and annual plans. Ultimately, this increases the odds for success and engages and empowers the organization's broader leadership team.

Attending to the New Executive's Success as the Months Go By   TransitionGuides experience and an unpublished exit survey of departing nonprofit executives I conducted while at NeighborWorks America reveal three reasons why executives leave prematurely:[10]

- The executive feels misled about the position; the work is not what he expected.
- The board and executive are not in alignment about the goals and direction.
- Compensation turns out to be unacceptable.

The organizational review process noted above, done *before* the search, combined with a social contracting process of clarifying priorities, expectations, and roles *after* the new executive is hired significantly reduce the risk of premature departure. There are a number of ways to do the social contracting (described later in this chapter). The important decision is a commitment by the board chair, board, and new executive to put in writing their expectations of one another and define success. This greatly enhances the likelihood of a positive and long relationship.

Process Decisions

The following are key decisions about process and the organization's approach to transition that are essential for success:

Not Rushing/Taking Time   It is normal to want to get out of a transition as quickly as possible. To do that, when one is informed an executive is leaving, the normal reaction is to think about possible successors and place an ad. Unfortunately, this perfectly normal instinct often leads to wrong hires and undermines the transformational power of leader transition. A consultant colleague is fond of saying that during transition "we make haste slowly." Rushing too much threatens the good ending with the outgoing executive; the appropriate engagement of board, staff, and stakeholders; and most important, the opportunity to consider the health and direction of the organization and make a decision on the future and the leadership team needed to head into that desired future.

Deciding to Focus on Both the Transition and the Search It is easy to give lip service to the need for the dual focus on transition and search. It is harder to actually do it. It is important that board and staff leaders discuss the difference between transition and executive search and clarify that they are committing to both. This commitment shapes the decisions about who leads various transition processes. More important, it will increase the benefits to the organization from the leader transition. Done well, the organization will be more focused and better led as a result.

Deciding on What Help the Leaders and Organization Need for a Successful Transition Until recently, most nonprofit organizations either managed the transition and search themselves or hired an executive search firm to do the search. The focus by national and local foundations over the past fifteen years on how to get better outcomes when nonprofit boards experience executive transition has significantly broadened the options. In many communities there are now consulting organizations (management support organizations) and consulting companies that specialize in executive transition management. These entities offer assistance with the transition planning and management and with the executive search. There are also numerous organizational development consultants who can bring independent skills in facilitation, organizational assessment, and relationship building to the transition and search. Because of their commitment to mission and the tendency to underestimate the complexity and opportunity of executive transition, many boards are reluctant to pay for consulting services. Experience shows that many organizations are successful in securing one-time grant support from their funders to support the transition and search process. Some boards are fortunate to have access to a facilitator who can assist pro bono. Where that doesn't exist, the cost of outside help is minimal when compared to the cost of time and money with a flawed or failed transition. (See Appendix B—also available online—for more on finding and selecting a consultant.)

The Executive Transition Process

Having looked at the most common types of transition and key decisions leader face, let's walk through the process. The executive transition management (ETM) process is best practice for organizations to attend well to both the transition and search. This model, as described in the process step summary found on the following pages is organized into three phases: Prepare, Pivot, and Thrive.

The *Prepare* phase involves planning for the transition, conducting the organizational review, and planning the search. The *Pivot* phase focuses on successfully completing the search and making progress on any agreed-on capacity-building goals that will improve the odds of the new executive succeeding. The *Thrive* phase ensures a positive entry for the new executive by attention to welcome, orientation, priorities, roles, and performance accountability. What follows summarizes the steps in each phase and then offers a few illustrations of the model's application in different types of transitions. Examples of worksheets and tools used in the process are found in Appendix A (also available online). For a more detailed treatment of the ETM process, see *Chief Executive Transitions: How to Hire and Support a Nonprofit CEO* (Tebbe, 2008) and *Managing Executive Transitions: A Guide for Nonprofits* (Wolfred, 2009).

The Prepare Phase

The way things begin is often the way they end. A rushed hire often results in a short tenure and the need to hire again. The Prepare phase calls attention to the key decisions and actions that reduce this risk. Furthermore, the Prepare phase increases the gains in capacity and leader development for the organization during and after transition. The investment in the Prepare phase may lead to transformational change and greater mission impact. This is accomplished by doing the following:

Planning the departure, transition timeline, and departure communication. A well-managed transition starts well by ensuring the departing executive and board clarify the departure plan, the executive's role during transition, and how and when the departure will be announced. This is important to the organization in having the good ending described above. (There may be poor consequences if, in contrast, word of imminent departure leaks out without a message.) The transition timeline is worked out through discussions between the executive, the board, the transition committee, and any outside consultant; these groups assess how much time is needed for each of the three phases given the circumstances of this transition. Typically the period from departure announcement to new executive selection takes four to six months, sometimes longer. In situations where the departure is positive, a decision is made fairly early about how to best say good-bye and thanks to the departing executive.

Deciding who is in charge. As noted above, selection of the transition and search committee chair and committee and agreement on the committee's charge is a key decision. Vagueness about who will make the ultimate hiring decision and the roles of the transition and search committee, board, and in some cases the executive committee creates confusion and undermines the process. Additionally, the organization must decide if an interim executive is needed, for what purpose, and when.

Announcing the transition. Typically it works best to announce the departure to the board, staff, and key stakeholders within a one- or two-day period. The guiding principle is to be sure key figures are informed directly rather than secondhand. A carefully orchestrated set of phone calls to key funders and stakeholders and back-to-back board and staff announcements work well to accomplish this goal.

Reviewing the organization and its direction. Lack of alignment between all the board members and the staff threatens an organization's ability to hire and retain an effective executive. The focus and intensity of the organizational review depends on how recently the organization has taken stock through strategic planning or a similar process; contrary to some board members' apprehensions, it does not need to be an overly long review.

Building on available data, the review typically takes six weeks or less. Using input from the board, staff, and usually some key stakeholders or customers, the review uncovers:

- Perceptions of the organization's effectiveness and health
- Primary customers or clients
- Organizational strengths
- Perceived challenges for the organization and new leader
- Values or practices to be preserved
- Programs or practices to be discontinued during the transition or permanently
- Twelve- to eighteen-month and three-year priorities and success measures
- Key competencies and attributes of the next executive

Stabilizing the situation. Sometimes the review reveals that the organization is not ready to begin a search or finalize its position profile. There are pressing critical issues that require attention before the organization is stable enough to attract qualified candidates and begin a new relationship with an executive. A major budget deficit or funding crisis, a scandal involving a board or staff member, and a sudden departure of one or more key staff or board members in an already unstable situation are among the most common reasons organizations need to slow the search down and invest time in stabilizing the organization. This often requires an interim executive or outside assistance with expertise in the area of crisis.

Aligning Board and Staff—Strategic Leadership Planning Session

Each organization has its way of planning. Building on that experience, it is important that staff and board have the opportunity to have a conversation about the direction and top priorities for the organization. Without this conversation, there is a high risk that in the interview and after being hired the prospective executive will receive mixed messages about what is important, often resulting in a short tenure. This is typically done by a strategy and leadership review session with the board in a half-day or full-day meeting. Often staff (or senior staff for a larger organization) hold their own planning session prior to the board session and participate in part of the meeting with the board. The board has some executive session time to complete its planning of direction and requirements for the next executive.

Exploring the Culture and Diversity Considerations Important to Success

The discussion of leadership requirements involves understanding the current values of the organization and how these values are manifested in day-to-day behaviors and decisions. Each organization has a set of habits, patterns of behavior that shape what the organization is and what it feels like to be a leader there. Top leadership change is a great time to review these habits and see what is working and what changes current leaders aspire to.

One area in which organizations have a conscious or unconscious way of operating is around how difference—in background, age or generation, race, class, sexual orientation, physical ability—is addressed (or not addressed). For example, some organizations espouse a value of diversity but consistently hire and recruit leaders who look like the dominant group. Each organization has a community or constituency to serve. Attention to leader diversity and inclusiveness is known to influence mission capacity. For that reason part of the leadership planning conversation is about what inclusiveness and diversity needs are in play and how the organization and search committee will ensure attention to these needs in its outreach and in welcoming the new executive. Leadership transition is the perfect time to review the realities of who is involved in leadership and how representative the leaders of the board and staff are of the communities and constituencies served. (Leadership transition offers many leverage points for improving diversity and inclusiveness. See Chapter Four for specific guidance.)

Finalizing the Position Profile and Search Plan

Writing down the results of the strategy and leadership planning gives everyone an opportunity to review and sign off on the important pieces of communication to candidates. These results are the description of the organization and its history, the direction and priorities, and the competencies and attributes required for the next executive. This typically results in a three- to four-page position or search summary used with candidates. A shorter one-page announcement is used to market the position. (See Appendix A for examples.)

Prepare Phase Examples

To help you better understand what the Prepare phase feels like, the following fictionalized examples show how the phase unfolds in each of the five types of transitions introduced at the beginning of this chapter: Sustained Success, Hard-to-Follow Executive, Underperforming Organization, Turnaround, and First Hire. (These examples will be continued through the next two phases of the ETM process.)

Sustained Success—Shelters Midwest served homeless people in the Midwest. It had developed a steady flow of contributions from individuals, foundations, and government and had a strong and aligned board and staff. Homeless Midwest used the Prepare phase to better understand their strengths and to look at where they would be vulnerable during transition. They also discussed expectations of the new executive and developed three priorities that were important, doable, and possible for a new executive in the first year. Having done this careful planning *before* they hired an executive, this organization was able to serve more homeless people and expand its role in advocacy over the next five years. Without this preparation, the risk of a downturn and a much longer road back to past success would have been increased.

Underperforming Organization—Northeast Wellpeople was a mental health nonprofit agency. It looked strong and vibrant. The executive was well known and had won a major regional award for outstanding leadership. Government agencies trusted the executive and awarded contracts based on that trust. However, in the last three years of his tenure, the state agency that provided much of the funding initiated performance-based allocation of funding. The agency received warnings and requests for improvements in care. Shortly after the executive gave notice of his intention to leave, the state agency asked for a meeting with the board and reviewed the list of deficiencies in service and suggested that funding might be reduced by as much as 30 percent without immediate change. The board used the Prepare phase to better understand the deficiencies, to assess staff capacity to address them, and to develop with the outgoing executive a new senior management structure. This resulted in the hiring of a new chief operating officer from among a pool of two internal and three external candidates. An internal candidate was selected. The board made this hire before the new executive was hired based on the need to respond immediately to the state agency. By taking these actions while preparing for transition, the agency rebuilt its positive reputation with the government funders and was able to attract a stronger pool of candidates for the executive position than would have been possible with declining funding and lack of confidence from its primary funder.

Turnaround—Southwest Arts had been consistently struggling to keep its doors open. When the third executive left in five years, the board called a time-out. They engaged a local consultant to better understand what they needed to do differently in preparing for a hire to be successful. Fund-raising, board development, and poor service delivery were identified as the main barriers to success. During the Prepare phase, the board stepped up and committed to raise enough money to keep the organization operating for two years to allow time for transition and for a new executive to build relations and get oriented. This was a major change for the board. Until then, they had relied heavily on the executive and staff to lead the fund-raising. With this commitment in place, the board hired an interim executive with skills in fund development and management for one year. During this time, the organization exceeded its fund-raising goal, recruited three new board members who could assist with fund-raising, and completed the Prepare phase. The final step in the Prepare phase was a strategy and leadership session in which board and staff discussed what funders and customers valued about the organization and finalized a vision and top priorities for the next three to five years. The new executive has served for seven years, and the organization is the statewide leader in creative program design and delivery.

First Hire—BetterParks South was an all-volunteer organization focused on park improvements in the South. It was moving from an all-volunteer effort to hiring its first executive. The organization was fifteen years old, so the volunteers were very experienced in getting the work done. As the organization grew, the work was outstripping the volunteer capacity. A large grant from a regional corporation and gifts by board members were financing the hiring of an executive and an administrative assistant. The Prepare phase focused on this big change from volunteer to staff and what it would mean for the volunteers and for the executive and staff. This phase was also used to learn more from volunteers about what they valued and any concerns the volunteers had about the growth of the organization. This work informed both the requirements for the executive and the message to candidates in interviews. By thinking ahead with the board and volunteers about what they wanted to preserve and what role they wanted the new executive to play, the staff was able to hire an executive who stayed five years and grew the organization. Without such preparation, it is common for volunteers to struggle with letting go and for the first executive's tenure to be short.

Hard-to-Follow Executive—World Village Builders was a large international development organization in the West. It was facing the retirement of its founder and executive of thirty-five years. While the board had expected her retirement for some time, it took them three months to organize a search committee after the executive informed them of her intention to retire in a year. Once the board got over its shock, it became zealous about the transition. The executive committee made up of six board members and the past board chair led the transition planning and Prepare phase. Three of the executive committee members also served on the search committee. The executive committee used the transition preparation time to review the finances and sources of revenue, meet personally with the executive with their top ten contributors, and survey members and staff to get input on what was important for a successful transition. This stepped-up involvement by the board and increased communication with the staff reduced anxiety and allowed the organization to make the change to a new executive without stumbling. Organizations with long-term executives or founders who rush to hire a new executive without any attention to what people are feeling and the impact of the change on the organization's relationships in the community risk taking a Hard-to-Follow Transition and making it into a Turnaround.

The Pivot Phase

The Pivot phase builds on the Prepare phase. If the Prepare work is done well, the leaders of the organization have the necessary information to make two major decisions that define their "pivot":

- What does organizational success look like three to five years from now and what are our twelve- to eighteen-month priorities to achieve that success?

- What competencies and attributes do we need in our executive and board and staff leadership team to achieve these priorities and head toward our vision of success?

There are two sets of activities in this phase: 1) the *search,* which is the burning issue for most board leaders and the singular focus of a search firm; and 2) *organizational strengthening,* which is the unique opportunity for change and transformation that the ETM approach offers. The outcome of the activities that constitute this phase is to position the organization for the desired "pivot" by strengthening the organization while carrying out an executive search that produces a pool of finalists meeting the leadership requirements and attributes defined in the Prepare phase.

Organizational Strengthening

As noted earlier, this chapter provides an overview of the ETM process, not a step-by-step guide. The intensity and type of internal strengthening will determine the process steps. If the organization is not ready to successfully recruit a new executive until certain issues are addressed, the process may include an agreed-on slowing or delay of the search. This allows time for the board and staff to take the actions needed to position the organization for a successful search and hiring. Where a financial crisis or major system weakness exists that would derail the new executive, it is critical that this time-out and capacity building occur.

More typically where the organizational strengthening does not threaten the success of the search, the process steps include the following:

- The transition committee reviews the findings of the organizational self-assessment and decides which issues need attention before the new executive is hired and which ought to wait. The committee also clarifies what the priority issues are for either timeline.

- The priority issues to be addressed before the new executive is hired are assigned to board committees or staff with milestones and reporting expectations.

- The transition committee reviews the progress on issues monthly and prepares a short report for the new executive on key issues, progress, and expectations of the new executive in the first ninety days relative to these issues.

- The transition committee and new executive meet in the first thirty days and agree on the priorities for the executive and board to include in their six-month work plans.

- The ninety-day check-in and six-month review of the new executive include attention to priority transition issues as agreed.

Highlighted here are some of the key issues that arise during organizational strengthening.

Attending to the Transition Issues   In the Prepare phase, the organizational review sharpens the picture of the strengths of the organization and the areas where change is desired. The change agenda usually includes items that are critical and have to be done now, items that the new executive would appreciate not having to deal with, and items that are important but should best wait until the new executive is on board. The challenge for the board and staff is that it is difficult to stay focused on the right issues with all the extra activity and uncertainty that come with leadership change.

For that reason, in most cases the transition committee takes responsibly for being the gatekeeper (and nag) about key issues. If an organization is financially struggling, the committee keeps an eye on progress toward strengthening financial health. In some organizations, this means having a leader from the development committee and one from the finance committee on the transition committee. These leaders keep the committee informed about progress. In other organizations, the executive committee is the place where most issues get addressed. In that case, one or two members of the executive committee serve on the transition committee so there is coordination and communication. The point is to be able to accurately inform candidates about the organization and to make any possible changes that will strengthen the organization and its appeal in attracting and retaining top candidates.

The transition committee reviews the list of issues and decides which need attention and which leaders or committees to address. The committee makes sure progress is reported to the staff and board and makes any adjustment in priorities as the situation unfolds.

Making Tough Choices Many transitions involve difficult decisions as the process unfolds. An obvious area is what to do about managers or key employees who chronically underperform or whose strong personality has been managed by the departing executive. The guiding principle here is: "What is best for the organization?" Organizations with human services or social change missions sometimes find it hard to terminate employees who are by all standards underperforming and for whom finding a comparable job and salary may be challenging. Departing executives give their successors a great gift by dealing with any unresolved personnel issues before they go, as determining who is underperforming will be much more difficult for the successor and a major distraction. The transition committee can serve as a sounding board for the executive in addressing challenging questions like those related to personnel.

Similarly, during some transitions managers who have been thinking of moving on may begin to actively search—and eventually they do depart. This can be devastating when one or more of these managers is key to the organization. In some organizations, incentives are offered to key managers to stay for the first year or so of the new executive. (This is highly situational as the board does not want to limit choices for the new executive.)

When a key manager does depart, the executive typically consults with the transition committee about the decision to hire or not. In normal times, the executive makes this decision on her own. During a transition, it is important to consult the board. This discussion focuses on the advantages of waiting and letting the new executive hire and build her team versus the cost to the organization of waiting. There is no right or wrong answer; it depends on what is best for the organization.

Clarifying Future Priorities for Action   Effective leaders continuously balance both the degree of change and its timing. Some executives and boards want to deal with twenty years of deferred maintenance in a few months. Others want to solve the one biggest issue that has confounded the organization forever. Yet others want the organization to continue without any change. The transition committee, often with consultant help or a facilitator leader from the board or allied organization, paces the attention to issues and the change agenda. This includes providing guidance to the board about priorities for the new executive in the first six to twelve months of tenure. When, for instance, should the next strategic planning process be undertaken? Does it need immediate attention from the new executive or is it best deferred for a year or so to provide time for the executive to better understand the organization, its people, and work? How about the ramping up of a major capital campaign or beginning online fundraising? Effective board leaders guide the organization and work as a partner with the departing and incoming executives around these decisions.

Executive Search

Successful hiring is part science, part art, and part luck. If you have done a lot of hiring, your own experience will inform your beliefs about the mix. I have not met anyone who has done hiring who hasn't made an inappropriate hire. The pricey executive search industry would not exist and be so resilient even in tough economic times if there weren't risk in search and selection. Private sector boards protect their risk by hiring a handful of prestigious search firms. Nonprofit organizations manage the risk by networking and trial-and-error. With a third or more nonprofit executives resigning involuntarily, hiring is clearly an imperfect art.

As noted, there are a number of excellent books that detail the search and hiring process for a nonprofit executive. They include Don Tebbe's *Chief*

Executive Transitions and Wolfred's *Managing Executive Transitions.* Tom Gilmore wrote the classic on this topic, *Making Leadership Change,* which is also a useful resource. Readers should best consult these publications for the details of a search. What follows are a few key issues that in our experience can make or break a search. The key process steps during an executive search include the following:

- The board, staff, and any key stakeholders ensure that the position and the required competencies are clearly defined and agreed to.

- The search committee launches an aggressive networking and outreach campaign that reaches a broad and racially diverse mix of people who will refer candidates, leaders, and potential applicants.

- The committee reviews all applicants against the agreed-on competencies and ranks them as "definitely consider," "maybe consider," and "not qualified."

- The board committee completes interviews and reference checks and narrows the field to one to three finalists.

- The finalists meet with staff, have a second interview with the committee, and may meet informally with other board members or stakeholders.

- The search committee recommends one finalist to the board, and the board accepts or rejects the finalist.

- The board chair is authorized to negotiate and finalize a written hire offer to the selected finalist with appropriate legal review of the offer.

- The board and staff begin planning for on-boarding and the welcome and orientation of the new executive.

Clarity About Successful Candidates Most boards are highly skilled at developing a position description and profile for their next executive. In sum, all boards want "God on a good day." The thoughtful search committee goes deeper and works to understand the behaviors and experiences that are important to the situation a leader will face. Some search firms develop a set of organizational challenges and work backward to sharpen the picture of the competencies and personality needed to be successful. It is quite easy for even the most experienced employer to be distracted and snowed by a highly skilled and personable interviewer: presence and charm are important attributes of a leader, but they are not enough. In work with search committees, our consultants seek to ensure clarity about the four or five executive characteristics critical to success. If the organization needs a turnaround, then the capacity to be strategic and decisive is critical; an otherwise solid leader who is too methodical and incremental will fail in such a situation. Once clear about the characteristics of success, behavioral interviewing (tell me about a time when you . . .) helps identify the candidates you want to consider.

Allow Enough Time to Network Most boards and their staff are in a hurry to fill the executive position. It makes sense. There is a lot of uncertainty, and the organization will run better when the right leader is fully on board. Most searches take four to six months. The best candidates often don't apply right away. Rushing the process runs the risk of missing great candidates. Achieving a racially diverse pool for organizations with predominantly white leaders will take more time. Effective searching is about social networking. It is not about advertising or being on the right Web site, although those actions can help. Effective searches have an organized approach to personally reaching out to extensive and racially diverse networks of leaders to ensure a talented and diverse finalist pool. It's better to spend four to six weeks more than a board had hoped to spend and get the executive you want and need than to rush and settle or fail.

Avoid Perfectionism, Overcompensating, or Settling Hiring involves risk management. Some companies and nonprofit boards manage risk by hiring leaders with Ivy League credentials. If you made it through there, the thinking goes, you can do most anything. Wrong. Success in school is an indicator of intelligence, ability to write, and ability to focus. While these are all very helpful traits, they may or may not be enough to lead your nonprofit at this critical time.

Most nonprofits don't hold out for Ivy League candidates. However, there are three related risks that are more prevalent for nonprofits. One is to hold out for the perfect candidate. Boards without much experience in nonprofit hiring may look for a level of experience either the organization can't afford or can't attract. There is a mismatch between the vision of the perfect candidate and the health, finances, and standing of the organization and its ability to attract those candidates. Holding out for a perfect candidate while rejecting candidates who can succeed undermines some searches.

The opposite behavior—desperately or impatiently settling for a candidate who does not meet your requirements—is equally risky and costly. This usually leads to an extended period of underperformance by the organization or a second search within a year or two.

In other situations, boards manage risk by overcompensating for the perceived weakness of the departing executive or the most pressing issue of the organization. Typical lines of thought in such cases are: "We were ineffective as a lobbyist so let's hire an attorney who is a skilled lobbyist as executive." "Our finances are a mess. We trust our CFO. Let's hire the CFO as executive." "We need to raise more money to survive. We don't know her well, but the new development director is bright and energetic; let's make her the executive." Though these decisions *may* work out, more is left to chance. The current deficit is only one of the issues the organization faces. Although the skilled attorney-lobbyist-executive may indeed correct the organization's lobbying deficits, it's a matter of chance as to whether he or she can lead the organization to a bigger future (if that future includes more than lobbying).

When a board is overcompensating, the risk of stalling the future growth of the organization is high; hence the importance of understanding the long-term needs of the organization as well as its current deficits—which is why such deficits should be addressed (or remedial plans developed) during the organizational strengthening portion of the Pivot phase.

Be Organized and Clear About Your Offer Boards in which power and authority are not clear have a hard time closing the deal with the finalist. It is important to be clear about the offer—salary, benefits, start date, and any other important considerations, like the role (if any) of the outgoing executive—and decide what authority the board chair or search chair has to negotiate. If there is a consultant involved, she can assist in brokering a win-win agreement without straining relationships. Hard negotiations at hiring often lead to unexpressed concerns or resentments and undermine the building of a positive relationship. A legal review is essential for any offer letter or contract before it is made. (Most nonprofit executives do not have contracts unless they are in an association or industry where that is a common practice.)

Pivot Phase Examples

To help you better understand what the Pivot phase feels like, the following examples show how the phase unfolds in each of the five types of transitions introduced at the beginning of this chapter: Sustained Success, Hard-to-Follow Executive, Underperforming Organization, Turnaround, and First Hire.

Sustained Success—Shelters Midwest, as noted earlier, had enjoyed enduring success. During the Prepare phase, it found that its infrastructure was solid and its strengthening requirements amounted to tweaking and updating. The executive and the board chair or a member of the development committee met personally with all the funders and government agencies to update them on the transition and request continued support. The major infrastructure change was a shift to new customer relations software, completed ably during the Pivot phase by the skilled staff. The search was led by the five-person transition and search committee. The transition consultant provided staffing support to the committee and was the list keeper for outreach. Outreach was the responsibility of the committee. Two members of the committee hosted teleseminars with social networks to which they belonged to increase the diversity of the pool. There were three finalists; the board selected an advocacy attorney who had been chief operating officer for a nonprofit in the community.

Underperforming Organization—Northeast Wellpeople, after years of success, had fallen into decline; government agencies that contracted with the organization gave a serious warning that they might soon send business elsewhere. During the Prepare phase, the organization had focused on understanding the concerns of the funding government agencies and on assessing staff capacity to address the concerns. In the Pivot phase, the organization began to address those concerns, so the incoming executive would be less burdened by them. The chief operating officer, who had been appointed at the end of the Prepare phase, led a staff task force and worked with the transition committee to oversee this work. Because of the nature of the organization's problems, the transition committee included two staff and three stakeholders from outside the organization who represented consumers and government. Because of its size, the board decided to have a search subcommittee of five persons. This search committee managed the search with help from a pro bono HR consultant who served on the board. Outreach was focused on comparable agencies in the region and produced a pool of four finalists.

Turn Around—Southwest Arts used its year with an interim executive to address a crisis of confidence by funders and customers. This was achieved by organizing a group of well-respected leaders as an advisory group and engaging their assistance in strengthening the fund-raising capacity and improving the quality of the productions. This resulted in the board meeting its commitment to raise two years of operating funding, recruitment of four new and energized board members from the advisory committee, and four sold-out events with positive publicity. Given the interim executive's knowledge of the arts community, she supported the board's search process through her own expansive network. The search committee was a nine-member committee with three members from the board, three from the advisory committee, and three from the community. The committee referred two finalists to the board who selected between the two.

First Hire—BetterParks South had completed its Prepare phase by sorting out which duties would still be done by volunteers and which by the new executive and staff. A volunteer appreciation party was organized by the transition committee at which the "old days of all volunteers" was celebrated and the new era with staff was introduced through a humorous skit. Involving key volunteers in the skit deepened their understanding and commitment to the change in roles. The search focused on environmental leaders from the region. Managed by the transition committee, it resulted in five semifinalists and the referral of one candidate to the board.

Hard-to-Follow Executive—World Village Builders completed its Prepare phase with the realization that its key issues were 1) strengthening the financial system, and 2) building funder and stakeholder confidence in the organization independent of the departing founder executive. During the Pivot phase, the organization reorganized its board finance committee and appointed a new chair. It added a comptroller under the CFO to increase capacity to stay current with and understand organizational finances. With the founder executive, the transition committee developed a list of ten funders and six government agencies critical to long-term success. Board members and senior staff organized a series of group and one-on-one meetings with these stakeholders. The search was led by the five-member transition committee and was staffed jointly by the transition consultant and an executive search consultant. Given the unique pool of people working and living internationally the board wanted to reach, they retained a search consultant with expertise in international recruiting to work with the transition consultant who facilitated all three phases of the transition. This approach resulted in a positive ending for the founder and an ethnically and racially diverse pool of six semifinalists who met with senior staff and the board. One finalist was eventually hired to take over for the beloved founder.

The Thrive Phase

The mystics have a saying that "the way things begin is the way they will end." The Quakers have a slightly different perspective when they say: "The way will open." Successfully beginning a new relationship between an executive and a board and staff is a balance of both of these views. It is part science and part art, like the entire transition process. The Thrive phase is marked by the engagement and, hopefully, success of the new executive.

The two biggest risks organizations face as a new executive enters and takes charge are:

1. Overreliance on the new executive, sometimes bordering on abandonment by the board

2. Failure to make room for the "pivot" and to act as if nothing has changed

The new executive walks a tightrope of needing to appear confident and capable and at the same time admitting the need to learn and adapt to a new organization and position.[11] Executives who are not by nature extroverts or lean heavily on technical expertise in exercising leadership may underinvest time in relationship building. This is dangerous, potentially fatal, for it is the quality of the relationships with the board and direct reports that will limit or enhance the potential for success. Since over 60 percent of new executives have never been a nonprofit executive before, finding this balance can be challenging.[12]

The board's challenge is to provide guidance and an orientation to the new executive while making room for the new leader to lead staff and enter into a partnership with the board that will look and feel different from the relationship with the previous executive.

The direct reports and staff want to get to know the new executive and figure out what the new leadership means to their day-to-day responsibilities.

Negotiating this web of relationships successfully so that it optimizes success for the organization and leaders is the work of the Thrive phase. Because in the writer's experience this is the hardest part of the process to do consistently well, what follows looks at the mechanics of a process that advances the change desired in the organization and a positive entry for the executive. There are four key components to a successful executive entry and Thrive phase: 1) plan for and facilitate a positive beginning; 2) ensure clarity of goals, roles, and expectations between the board and the new executive; 3) offer support to the new executive; and 4) establish a performance review process and agreement about mutual accountability between the board and the executive. Let's examine each component.

Plan for and Facilitate a Positive Beginning

The nonprofit executive director position is very challenging. For-profit executives who cross over report amazement at the complexity of the challenges, skills required, and the limits of resources and power. Sixty to seventy percent of nonprofit executives are in this top leadership position for the first time. From a risk management point of view, it makes sense for the board to pay careful attention to a positive beginning in their relationship with the new executive.

Unfortunately, this logical decision to pay attention to the new executive entry is offset by the emotional tug to withdraw, by fatigue from the hiring process, and by the added pressures and demands of transition. Board leaders are typically more engaged during the Prepare and Search process. Staff also are often doing extra duty due to the executive transition. As Bridges reminds us in describing the neutral zone, everyone is a little off balance and anxious. It takes a decision and commitment by the board leaders to pay attention to the new executive entry for it to go well. The alternative is the familiar: "Welcome aboard. Here are the keys to the office. The restroom is over there. Have at it."

Fortunately there are some practical actions that support a positive entry for the new executive. One of the most appreciated and simplest is to prepare a briefing book or orientation CD that makes it easy for the executive to learn about the organization. Such a "file" typically includes organizational documents (bylaws, articles, membership agreements, or other relevant documents); budgets and financial reports; fund-raising and funding information and contracts or agreements; a list of key leaders to meet with and get to know; personnel information and organizational charts; board and staff lists; an annual calendar of key events and deadlines; and so forth.

A second practical action is to assign a board leader and staff member to pay attention to helping the new executive learn about the community (if the executive is relocating or commuting a distance). Such assistance can be tailored to the executive's specific needs and may include neighborhood orientations, house hunting assistance, and connections to services needed in settling into the community like schools or day care providers. Most new executives warmly receive early acts of hospitality.

The orientation book should also provide a road map to the key relationships required for success. This includes key funders, government leaders, collaborators, and others. This speeds up the most important new executive responsibility: building positive relationships.

The first day is another opportunity to extend a welcome. For example, a board member should come by the office and welcome the new executive to join a breakfast or lunch hosted by the staff. This simple practical step says "we are glad you are here."

Finally, the organization should host a series of meet-and-greet events that introduce the new executive and speed up forming important relationships. A subset of the transition committee working with senior staff or (if appropriate) the departing executive can think through what's the best mix of small events and one or two larger community events. The new executive will have a point of view and ought to be consulted in finalizing these plans. Done well, they speed up the entry and support attention to the pivot that the organization desires.

Ensure Clarity of Goals, Roles, and Expectations Between the Board and the New Executive

Agreement about what is important is essential for a good beginning. During the hiring process, the board and (potential) new executive should discuss how to best develop a ninety-day work plan. If the new executive knows the organization, she may take the lead in developing the work plan. If new to the organization, the committee (with help from a consultant if one is involved) might prepare a draft for the new executive to review and amend. The work plan provides the board with an opportunity to emphasize the importance of relationship building and to communicate to the executive support for making time for this activity. First-time executives often tend to put off relationship building—at their own peril. Making it a key objective in the work plan reinforces its importance.

Typically the transition committee (or a posthire subcommittee or the executive committee) works with the new executive to provide both support and direction about priorities. For new executives, regular communication with the committee chair and meetings every two to three weeks with this small committee as a sounding board can be very helpful. The exact nature of the support is negotiated between the executive and the committee. For more experienced executives, it will be different and less intense. Either way, providing a forum for the executive to meet and build consensus with the board on goals for the first year with six-month milestones and expectations about the roles of the executive, board, and staff in achieving these goals is a key early step. As this clarity takes shape, the board is involved in reviewing, amending, and ratifying the agreement, sometimes referred to as a *social contract*.[13]

Finally, the new executive should clarify communication expectations with board chair, board, direct reports, and staff. The goal should be to ensure agreement on how important information is communicated.

Offer Support to the New Executive

Taking the steps above helps the new executive craft a working partnership with the board and reduces the sense of isolation that comes with the executive position. Board leaders who acknowledge there is a lot to learn and there are multiple priorities help relieve some of the inevitable pressure of a new position. Recognizing that we all learn differently and being patient with the executive's learning process is also helpful.

This may be the first time the executive has worked for a board. It certainly is her first time working for this particular board. Boards don't always speak or act with one voice. The activities mentioned above—especially frequent and regular meetings with the board chair and a small entry committee for the first few months—are important ways of supporting the new executive.

Encourage the new executive to learn by visiting peer organizations, attending national or regional meetings, or doing other activities that speed up the learning curve unique to that executive and provide opportunities to develop a support network external to the organization. Some executives may be hesitant to take time away from the office, so encouraging such activities in the first ninety-day work plan and budget is helpful. For others, perhaps more experienced and practiced, all that is needed is understanding and support for this time away from the office.

Another small shift that advances the practice of leader development is to make sure there is a professional and organizational development line item in the budget. Executive coaching works best when it is not seen as a remedial effort for the struggling, but rather a learning tool for leaders. Similarly organizations and executives benefit from outside consultants with expertise in organizational development during times of change. Budgeting for these and other learning opportunities by the executive and organization supports the positive entry and a leaderful organization practice.

Establish a Performance Review Process and Agreement About Mutual Accountability Between the Board and Executive

Creating a positive learning environment and a performance review system that is focused on growth and development as opposed to a scorecard of successes and failures is challenging for any organization. For nonprofits, where a volunteer board reviews performance, this challenge becomes more acute. The result is a range of practices from no evaluation to a superficial board chair review to a comprehensive review with input from the board, staff, and stakeholders.

Before the executive begins, the transition or post-hire committee takes a look at how the executive performance review has been done in the past and what worked and what didn't. At the same time, the board looks at board self-assessment and how well the board pays attention to accountability and learning.

Once that is done, the first step is to agree on a process for an informal check-in on executive progress and performance after ninety days. Typically the executive and the board committee discuss progress on the work plan, how the relationship feels, and the degree of mutual satisfaction with communication and support. This conversation, sometimes facilitated by a transition consultant, provides needed feedback to the executive and learning to inform the next ninety days.

At the end of this ninety-day check-in conversation, typically there is a discussion to review the agreement about how the six-month review will be handled and any implications for the compensation of the executive. Sometimes there is a salary adjustment after six months; other times it comes after the first-year review. If it has not happened before this meeting, a time is set for a specific discussion of the performance review system for the executive. In addition, the board discusses how it will measure its own performance as well as its future needs for leadership, talent, and annual self-assessment.

Paying attention to these key steps is difficult because of the compelling pressure to deal with organizational priorities and crises. Though it is possible to set the steps aside and come back to them in the future, more often organizations set the steps aside and forget about them. That's unfortunate, because inattention to the steps above reduces success. In contrast, attending to each step, regardless of other organizational imperatives, builds positive long-term relationships and the clarity of focus that leads to more mission results.

Examples of the Thrive Phase by Transition Type

Sustained Success—The new executive for Shelters Midwest (the homeless organization) had been a chief operating officer of another nonprofit in the community and was an attorney. His entry challenge was learning about Shelters Midwest and adjusting to being the executive for the first time. His training and experience made learning the operational aspects of the new position relatively easy. He knew the external relationship building and fundraising would be new roles and a big change for him. He asked the chair of the development committee to meet with him biweekly for the first three months to speed up his learning. He also joined a new executive's brown bag group hosted by his trade association and signed up for a course in development that began in month three. He found some of the ways that the organization did things different from his experience. He decided that most of them didn't matter and picked out three changes he thought would improve results to explore with the board and staff. His openness and the willingness of the board to have a discussion about goals and roles resulted in a positive start.

Underperforming Organization—Northeast Wellpeople had three challenges in its post-hire process:

- The chief operating officer had served as interim executive. He now had to step back to the COO role (which itself was a relatively new role for him). This meant that the new executive and the COO had to clarify their respective roles and build a positive relationship between each other, as well as with the board.

- The government agencies with which Northeast Wellpeople had lost credibility needed intensive contact as well as documentation of improved results. The new executive focused on continuing to meet the commitments to government agencies and rebuilding credibility.

- The board and staff had formed strong bonds while overcoming the crisis of underperformance. Now the organization had to make psychic room for the executive to provide leadership and new ideas while maintaining the power of the deepened board and staff relationship.

The executive and board focused on these issues through continued work with the transition consultant. The entry process and relationship-building activities were all designed to achieve these three goals. This resulted in a positive entry for the executive and a successful transformation into a positively performing organization. Gradually, government agencies, funders, and others reported improved satisfaction, and the organization's reputation followed suit.

Turn Around—Southwest Arts's board, staff, and stakeholders were delighted with the work of the interim executive to address a crisis of confidence by funders and customers. The staff had encouraged the board to offer the position to the interim, which they did. He was not interested. He attempted to engage the board and staff in discussions to prepare them for working with the new executive. These conversations had limited impact. The new executive was a proven fund-raiser. In his first three months he focused heavily on sustaining the fund-raising that had been started by the interim executive. He invested limited time in getting to know board and staff. Most of his interaction with staff was in meetings or about fund-raising. By his third-month anniversary, there was significant grumbling from the staff and from board members who were not involved in fund-raising. The board chair confronted the executive about the concerns. At first he was hurt and angry. After a weekend to reflect, he called the board chair, acknowledged he needed to look at the concerns, and told the board chair he had found an executive coach he would like to hire. Through work with the coach, he was able to back up. He recognized that a significant gap in his work had been the necessity of building relationships with all staff, board, and stakeholders, not just those involved in development activities. After some time, he gained the confidence of these groups and began to have success beyond his role in fund-raising.

First Hire—During the Pivot phase, BetterParks South had had focused on helping its all-volunteer staff prepare for their changing roles. The board treasurer was a retired mail carrier who spent a part of each day in the office. As treasurer, he had attended diligently to the budget. When the new executive started, the treasurer continued to come in daily to review and approve spending. At first the executive saw this as helpful. By the second month, he found himself arguing with the treasurer about every expense and check. The new executive was experiencing a similar difficulty with the volunteer who had always run the "Auction in the Park" fund-raiser, who tried to work closely with the executive but could not let go of doing things the way she had always done them. The executive brought these concerns to the board chair, who listened, smiled, and said: "Change is hard." The executive raised his concerns at the next board meeting. Several board members were offended and defended the other board members. The executive resigned the next day. The Pivot failed, and the board had to restart its search.

Hard-to-Follow Executive—The Pivot phase for World Village Builders was a classic success. The work that was done to prepare leaders and funders for life without the founder had been a success. The new executive had worked with a founder in her previous organization. She had a lot of empathy for the founder and the leaders adjusting to the loss of the founder. She was patient, reassuring, and focused on the results everyone agreed they wanted. She spent half her time building relationships with the board, staff, and funders and asking them what she could do to preserve and build on the organization and founder's legacy. She reported at the board meeting on what she learned in these visits and involved the executive staff in how to best use this information. The transition consultant facilitated a social contracting session with the board and executive that increased the executive's ongoing relationship building with stakeholders. Her six-month review was stellar, and she went on to lead World Village Builders through a three-year expansion.

Conclusion: Leader Development Through ETM

An executive transition presents the best opportunity to advance a leader development culture and to strengthen organizational effectiveness. The executive transition management process (ETM) is designed to ensure the maximum possible benefit from this opportunity. A well-executed executive transition can advance leader development in the following ways:

Hire an Executive Who Satisfies Organizational Needs and Commits to Building an Effective Management Team, Staff, and Board

The organization's leadership needs change as it moves through the organizational life cycle and as the mission and strategies change. Defining that change clearly before the executive search increases alignment between the executive, board, and organizational needs. Up until the year 2000 or so, particularly from 1970–1990, many new organizations were being formed. Entrepreneurial leaders committed to a mission built much of today's nonprofit sector. While organizations still value the skills of the entrepreneur, most hiring boards need both a leader and a manager. This means a commitment to leader development. Similarly, for many years, more than a few nonprofit executives took the position of seeing the board as a necessary evil to be worked around. Those days have also gone. Organizations demand involved boards to adapt and survive.

Leverage the Board's Involvement in Transition and Search to Intentionally Cultivate and Educate Board Leaders and Future Officers

Board members who serve on the transition committee are involved in a crash course on the organization. In order to search for and hire an executive, this committee needs to know what the organization does, why, and what competencies and mix of leaders among managers and the board are needed for the organization to thrive. Potential board chairs often serve on the transition committee to have a hand in selecting the executive they may one day partner with in leading the organization.

Make Diversity and Inclusiveness a Priority for the Organization, Especially with Regard to Leader Development

How a committee is selected, how candidates are sought and recruited, and who makes it to the finalist pool all provide opportunities for organizations to clarify and advance a commitment to diversity and inclusiveness. The nonprofit sector struggles to recruit diverse boards and executives, as noted in Chapter Four. Diversity considerations for organizations and communities vary widely. For some it is about race and ethnicity; for others, age; and for others, disability or the capacity to make a commitment to a cause or issue. There is no quick fix. Whether an organization is having its first conversation on the issue or revisiting and deepening a long-held commitment, executive transition is a powerful time for leaders to reflect on what a commitment to diversity and inclusiveness means and to advance this goal. (See Chapter Four for more on this topic.)

Model New Behaviors That Advance Leader Development

A transition also provides the opportunity to model new approaches to leading and for managers and staff to step up and lead in new ways. Unfortunately, some organizations have never had the experience of being well led. For underperforming or distressed organizations, this is often true. Hiring an interim executive who has a vision for how to build an effective relationship with the board and empower staff while getting the critical work done is an eye-opening experience for many boards. In other situations, a senior manager or in smaller organizations a manager or high-potential staff member is asked to take on expanded duties. These stretch assignments and opportunities to work more closely with the board provide another important leader development opportunity.

Through the process described above, leaders grow and organizations broaden their pool of current and future leaders. In this way, they become leaderful organizations.

REFLECTION QUESTIONS

For the Individual Leader

1. Have you observed any organization get stronger or weaker as a result of an executive transition? If so, how, and to the extent you have enough information to know, why?

2. If you have been involved directly in an executive transition, how did the organization handle the seven important decisions described above? What was the result?

3. If you are involved or soon to be involved in an executive transition, what are the top three ideas you want to pay attention to from this chapter?

For Executive Directors and Board Leaders of an Organization

1. If you are facing a transition or involved in one now:

   a. Does the three-phase approach presented here seem relevant? If yes, why? If no, why not?

b. How will this transition if successful grow organizational capacity and leadership?

2. What are the biggest risks your organization faces during transition? What can you do to reduce their threat?

3. If you are not facing a transition:

a. What might you do to be better prepared for when one occurs, given this chapter?

b. Do you have leaders on your board who have experience with executive transition in nonprofits? If so, what can you learn from them? If not, might you recruit a member with that experience?

For Funders, Capacity-Building Providers, Association Staff, and Other Supporting Stakeholders

1. Does your organization step up or pull back when an organization you care about is involved in executive transition? Does your behavior add to or detract from the success of the transition?

2. Given what you have read, how might you be most supportive to organizations you are involved with when the organization faces executive transition? Please be as specific as possible.

6

Getting Started on Succession Planning

IN MY WORK AS A NONPROFIT CONSULTANT, I've witnessed all of the following events:

The executive director of an advocacy group in the West was driving home on slippery roads from a late-night legislative meeting. His car skidded and he was in a serious accident. He was not in the office for four months and in physical rehab for months after that.

A board chair who was the key fund-raiser for a human services organization was promoted and abruptly relocated to a city two thousand miles away.

The development director for a leading arts organization in the Midwest was in the middle of a $10 million capital campaign. Her spouse was diagnosed with terminal cancer, and she resigned immediately.

The chief financial officer for a $150 million nonprofit had a heart attack in the middle of the audit and was out for over a year.

The executive director of a community development organization was a healthy forty-something whose organization was involved in three major projects to expand affordable housing in a southwest city. She was heading to work in the spring of 2005, was hit by a car while crossing the street, and died.

These anecdotes come from real stories. You can most likely add to them. The philosopher Heraclitus wrote 2,500 years ago: "Nothing endures but change." Change—sometimes surprisingly fast change—remains the one constant we can count on. Despite this, many nonprofits fail to prepare for the most predictable change of all—the departure of their executive or other key leaders.

In the for-profit world, *succession planning* is the answer to preparing for leadership change. Generally there are two approaches to succession planning: replacement planning and leader development planning. *Replacement planning* is simply a plan to replace leaders or managers who will be out for a short term. *Leader development planning* is more complex and includes a variety of activities to develop new leaders in the organization. This book will address leader development planning in Chapter Eight.

Most businesses do some sort of replacement planning, if nothing more elaborate than stating who takes care of key duties when leaders and employees are on vacation or out sick. These plans vary in complexity and purpose.

A few organizations go beyond identifying potential replacements to create a proactive plan for offering these leaders the opportunity to round out their skills and professional experience in various ways. This may include mentoring and coaching in preparation for their next leadership position. This approach is illustrative of the leader development approach to succession planning. For example, one of the past CEOs at UPS started his career there as a truck driver. Or consider Jeff Immelt, who followed the legendary Jack Welch as CEO of GE after years of leader development opportunities within GE. One of his first acts as CEO was to create a four-day Leadership Innovation and Growth seminar. Immelt met with each class of graduates of this program to discuss what they learned and its application to a specific project that would contribute to GE's growth and success.

Prior to 2003 or so, it was very rare for any nonprofit board or executive to discuss succession planning. They avoided the term itself, which conjured up a host of feelings and fears, mostly negative, for both boards and executives. Executives were often concerned about bringing up succession planning for fear of prematurely sending a signal that they were planning to leave. Worse yet, they worried that discussion of succession might result in the executive being forced to leave before he or she intended. Boards whose executive was performing well did not raise the topic because the last thing any board chair or board wants is to lose an effective executive during their leadership tenure.

Fortunately, through education, experience, and the sheer number of Baby Boom era leader departures, the nonprofit sector has moved forward significantly in its acceptance and use of succession planning practices. In 2006 the *Daring to Lead* study found that 29 percent of the two thousand executives "had discussed succession planning" with their board. Having a discussion is different from developing a plan, but it is a start![1]

This chapter is about how your organization can begin the discussion and then begin to plan. The time for such planning is *now,* before the executive director or other key leaders leave. We call this *succession planning.* As you will learn, succession planning is a catchphrase for a variety of actions. At a minimum, good succession planning includes the development of positive language and attitudes about succession, good emergency backup plans, a succession policy, an organizational culture that encourages the growth of new leaders, and adequate preparation for the planned departure of an executive. The steps and tools that follow will increase the odds that your organization will sustain effective leaders—and success.

This chapter is divided into three sections: "Prepare for Succession Planning," "Create an Emergency Backup Plan," and "Develop and Adopt a Succession Policy." Having completed this work, your organization will have the succession planning basics (an emergency backup plan and succession policy) in place and be less vulnerable to leadership change whenever it occurs.

While succession planning may sound like a daunting task, there's good news: you can complete the basics—an emergency backup plan and a board-adopted succession policy—in one to three months. The time investment is as follows:

- Eight to twelve hours of executive time
- Six to eight hours of the board leader's time
- One to four hours of full board discussion

Prepare for Succession Planning

Agree on Terminology

Typically, executives and board members each carry their own notions of what succession planning is—ranging from immediately filling a vacancy to long-term leadership planning. The goal, regardless of the words you use, should be agreement that *the organization seeks a plan to sustain effective leadership over time and multiple leadership changes.* Because succession planning can make organizations "nervous," your executive and board should start by agreeing on the language that best fits its situation.

Here are some of the terms boards have employed to frame succession planning in ways that help everyone feel safe:

- *Succession planning.* Planning to ensure that there is preparation for planned or unplanned leadership transitions for key positional leaders, especially the executive director. Succession planning includes the subpractices of *emergency backup planning, departure-defined planning,* and *leader development/talent management.* However, succession planning is an umbrella process that occurs regardless of whether there is a known future departure.

- *Leadership sustainability planning.* This promises a goal of ensuring effective leadership over time by preparing the organization for both planned and unplanned leadership changes. It emphasizes building an organizational culture that supports and nurtures existing and potential leaders. We call this a leaderful organization.

- *Emergency backup/emergency succession planning.* Planning to facilitate rapid transfers of duties and authorities to designated individuals in the event that the current executive or other key leader is unable to function. Includes a cross-training element, so those who would temporarily assume duties are prepared; this cross-training also helps expand the leadership capacity of the organization.

- *Leadership planning.* This frames succession planning as readiness for staff and board backup and succession. This approach emphasizes defining who leads in your organization and how existing and potential staff and board leaders can learn more about opportunities for advancement and development within the organization.

- *Talent management and development.* This term frames succession planning as a human resource process. In this process, top leaders in an organization assess its key leadership needs, current capacity, and "bench strength" (potential leaders ready to move up). This usually results in an annual review of talent and individual and departmental plans for building additional bench strength and backup capacity where needed. It is similar to leadership planning with the focus more on the top leadership and key positions.

- *Leader development.* The process of supporting the ongoing development of leadership through performance management, educational opportunities and the use of assignments, and peer support and coaching, among other tools, to expand the capacity of current and potential leaders.

All of these terms are helpful. The act of talking about the meaning and implications of each will get you started in the right direction and help the board get comfortable with the topic. If the term *succession planning* creates anxiety or confusion in your organization, pick a term that works for you and define it so that everyone is clear about what you hope to achieve by the planning.

Reduce Anxieties

Succession planning is about change. Change makes people anxious—which is why they so often put off planning. Clarifying your terms is a start toward reducing the anxiety, but there is more to be done. First, you must check in with your mission to be sure you have broad agreement. Then you must check in with each other to be sure you have adequate trust within the board and between the board and executive.

Begin by checking in on your mission and strategic direction. Review your most recent strategic plan, vision, and mission statements. Be sure that your mission and strategic direction are clear. If there are wide variations in opinion, you need to build consensus on mission and direction before moving into leadership planning. That's normal—and it's fine, because as you reach (or rediscover) agreement, you also build trust. (See the section on sustainability planning in Chapter Six and Appendix C for more details on this step.)

Checking in on trust is more difficult than checking in on mission, so take it slow. Honestly assess whether you have good trust and communication among board members and between the executive and the board. If there is some doubt, discuss the issues and take steps to improve. You may need to delay succession planning for a few months while you sort through any performance issues or lack of trust among the top leaders. Consider one example:

> Jane Jones had served as executive director of Community Service Inc. for fifteen years. She was in her mid-fifties and in generally good health. Over lunch, her board chair inquired, "Jane, do we have a succession plan in place? We're working on those at the bank and I think we ought to have one for Community Service."
>
> Jane caught her breath. "I haven't thought much about that and don't have any plans to go anywhere. I'd like to learn more about it and see how it might help us."
>
> As she drove home, she thought back over the past few board meetings and her last performance review. "Did I miss something? Is the board unhappy with me?" The voice of self-doubt festered for days as she relived the conversation.

Board members may have similar doubts when the executive raises the topic. For example, the executive director says, "Several funders have asked us if we have a succession plan, and I think it is a good idea for us to develop one." But some board members hear "He's thinking of going somewhere else and we better get ready."

Successful organizations are built on positive, open relationships between the executive and the board. Even where that trust exists, the worm of doubt can show up when the delicate topic of succession comes up. Imagine the fear that arises where there is already some strain in the executive-board relationship.

Take care not to create unnecessary fear and anxiety when you bring up succession planning—on the board, on the staff, or for the executive. To begin, the executive director needs to reflect on his or her readiness to talk about leadership sustainability and succession. Those who have been a founder, a long-term executive, or recently turned around the organization will likely be deeply attached to it. In some cases, the executive's identity and that of the organization have become one. The executive may or may not be ready to begin this work with the board. If not, he or she should take the time to understand the resistance, learn about sustainability and succession planning, and clarify personal intentions. (See Chapter Three on founder transitions and Chapter Two on the emotional dimension of succession and transition planning.)

Because of the emotions and possibility for misunderstandings and the benefit to the organization of buy-in by the board and staff leadership, many organizations find it helpful to form a team with the executive and board chair or other board leaders. This team collects information, may attend training, and learns more to help lead and begin the conversation. Other boards choose to form a small sustainability or succession planning work group from the board and (with or without consultant help) begin the conversation. The important thing is to check in to make sure no one feels undue fear and everyone clearly understands the intention of the process.

Where the board has performance concerns or the executive-board relationship continues to be strained, the stressors need to be addressed *before* succession planning. Resolution of such issues may require help from a board member or community resource skilled in board-executive relations or conflict resolution.

Plan to Follow Through

It's easy to get hung up on this process—even to make too much of it. A real problem for organizations that face succession is *failing to start* or *failing to finish.* One executive we know had served as leader of a community building organization for many years. She and her board began talking about leadership sustainability as part of strategic planning. She attended a workshop to learn more about the topic and clarify her personal plans. After the workshop, she drafted a tentative succession plan, required by the board so that she could take a three-month sabbatical to think about her next options. But when she returned, she got so busy that she never finished the plan. She told us, "It was on my 'to do' list for two years. Finally I realized I was stuck and asked a consultant for help. We finished a draft of the plan in two hours! I was amazed how simple it was once I decided to get help and get going."

The following steps have helped organizations start, complete, and maintain useful emergency backup plans and succession policies:

1. Recruit one or two board leaders with the interest and skills to champion this issue. These champions should recruit others to form a sustainability or succession task force (usually not a standing committee), or to make the tasks part of the governance or board development committee.

2. The work group should gather and review resources. They can keep the process simple by using existing templates and experienced consultants, rather than starting from scratch.

3. Set a timeline and completion date and stick to it. Often doing the work and finalizing it at the annual board retreat or a special board meeting helps move this process to a healthy closure.

4. Set a firm date on which the annual review of the plan will take place and a decision will be made about how to integrate leadership planning in the annual and strategic plans.

Build Support for Succession Planning

Persuading the board, executive director, and staff to begin succession planning may take some doing. If you have already enlisted one or two leaders to champion this work, and your executive director is enthusiastic or at least supportive of doing it, then your foundation for planning is taking shape. To broaden support (or build it if nonexistent), the board should discuss both the risks of failing to plan and the benefits of planning. Let's look at both.

Risks We know of an environmental organization that was founded by a strong leader. He was board chair, then unpaid executive, and then moved back to board chair. He could never find anyone to hire as a new executive who could meet his standards. After three tries to hire a new executive, the organization failed. It could not handle the lack of direction. As a result, it lost funder support, forward momentum, clients—and finally, it lost itself in bankruptcy. And that is the number one risk of failing to plan for succession—going out of business. Ask around. It happens.

A second risk is the sudden and unprepared loss of a director. People in an organization often feel their leader is essential, that the organization can't "live" without him or her. But leaders depart all the time—due to new job offers, dramatic and sudden life changes, accidents, and other unpredictable causes. For example, the founding executive of an arts organization was hit by a car crossing the street one morning and died. Fortunately, the board had already begun a process of identifying and developing new internal leaders—which eased the loss and transition. The organization didn't go out of business, but the road back was long and difficult.

A third risk could be called "the bloom is off the rose." Here, an organization becomes stale, out of touch, less effective. Perhaps its leadership needs have changed, or its community has changed. Leaders need to grow and change to stay relevant or a slow painful path to irrelevancy results. Consider the case of a social services agency that was led by the same executive for twenty-five years. At about year twenty, she decided to move to another city and work half-time. The board, all longtime associates and friends of the executive, didn't see the obvious problems with this decision and never challenged her. Others did: funders talked privately about the lack of leadership and direction, and the community began to grumble. Eventually, years of declining funding, service delivery, and reputation caused the executive to resign.

Benefits Successful companies and government agencies make annual, ongoing investment in growing new leaders, managers, and bench strength. The U.S. government, for example, has a plan that tells them how many senior executives will retire and when. The program offers fellowships and in-service training programs to prepare a pool of successors. Similarly, a national insurance company does a detailed "bench strength" report every year to its board. In this report, the CEO specifies who is being groomed to replace each of twenty senior positions. The CEO notes each candidate's readiness, strengths, and deficits that require further preparation.

This may seem impossible for organizations of limited size and resources. Regardless of size, you can adapt these practices and reap the following benefits.

The first benefit is that succession planning helps you "unpack" the executive and other top positions in such a way as to make them more sustainable. Often, longtime executives and managers have accumulated a mix of unrelated duties, suitable only for their particular background and experience with the organization. *This mix can render the position (as presently defined) impossible to fill.* However, when the organization begins emergency succession planning, it clarifies the key roles, functions, and relationships of the executive. Then, a plan is developed for cross-training other staff. Sometimes this process results in adding a part- or full-time position to make the position more sustainable.

Here are two examples of organizations that made changes as a result of emergency succession planning. One, a large, multiservice nonprofit, had a thirty-year executive with twelve managers reporting directly to her. After "unpacking" her job functions, hiring a chief operating officer was an obvious step to sustainability. Another, a small, mostly volunteer organization that served the homeless, decided to cross-train volunteers in certain key elements of its work and to hire a part-time executive assistant.

A second benefit of succession planning is the unleashing of new energy and talent. Younger staff has a deep hunger to grow and take on new responsibilities in the nonprofit workforce. For example, a Latino advocacy organization invested in leader development planning with its managers, most of whom were in their late twenties and thirties. In the process, the organization clarified roles, increased its impact, and trained managers in new skills. It was, in fact, becoming a more leaderful organization.

A third benefit of succession planning is that the process tells all employees what leadership is and how to advance in the organization. For example, in a small environmental nonprofit, staff frequently deferred to the executive. He took a sabbatical, and during that period the staff had several discussions about the nature of leadership. When the executive returned, staff had determined that leadership could occur at all levels. Rather than deferring to the executive at all times, they became more assertive and self-starting. Managers achieved more and felt better, the executive began delegating rather than micromanaging, and the organization's impact improved.

Or, in a larger mental health agency, staff felt that a person had to be "known" by the CEO to get promoted. Through sustainability and succession planning, the organization identified attributes and competencies required for leadership at all levels of the organization. The organization then created management and training opportunities to help staff develop these competencies. The result was greater retention and internal advancement, and ultimately, a more sustainable organization.

Create an Emergency Backup Plan

Most organizations ease into succession planning by developing an emergency backup plan for the executive director.[2] The executive is often the glue for the organization, so it makes sense to first ensure there is a plan in case of a sudden absence.

The purpose of the plan is to:

1. Define a short- and long-term unplanned absence

2. Clarify who decides such an absence is occurring

3. State who assumes the functions and roles of the executive during the absence

(In larger organizations with a management team or smaller organizations where the board volunteers carry out key duties essential to the mission, often it is important to develop additional emergency backup plans for other key positions. The board should ask the executive to determine whether such backups are needed, and if so, get them in place after the executive backup plan is complete. In some larger organizations, the executive may decide to complete emergency backup plans for herself and the entire executive management team at the same time.)

In some instances, emergency backup planning is initiated by the executive director and is mostly staff-led. In others, it is initiated by the board or a board member and acted on by the executive and a few board members. Much depends on the size and operating style of the organization and its board. Either process works as long as the executive and the board communicate clearly about their respective roles.

Regardless of the starting point, the board should review and adopt the emergency backup plan as a policy. At a minimum, the board should expect to be oriented to the fact that an emergency backup plan is being developed and that it will be brought back for board action. In cases where a founder or long-term executive is involved, it is quite helpful for a small group from the board to work with the executive on the emergency backup plan. This same work group also typically takes responsibility for developing the draft policy for the board to discuss and adopt.

The circumstances that bring up this topic and the group dynamics of the organization influence how to best get it done. In smaller, simpler situations, almost anyone in the organization can craft a helpful plan as long as all the stakeholders are appropriately engaged. In more complex situations, a consultant with experience in emergency backup plans and succession planning may be helpful.

To get oriented to what an emergency backup plan looks like, view and download templates of emergency backup plans at:

http://www.compasspoint.org/assets/520_emergencysuccessionplanmo.pdf

http://www.nonprofitadvancement.org/usr_doc/Emergency_Succession_Plan_Template.doc

http://www.transitionguides.com/about/publications.htm

The backup plan should include the following items:

- A written emergency backup plan
- Contact information for key stakeholders

- Instructions for informing key stakeholders of the unplanned absence

- A cross-training plan for designated executive backups

- An updated or new executive job description (if needed)

The process appears simple, but the time commitment and the possibility of emotional resistance is the main barrier. Some organizations send a team of the executive director and a few board leaders to one-day workshops (when available) or a consultant-facilitated retreat. The goal of either is to get the plan done quickly so that something is in place for an emergency.

Whether in a workshop, retreat, or the board conference room, move ahead briskly with the following steps:

Step 1. List the Executive's Key Functions

The executive needs to list the five or six most important functions she plays in the organization. To complete this step, the executive can generate a first draft, or a consultant or trusted colleague can interview the executive and write a draft for the executive to review. *Functions* are the major tasks the executive performs within the organization to ensure its efficiency and success—what the executive does and who she oversees, for example. A review of the executive's calendar of activities over the past six months and of her position description may help inform the listing of key functions.

Once there is an initial list, other managers, staff, or board members (depending on the size and culture of the organization) may review and comment on it. Other people can often add or see key roles or functions in ways the executive misses or takes for granted.

Step 2. Determine Emergency Backup Staff

The executive (or working group) should now proceed to a) list individuals who now or with training could carry out high-priority functions; and b) select a person to serve as acting director in an emergency backup, plus one or two alternatives if that person is unavailable.

Listing individuals who can do *parts* of the executive's job is relatively straightforward and is usually led by the executive in consultation with the management team or participating board leaders. The second task—picking a standing appointee and alternatives—can be more complex. In smaller organizations, there may be no single person on staff with the capability to do the job. In larger organizations, multiple possibilities may exist, and thinking through who is selected and how others will interpret the selection needs to be done carefully.

Keep reminding those involved that emergency backup planning is not a process for selecting a long-term successor or heir apparent; the goal is to ensure continuity of leadership in an emergency. While having one designated person is simplest, some organizations opt for coleadership and others turn to a board member or consultant who works closely with the organization. Focusing on the functions of the executive and who can best assume those for the short term helps guide this decision. Some organizations think it better to avoid naming a specific person and want to state that the designated backup is to be named at the time of the emergency. This defeats the purpose of being ready when an emergency occurs. Other organizations prefer stating the title of the position of the person who will serve as backup rather than the individual. Because it is the experience of the person designated as acting executive that is important, in most cases the plan is stronger if a specific person is named, not just a position title. If that person leaves and a less experienced person succeeds her, the plan can be updated as needed.

Step 3. Create a Communications Plan

The communications plan involves creating a regularly maintained contact list of which stakeholders need to be informed (along with how quickly) in case of an unplanned absence. Most organizations inform board and staff within two to three days. If clients need to know, they are also informed. Depending on the nature and expected length of the absence, funders, government officials, and other stakeholders may or may not be informed. Most communication occurs initially within a week and then on a "need to know" or update basis, depending on the circumstances and length of departure.

Step 4. Create a Cross-Training Plan

The cross-training plan is aimed at ensuring that the designated backups receive orientation and training in any areas deemed essential for carrying out short-term leadership. For example, the person who will take over communications with key stakeholders needs to learn a little background about the most important of those stakeholders. Or, the person who will take over representation of the organization in collaborations and coalitions needs to learn about the history and relationships involved in those activities. Keep the list short, and ensure that the process and timeline for completing the training are realistic. Put someone in charge of making sure it happens.

Step 5. Finalize the Plan

The final section of the backup plan should suggest an annual review of the plan and designate who gets a copy—usually the board chair and vice chair or secretary, the executive, those named as backups, and in larger organizations, the human resources director. During this final step, most organizations also review who knows where key documents and passwords for computers and bank accounts are kept, to ensure backup for day-to-day operations.

The team working on the emergency backup plan should then finalize the language and prepare a draft for the board to discuss and adopt. The board should focus its discussion on the thinking that went into the plan, the decisions in the plan, and the implications for the organization in terms of long-term sustainability.

Develop and Adopt a Succession Policy

Every organization should have a written succession policy.[3] First, it provides a framework for important conversation and planning *before* a leadership change happens. Second, it provides a structure and process to guide the organization when the change occurs. When an ending of any kind occurs, it is human nature to want to get out of the confusing time of ambiguity as quickly as possible. Our experience as nonprofit transition consultants has taught us that this urgent need to act is among the leading causes of failed transitions. The written policy adds security at a very insecure time.

A written succession policy usually addresses the following questions (often as separate sections of the policy):

- What are the roles of the board, the outgoing executive, the staff, and (in some instances) external stakeholders in planning for and hiring a new executive?

- Is the organization committed to managing both the transition and the search by setting up a transition and search committee (a recommended best practice)? What is the size and makeup of the committee?

- Will the staff be a part of the committee? How will staff be involved in the process?

- What is the committee's authority to recommend one or more finalists and what is the board's process for making the hiring decision?

- What is the organization's philosophy and practice in terms of filling key vacancies such as an executive director? Is there a culture of encouraging the development of leaders internally? Are internal candidates encouraged to apply? Is there always an external search?

- Will the organization consider using an outside consultant to assist with the transition planning and management or the executive search?

- What is the organization's commitment to diversity and cultural competency in its recruiting and selection process?

The answers to these questions result in a one- to two-page document, which is reviewed and adopted by the board. The process for developing the draft usually involves a small work group of board members, the executive director, and, in some larger organizations, one or more representatives of the senior staff.

Holding this discussion and forging a written succession policy is helpful for all organizations. It is essential for organizations where an executive transition is anticipated in the next one to five years.

WHAT IS A SUCCESSION PLAN?

Some leaders ask to see a sample of a "succession plan." That is a logical and appropriate question. Our response is that there are a number of documents that are part of a succession plan. The kind of succession planning you are doing will determine what is in your plan. Succession plans may include the following:

1. An emergency backup plan for the executive director (and in some cases executive managers)

2. A succession policy

3. A sustainability review or audit report that highlights organizational strengths and aspirations or goals for making the organization more sustainable

4. An executive transition plan and timeline, typically part of a departure-defined succession plan, which may include options for departure and address any future role for the departing executive with the organization

5. A leader development or talent management plan that may include a bench-strength review report to the board

Conclusion: Gentle Paths to Succession Planning

The steps in this chapter move you far along the road toward preparedness for an executive transition and increased leader development in your organization. Grappling with the *idea* of succession is sometimes the first and hardest way for organizations—especially boards and executives—to face the inevitable. But this chapter provides you with three different ways to enter gently into the discussion of executive transition. The succession policy and emergency backup plan are both must-haves for *any* organization—as important as your strategic plan, your fund-raising plan, or your back-office database. They are simply elements of good management hygiene. And the succession plan itself is a quick step behind those two in terms of essential management practices. Start with any of these, and you will move more easily into the more complex processes outlined in the next two chapters.

REFLECTION QUESTIONS

For the Individual Leader

1. If you were suddenly unable to carry out your role as a leader, what would be your biggest concern about important priorities that would not get sufficient attention?

2. Have you prepared anyone to assume your duties in the event of an unplanned absence? Who would step in to carry out your leadership responsibilities?

3. What actions might you take now to prepare yourself for a planned or unplanned transition?

For Executive Directors and Board Leaders of an Organization

1. Is there a written emergency backup plan for the executive director? If so, when was it last reviewed?

2. Are the key documents, pass codes, financial information, and other critical organizational information securely kept and accessible to more than one person?

3. Has the board talked about leadership succession? Is there a written succession policy to guide planned transitions?

For Funders, Capacity-Building Providers, Association Staff, and Other Supporting Stakeholders

1. If you provide grants or contracts to organizations, do you require that there be an emergency backup plan and succession policy in place before finalizing a grant or contract?

2. To support grantees or members in developing succession basics—an emergency backup plan and succession policy—what actions might your organization take?

3. What actions might your organization take to model attention to succession planning? What would support you in making that commitment?

7

Departure-Defined Succession Planning

IN THE PRACTICE OF REAL ESTATE APPRAISAL, appraisers are trained to ask: What is the highest and best use for this tract of land or property? In succession or leadership continuity planning, many executives and organizations have the opportunity to ask themselves a similar question when the executive has a general or specific time in mind for departing from the executive position. That question is: What is the highest and best use of the remaining years of the executive's tenure which results in an organization that has more capacity to achieve its mission and is prepared to sustain success with a new executive?

The reason for a planned departure varies in length and specificity. Some executives have a definite date or year for retiring or transitioning to a new or less intense position. Others have a range in mind, and the specific date evolves based on circumstances and opportunities. Typically, the time period ranges from one to four years. (The public announcement of the departure timeline occurs later in the process—typically six to twelve months before departure unless it is an unplanned and rapid departure.) Making the most of this planned transition is called *departure-defined succession planning*.

Andy James was nationally recognized for his expertise in health and tax policy. His statewide nonprofit, Health Care for Everyone, was the go-to organization for advocates, policymakers, and legislative leaders for data-driven information and research on health issues. James founded Health Care for Everyone with two other advocates and three health care providers in 1990 when health care reform was hot.

Health Care for Everyone has grown from a three-person think tank to a $3 million, twenty-person research and advocacy center with both a statewide and national focus. James is now sixty, has four grandchildren, and is tired of raising the budget and managing staff and administrative details. He added a deputy director three years ago, but still feels burdened by details that get in the way of his passion for research and working for change. James wants to step down as executive and stay with the organization as a part-time writer. Departure-defined succession planning assisted James and his board in deciding if this was a good idea for the organization and for him.

Frances Brooks built the Prison Reform Coalition from scratch after her two nephews were incarcerated for violations that in most suburban white communities would have resulted in no trial, let alone incarceration. She was tired of the oppression of African-American and other youths of color by the judicial and penal system. In 1983, she put a second mortgage on her home and organized people from all over her Midwest city to form the Prison Reform Coalition. As the Coalition grew, she went to the Highlander Center to learn organizing and advocacy and became the first paid executive of the Prison Reform Coalition. Twenty-five years later she is seventy-three years old and ready to hand the organization off to the next generation. She tried to retire twice before and it didn't work. Departure-defined succession planning helped Frances and her board to develop a real three-year plan for her stepping down as executive and making room for new leadership.

Juan Rodriguez grew up in a privileged family in Puerto Rico. He came to Washington, D.C., to go to college and stayed for law school. Throughout his education, he became more interested and involved in immigration issues and Latino civil rights. In 1990 he and three law school friends organized the Latino Justice Center. They operated like a law firm except they charged minimal fees and took a small percentage of fees from the settlements of lawsuits. They quickly built a positive reputation in the community and among funders. By 2000 the Center employed fifteen attorneys and eight paralegals and was working with 240 clients a year.

Juan was thrilled with the growth, but concerned about the time he was spending away from his three children and wife. The intensity of combining legal cases with national travel for the organization left him little time with his family. Juan decided it was time for a change. He was conflicted and decided one day to leave, another to work part-time, and yet another to stay and reorganize the management team. Departure-defined succession planning assisted Juan in becoming clear about what he wanted to do and about working with his board to implement the transition.

In each of the examples above, the executive is trying to understand the best way—for the organization and for him- or herself—to depart or change roles. This *departure-defined succession planning* typically occurs when an executive has a private plan to carefully transition from leadership in one to four years, sometime a little longer. Many of these executives are founders or long-time executives. Often such executives are retiring, moving to part-time employment, or preparing to enter a new field or make a career change after some time off. (Just to be clear, departure-defined successions are *not* immediate transitions where the executive decides to take another job and plans to leave within thirty to sixty days of securing a new position.)

The depth and breadth of this type of planning is heavily influenced by the length of time before the executive plans to depart and what else is going on in the organization. Planning that happens more than two years in advance can address issues that cannot be addressed when the executive is leaving in a year or sooner. Similarly, if the organization is in the midst of a major capital campaign, experiencing major growth, or downsizing, doing much additional planning may not be possible; those issues take priority.

The name *departure-defined* might imply that there is an announcement of an executive departure years before the executive is leaving. Usually this is not the case. Typically there is a completely private period when the executive is clarifying her plans and timing on her own or with the help of a trusted mentor or two or a coach or consultant. Once the executive has some degree of certainty about her plans, she may encourage the organization to engage in succession and sustainability planning. Depending on the circumstances, she may or may not have a conversation with the board chair or a trusted member of her management team about her general intentions. Some executives say something like: "I'm not getting any younger and won't be here forever. I don't have any imminent plans to leave. It is best practice to have a succession plan and invest in leader development—and I think we ought to begin that process."

Other executives might say: "My spouse is retiring in three years and I'd like to begin planning to retire within a year or two of her retirement depending on our circumstances." A few are more precise and say: "I'd like to retire in three years on such and such a date. I think we ought to begin planning."

In yet other cases, the board initiates the conversation and asks the executive in his annual review how long he plans to be in the position, and if he doesn't know, asks him to think about it and plan to discuss it in a few months.

For example, in a community development and service organization, a founder had left to take a national position and returned six years later to lead the organization through a rebuilding process. As she approached retirement, she wanted to make sure the organization was in excellent health when she departed. She and the board contracted with a management support organization to conduct a full organizational review of the financial health, viability, systems, and leadership for each program area of the organization. This resulted in a plan for increasing funding, strengthening systems, and expanding the leadership team, to be carried out over the three years before the executive retired.

Certain factors influence the success of departure-defined succession planning. There are also numerous benefits to such planning. Before we move into the actual planning process, let's explore the success factors and benefits.

Success Factors in Departure-Defined Succession Planning

The purpose of departure-defined succession planning is to prepare the organization and its leaders for a successful executive transition. The executive transition typically occurs one to four years from the beginning of this type of succession planning. There are six areas of readiness that form the basis for defining success for this planning. The executive, managers, and board are encouraged to begin planning with the end in mind and discuss and deliberate with facts and data what readiness for transition would look like in these six domains. The domains or areas to explore and examples of typical key questions include the following:

1. Strategy readiness:

    a. How current is our strategic and business plan?

    b. What has or is changing in the environment that will influence our strategy or business plan over the next few years?

2. Financial readiness:

    a. Do we understand our current financial health: income, expenses, assets, and liabilities?

    b. Has our operating budget ended balanced or with a surplus the last three years? What is the trend in our income and expenses and capacity to sustain a balanced operating budget?

    c. What capital, facilities investment, or other financial requirements are relevant to achieving our mission? How are we doing in achieving our goals in this area?

3. Systems readiness:

    a. Do we have in place up-to-date policies and procedures to guide and protect our organization? Where are we vulnerable?

    b. Does our technology infrastructure support the work required to achieve our mission? Are there mission-critical investments in technology, equipment, or staffing required to sustain success or growth?

4. Management team/staff readiness:

    a. Depending on the organizational size, do we have competent managers or staff in positions essential for our success?

    b. Are there key managers or staff who are doing more than one person's job —and which if they left would result in a crisis for the organization?

    c. Is there a culture and morale among managers or staff that results in retention, growth, and ongoing advances for the organization in a capacity to achieve its mission?

5. Board readiness:

   a. Does the board have effective leaders as chair and treasurer, and leaders of key committees like development, finance, and program?

   b. Does the board have a process to regularly review its performance and any changes in competencies required in board members?

   c. Does the board plan for leader succession on the board and have systems to support board regeneration and succession?

6. Executive readiness:

   a. Is the executive clear about her plans for departure or engaged in a personal process to become clear?

   b. Does the executive support this planning? Is she ready to begin to prepare the way for a new leader and let go or support others in learning key responsibilities?

   c. Does the executive have the energy, commitment, and support to lead through the proposed departure-defined time frame?

The following process provides a path for leaders to follow in defining and addressing these six success areas.

Benefits of Departure-Defined Succession Planning

The benefits of departure-defined planning are many and include:

- *Control.* Emotional closure is in the control of the executive, which reduces the risk of top-down instability or "craziness" filtering through the organization. This is because the executive has done her or his personal planning, has come to grips with the meaning of departure, and has a clear timeline for leaving.

- *Time.* The executive has time to seek and find the support needed to address the infrastructure, management, and related emotional challenges of departure. This can include changes in approach to delegation, increased investment in mentoring other managers and sharing details of role with managers and the board, reorganizing the position to make it more doable for a successor, and so on.

- *Communications management.* The organization can privately prepare for executive transition without making any public announcements. As a result, the executive, board, and staff are prepared for transition, reducing or eliminating its trauma and risks to donor, funder, and constituent bases.

- *Strategic improvements.* The organization has time to complete an organizational review (sometimes called a *sustainability audit*). This helps staff and board understand the organization's strengths and develop a blueprint for improvements consistent with its mission, goals, and resources.

- *Stability and smooth sailing.* Issues or improvements that will distract or potentially derail the new executive are made a priority for action. Examples include resolving issues with underperforming or disruptive employees, out-of-date or nonexistent databases, poor financial records or outdated accounting practices, and so on.

- *Talent recruitment.* When the executive transition occurs, the organization knows the competencies, attributes, and "fit" it needs in the next executive. This helps the organization recruit and hire, which in turn improves the next executive's chances of success. The planning also clarifies how the organization can best nurture the internal leaders needed to sustain mission effectiveness over time.

Four Phases of Planning

This section provides a step-by-step path for departure-defined succession planning. The timing of the departure and the health and life cycle position of the organization will influence how these steps play out in each situation. The steps are a general road map to be fine-tuned to the specific situation. As we look at each step, we'll provide examples of these differences. For simplicity, we'll refer to early departure as one to two years and later departure as three to four years in the examples. At a certain point in the process, dictated by the timing of the planned departure, this process morphs into the executive transition management process. (The reader is referred to Chapter Five, "Executive Transition Management," for details on that part of the process.)

Most successful departure-defined succession planning follows predictable phases. What occurs in each phase and when it occurs varies widely based on the following:

- The executive's goals, needs, and departure plan clarity

- The organization's health and life cycle situation

- What succession planning and leader development systems are already in place

- The time available before the executive departure, if known

There are four typical phases in departure-defined succession planning, illustrated in Figure 7.1. These phases are:

1. *Prepare*—in which the organization readies itself for planning

2. *Review*—in which the organization assesses itself and gets its succession basics in order

3. *Plan*—in which the organization creates a sustainability plan that expresses the actions it must take to strengthen the organization for transition

4. *Implement*—in which the organization implements the plan

It's important to note departure-defined succession planning is *not* the process of selecting and anointing an internal candidate as successor.

Figure 7.1. Four Typical Phases in Departure-Defined Succession Planning
Source: Copyright © TransitionGuides Inc., 2009

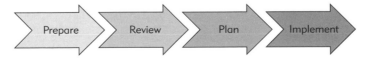

Some boards start out believing that the goal of succession planning is to decide two to five years in advance who the next executive will be. (This belief is especially prevalent among board members who are familiar with the corporate "replacement" planning, in which every senior manager is responsible for grooming a successor.) In most of the cases we have witnessed, this does not work. The reasons include:

- The departing executive is ambivalent about leaving and delays the exit. Meanwhile, the selected successor gets impatient and leaves.

- The board is not included in the discussion and does not support the executive's selection.

- The selected successor has a narrowly defined role or challenging role in the organization, and it is difficult for the board and the staff to imagine the individual succeeding in the broader role of executive director.

- The board wants the benefit of a full search and decides on an external or another internal candidate.

A more successful approach is to invest in developing the skills of a number of staff who might some day be the executive in your organization (or another) and to encourage all interested to apply when the position becomes vacant. This approach, similar to the for-profit method of *talent management,* is the subject of Chapter Eight.

Let's turn now to an in-depth look at the four phases of departure-defined succession planning.

Phase One: Prepare

The planning phase begins when the executive starts to consider whether and when she might leave the organization. Or, the board and executive might decide to focus on sustainability planning because there will be an executive change at some as yet undetermined date. There are three interconnected keys to this phase: executive readiness, board readiness, and executive-board-staff alignment about the process.

Executive Readiness The most important preparatory step in departure-defined succession planning is the work the executive does to decide when and how he wants to leave his position. Much of the pain of executive transition and the attendant disruption to organizations is caused by executive ambivalence or poor communication between the executive and the board.

Most people have anxiety and indecision about big decisions. Getting engaged, picking a college, buying a first home—these are big decisions. Leaving a position as an executive is like that. For the longtime executive or founder, it can be even bigger than those decisions. Where the executive and the organization identity are blurred and enmeshed, a decision to leave may feel like a life-or-death decision. (See Chapter Four on emotions and Chapter Three on founders for more details.)

Executives who send mixed messages to their boards on departure do themselves and the organization a disservice. For example, one Northeast-area executive told his board the following within a five-year period:

- "I'm done. I need to leave in two years."
- "I'll leave when we have an endowment of $10 million."
- "I'll leave when I can afford it and after the organization has completed payments on my trust account." (A trust account is a deferred compensation policy for executives used to provide additional retirement funds to the executive.)
- "I'll leave in five years."
- "I'll leave in seven years."

Eight years later he is still there, and it is no clearer when or if he will ever leave. As you might imagine, after a few years of being anxious and attempting to respond, the board and staff largely ignore what he says.

This is *not* succession planning. This executive and many who have less obvious manifestations of ambivalence about departure need to address their own plans before engaging others. Working with an executive coach or a trusted mentor, attending workshops on this topic, taking a three- to six-month sabbatical, finding and developing other or lost interests or hobbies, reconnecting with spiritual roots or faith, and in some instances therapy or help from a counselor are all tools used by executives to gain clarity.

Whether through a simple weekend of self-reflection or months or years of introspection and exploration, the executive reaches a decision: *I'd like to step out of this executive role either at a certain date or within a twenty-four-month window.* Most executives who have the opportunity to engage in departure-defined succession planning are well regarded and valued by their boards. (Departure for executives in trouble is a shorter and much different process.) Because of this respect from the board, if as it happens, the economy shifts and the executive wants to work longer, most boards are delighted.

This preparatory step is the same for early or later departures. It becomes more complex under several conditions: a) when the executive decides she wants to leave the executive position and stay in the organization in a different capacity, or b) when the executive wants to leave and the board asks her to join or stay on the board or to assist with fund-raising. (These complexities are also dealt with in more detail in Chapter Three, "Founders and Founder Transitions.") As the following example illustrates, the quick litmus test for this decision is: What is the motive? Who does this decision serve?

One executive of a large arts organization in the Mid-Atlantic region had been getting ready to leave the organization he founded eight years earlier. His first plan was to leave his position and start and run a subsidiary organization that would generate income for the organization he founded. While this seemed like a good idea, the unspoken motivation was troubling: first, he did not want to let go, and second, the board did not trust that any successor could raise money like he did and sustain the organization. With some outside help, the executive let go of this plan. He and the board began addressing the deeper issue of financial sustainability. As you can see, the questions "What is the motive?" and "Who does this decision serve?" ultimately clarified the situation and resulted in a proper planning process.

Board Readiness Two women started an environmental organization together. One left after a few years, and the other served as executive for fourteen years. The executive was a brilliant advocate and was involved with policy and legislative change in her state and nationally. But running the organization was something she "suffered through." Some health challenges caused her to realize she was spending too little of her time on the work she loved and did best.

She met with an executive coach for six months and explored a range of options, from leaving entirely to serving as an unpaid advisor. When she was clear, she and a transition consultant had a series of conversations with the board to look at sustainability, succession, and her role. The question of her long-term role was put on hold until the sustainability audit and emergency backup planning described below were completed.

At that point she and the board agreed together that she would take a one-year sabbatical and then serve at the discretion of the new executive as a senior advocacy advisor. The new executive would be told of this agreement before being hired and would have the right to terminate the agreement after six months if not beneficial to her. In this case the motive was the mission of the work and empowering the new executive—motives that worked. The new executive and advisor have worked together for four years now.

As this example shows, the next decision for the executive is *how to prepare the board chair and board for the coming change.* In some cases the board's concern about an aging executive or one with serious health issues causes the board to request succession planning with an eye on finding a mutually agreeable departure date.

Most executives fear becoming a lame duck. They don't want to talk about a specific date or go public until much closer to their departure. This is a healthy concern. Best practice is to engage in succession planning without any particular departure date announced. The executive needs to have some notion in order to guide him or her. He does not need (and in most cases it is unwise) to announce too specific a date too soon. An extended multiyear transition is exhausting and debilitating for the board and staff. Since for many leaders and organizations, leader change is an emotional process, there is a limit to how long leaders want to focus on any particular transition. A public process that exceeds twelve to eighteen months runs the risk of draining board, staff, and stakeholders, who grow weary of the anxiety of not knowing who will be in charge. Power begins to shift and relationships between potential successors or staff close to the executive can get strained. The board may begin to second-guess the executive or disengage from the executive and the organization.

A beloved leader of a social service organization announced he was retiring in two years at age sixty-five. The board and staff had just completed an exhausting year-long strategic planning process, their first in the agency's twenty years of existence. New board members were brought in. These same board members almost immediately began dealing with the executive transition process. By the time the executive departed, staff and board were burned out and ready to get back to "normal" again. This made it hard for the new executive to get much time or involvement from the board.

Most executives finesse the issue of date with general statements such as: "I have no plans to depart at this time." "I am not getting any younger." "I won't be here forever and have no imminent plans."

Executive-Board-Staff Alignment There is no right or perfect way to get ready for succession planning or to handle departure plans. The guiding principle is to look at motive and what serves the organization the best. *That is the point—to use however much time is available as wisely and effectively as possible to advance the organization's capacity and readiness for transition.*

In most instances where the departure is more than twelve months in the future, the simplest way to align board, executive, and staff is to talk about what each values about the work of the organization and the importance of sustaining those values. Since most leaders are motivated by the mission of the organization, a discussion about what these leaders have created together is a great launch to building consensus on moving forward with the next phase of succession basics and organizational review.

Phase Two: Review

Phase Two involves two key parts: an *organizational review* and *basic succession planning.* Circumstances, timing, the organization's culture, and leader preferences guide the starting point: either an assessment of the organization or the development of emergency backup plans and a succession policy (which constitute the most basic succession planning).

If the executive is leading the process and the departure is more than two years out or undefined, she may choose to begin with succession basics and the emergency backup plan. For example, one executive had a general discussion with the board chair about succession planning, let the chair know she was going to begin work on emergency backup plans, and agreed they would organize an ad hoc sustainability task force in a few months when the emergency backup work was done and the annual fund-raiser event was completed. This sustainability task force guided the board's work on a succession policy and the organizational review. The executive used her biweekly meetings with her senior administrative team for staff involvement, drawing on other staff at key milestones.

In situations where there are pressing organizational issues, major changes in resources, new organizational priorities, an antiquated infrastructure, or an aged strategic plan, it may make sense to start with the organizational review. This allows more time to build on strengths and address areas needing attention *before* moving into an executive transition process. Where the board has concerns about the performance of the executive, it is best to address those concerns before launching an organizational review so the two processes don't become inappropriately entangled.

In yet other situations, the board initiates the process out of concern about the pending succession of an aging long-term executive. In one example, the CEO and board chair of a larger nonprofit worked together to organize a process that charged the senior leadership team and a small board committee with addressing both the succession basics and the organizational review. In this case, there was no imminent transition, so the work was spread out over eighteen months with major reports at various board meetings. As this board was more focused on policy, they let the leadership and board committee handle most of the decisions, and the CEO was deeply involved.

In another large organization with a more imminent departure, the executive recruited four board members who served as a sounding board and helped him plan every step of the process. This board was hands-on, and the organization's executive team and infrastructure were less developed. The board was committed both to the agency and to the long-term executive. Over a two-year period, the executive and board group met regularly. The full board received reports on the emergency backup work, monitored the organizational review, and approved the draft succession policy. The discussions about the complex set of issues that were influencing the departure timing stayed confidential among the executive, a consultant, and the board group until it was time for the departure announcement.

In most situations, the staff and board are involved in the succession basics and the sustainability planning. The departure planning itself is a more private conversation with some exceptions, as described previously.

Organizational Review There are many approaches and tools for organizational reviews.[1] Once the executive and board agree to move forward with the organizational review, there are two fundamental questions in deciding on the approach for this organization in these circumstances: focus (the what) and process (the how). The specific questions will vary depending on the departure timing and circumstances and the age and life-cycle stage of the organization. For instance, preparing for the departure of an organization's first executive differs from preparing for the departure of the ninth executive. Length of tenure, organizational health, board capacity, current funding and staffing, among other factors, influence the focus of the review.

The most common approach for organizational review for departure-defined succession planning is a *sustainability review and audit*. Sustainability—of leaders and the organization—is the typical focus. The "how" decisions are about both what areas and systems to review and how deep the review needs to be. A quick look at all the basic systems is referred to as a *sustainability review*. A more focused and intense look at particular systems or areas determined to need attention is referred to as a *sustainability audit*.

In most situations, particularly for departures that are some years away, the process begins with a relatively light review of key systems and then selectively goes deeper.

Sustainability Review The initial sustainability review looks at assets and aspirations (strengths and areas of concern) in the following areas:

Board and Staff Leadership

- Do board and staff leadership match the present and future leader needs of the organization?

- Are board, executive, and staff expectations and roles clear?

- Are there mechanisms in place to ensure identification and cultivation to meet key future leadership needs and to keep the board effective and vibrant?

- Is the board you have the board the organization really needs?

For example, a children's services organization in the West was preparing for a planned departure two years out. There was an organizational culture of transparency and inclusiveness. The executive and board committee decided to do a survey of all staff and board and twenty key stakeholders and to hold focus groups with four sets of middle managers and staff. For this organization, there was an open question about whether to continue to attempt to be a comprehensive services agency or to become more specialized. This decision would affect both future resources and the background of the next executive. The process was designed to clarify the points of view and move to a decision on this issue.

Mission and Strategy Clarity/Organizational Positioning

- Is the mission clear, compelling, and agreed to by both board and staff?

- Is there an annual or strategic plan that lays out goals or results and strategies to achieve the same? Has this plan been reviewed and updated recently? Have there been major changes in the environment or organization that make the plan less useful or relevant?

- Are board, staff, and stakeholders clear about the compelling case for the work of the organization—its position or standing in the community?

For some organizations, the mission is clear and compelling. For others, a broad mission complicates efforts to sharpen focus or build alignment. Some organizations have a clear mission but lack effective strategies. Other organizations have too many goals and strategies, or have not updated them for some time. This review of mission, strategy, and position helps the organization align these elements.

Financial Health History

- Has the organization had a surplus or break-even budget in the past year? In the past three years?

- How many months of operating expenses are available in a reserve or cash account if needed?

- Has the organization had to lay off staff or reduce expenses due to reduced resources in the last year? In the last three years?

The finance and resource review requires an experienced individual who understands nonprofit finances. The review needs to include the current systems and health as well as an examination of the historical trends. In one case, what started out looking like a financially healthy organization turned out to be much more fragile when income and expenses over past five years were analyzed. The sustainability review made it clear that this organization was going to need to make some improvements in financial tracking, budgeting, and funding diversification. In yet another case, despite a financial review, surprises about resources and finances became evident later in the process. The review had not looked sufficiently at accounts payable and receivable and relied too much on assurances from the long-term executive. The next executive discovered major funding deficits as a result of the incomplete review.

Resource Development Trends

- What is the mix and amount of income for the past year? For the last three years?

- What are the trends in giving to the organization? What is growing? Declining? Stagnant?

- What are the resource development goals?

- What capacity exists or is needed to achieve these goals?

Similar to mission and strategy, how and from whom an organization receives its operating support changes over time. While conventional wisdom is to diversify resources, diversification is difficult. This discussion looks at the reality of where resources have come from over the past five years and in what amounts. What are the trends and interrelationships of these sources? Once the historical look is complete, a forward look is developed based on current reality and what is needed to sustain the critical services and work.

Internal Systems

- Are the basic organizational systems in place—HR, IT, finance?
- Are there systems issues that limit growth or success at the current operations?

Almost every nonprofit grows asymmetrically, with programs and services usually more formalized and sophisticated than infrastructure. So nearly every nonprofit has some catching up to do on systems as part of the departure planning. To bring focus to this, look at those systems that may be dependent on the departing executive's skill set or interests. For example, one organization's entire major donor tracking system was what the executive carried around in her head. It worked for her, but was clearly not a sustainable system.

This sustainability review is generally done through a series of conversations with the executive, senior staff, board committee, and some more formal data collection—short survey, telephone interviews, or focus groups. Timing, resources, organizational size, and culture guide what's the most effective approach.

Sustainability Audit The results of this initial sustainability review are discussed with the committee and as appropriate with the board. They may decide to go deeper in one or two areas, or to address issues identified in the review. To differentiate this from the sustainability review, we often call this stage a sustainability audit. (The meaning of *audit* here is not the same as its meaning in the term *financial audit*.) Here are some additional examples of the deeper work through a sustainability audit:

An advocacy organization in the Southwest had an obvious financial issue. The review sharpened the understanding of why: a combination of payment slowness from three major funders and the loss of two major donors. The audit looked at payment timing from all contributors, assessed the likelihood of retaining the other two dozen major donors, and stepped up research on major donor prospects.

An environmental group started out as a state organization and incrementally spent more time on national policy. National growth was never an intentional decision, and feedback from the surveys indicated concern among members about the lack of attention to state issues. In this case the sustainability audit took a deeper look at specific national and state issues and the issues that members felt were neglected. This resulted in the board and staff having a shared understanding of the connections and a policy for allocating resources to state and national issues.

A community-based health clinic in the East had grown quickly in the past five years. The sustainability review revealed that the financial system was inadequate and causing the board and staff not to know where they stood financially. The sustainability audit looked at options for a new finance system and an interim plan to ensure board and management had accurate and timely financial information.

The product of the sustainability review and audit is a written report that indicates the strengths, assets, issues, concerns, aspirations, and recommendations. A draft of this report is discussed with the executive and the board committee (see Appendix C—also available online—for an example).

Basic Succession Planning The most basic form of succession planning is the creation of an *emergency backup plan* and a *succession policy.* The emergency backup plan is a brief document that describes the process for appointing an acting executive in the event of an unplanned absence. The succession policy describes the guiding principles and procedures to be used in the event of a planned transition. (See Chapter Six for a detailed guide on developing the plan and policy.)

When an organization already has in place the emergency backup plan and succession policy, this step is simply a matter of reviewing them and updating if necessary. If these succession basics are not in place, typically the executive creates a backup plan while the board works out a succession policy. The exceptions are situations where the departure date is nine to fifteen months away or the sustainability issues are so critical that working on emergency backup planning is a distraction. For these situations, it makes sense to delay this step and get on with the transition planning.

The benefits for completing the succession basics during departure-defined succession include the following:

- The process of identifying key functions of the executive and management team clarifies strengths and vulnerabilities in the critical work of the organization. It also uncovers priorities for cross-training and professional development.

- The emergency backup planning puts a communication process in place that can be used for the departure announcement or any important communication.

- The board's discussion of the procedures and principles to be used in a planned executive transition reduces the risk of hasty or inappropriate decisions being made in the emotion of imminent transition.

Phase Three: Plan

Once the organizational review is complete, the board, executive, and staff need to listen to the results and revisit their goals, priorities, and leadership planning. This planning phase typically involves a series of meetings of one or more board committees and a parallel review process with the management team and staff. These discussions often culminate in an event that some call a *sustainability strategy session* or *a leadership and strategy review session.*

The sustainability strategy session may take many forms. For some organizations with a history of board-staff planning sessions, the committee, executive, and senior staff plan for and lead a board-staff planning session. The agenda includes a review of what has been learned, a discussion of the possible implications, and discussion and input on priority next steps.

In larger organizations, this planning might start with one or two facilitated sessions with the CEO and senior managers to clarify the information and issues that should be included in a subsequent session with the board or its executive committee. For another organization, the desired process might include a series of joint senior management and executive committee meetings. Ultimately the full board needs to be informed and involved.

The overarching result of the planning phase is that the organization knows what it must do to strengthen the organization for a transition. Some of the results and products from this phase include:

- A *sustainability plan* that details the areas of focus and priorities for actions to strengthen organizational and leadership sustainability

- Agreement on board and staff roles in moving forward and milestones for accountability and reporting

- A communications plan that describes the timing, stakeholder interests, key messages, and designated spokespeople

- If the transition is less than six to twelve months away, the formation of a transition committee (and preparations to move into *executive transition management,* the topic of Chapter Five)

One other product is less tangible: if handled correctly, the sustainability strategy session can begin the all-important process of creating staff ownership of the coming change. Ensuring organizational sustainability usually requires change. Change requires buy-in and involvement of those involved. Change is easier when those affected understand why it is happening. Therefore, some method of involving the rest of the board and staff in the results and implications of the review and audit is important. The sustainability strategy session can be that method.

The final sustainability plan serves as a road map for the executive, board, and staff and defines the big (and not so big) changes required for the organization to "pivot" to ensure long-term sustainability with the current executive *and* her successor. For boards that have up until now followed the lead of the executive and staff, this process and the report generally result in a new balance of board-executive leadership and increased awareness and commitment to the actions needed to prepare for and manage leadership change whenever it occurs.

If the departure is two or more years away, the focus is largely on sustainability and succession, with some attention to how executive transition will occur when it does. If the departure is less than two years away, there is more immediacy and therefore more focus on the executive transition planning.

Phase Four: Implement

How the plan gets implemented depends on timing and key issues. One result of the sustainability review session is clarity about actions needed *before* an executive transition occurs. These change items vary and might include actions that:

- Hire new managers or staff to reduce overreliance on one or two leaders or add capacity in a new area essential to sustainability

- Strengthen an essential part of the infrastructure (finance, IT, human resources, and so on)

- Launch a process to add a new strategy or a communications or branding campaign to sharpen clarity about who the organization is and what it does

- Expand financial resources through a campaign or new focus on fund development

- Advance leader development through increased attention to management and staff development, an annual bench strength review of key management positions in larger organizations, and attention to board recruitment and development

As noted, departure timing drives implementation of the plan. For early departures, the move into transition planning happens quickly and somewhat seamlessly. For later departures, there is more time to work on specific issues deemed essential. There is no immediate work on transition, and there is often a pause where the formal sustainability planning is completed and it is not time yet for transition and search. Let's look more specifically at how departure timing influences implementation.

Sustainability Actions   Most organizations have one or two actions that if completed will reduce the stress of transition and make the success of the next executive more likely. Organizations with later (two to four years) departures and more time can go deeper and work on bigger changes. Here are some examples of both:

Immediate Changes Possible for Most Organizations

- Rework financial reporting so the board and senior staff have a reliable and useful dashboard of key indicators that they understand and are covered in timely updates

- Increase attention to a particular fundraising effort to enhance revenue, for example, direct mail, an event, major donor giving, and so forth

- Update the Web site and communications materials with the current activities and focus of the organization

- Fill any agreed upon strategic positions or vacancies (in some cases some new hires may be deferred to the new executive if the departure is within six months)

- Complete a board self-assessment and recruit new members to fill vacancies or add needed competencies and leadership

- Work to strengthen results reporting and accountability

Deeper or More Substantive Changes When Departure Is Two Years or Longer in the Future

- Put a new financial or database system in place

- Hire a first or new development director or implement a newly developed plan for increasing revenues

- Make a major shift in services or activities as part of a new strategy and positioning of the organization

- Implement a comprehensive leader development program for managers and staff

- Change the bylaws and reorganize the board and organizational structure

- Revise and ramp up attention to communications and marketing

These examples are not exhaustive. Each organization will get clearer on actions needed and decide how to proceed given the current organizational realities and departure timing.

Executive Transition Actions   Executive transition actions vary tremendously, depending on the situation. Following are some of the implementation actions that occur.

Executive Transition Management (ETM)

- When the departure is within eighteen months, the sustainability planning process evolves naturally into an executive transition process (the subject of Chapter Five). In this case, the organization moves forward with the search and transition. The planning work already completed makes the executive transition process much shorter and simpler. The board puts in place its transition and search committee and reviews the planning work to make sure nothing has changed that impacts the competencies of the next executive and key transition issues. The communications plan for announcing the departure and plan for staff involvement are updated. In two to four weeks, the organization is ready to launch its executive search. (See Chapter Five for details of the ETM process.)

- Actions are taken to create a positive ending for the departing executive and to recognize her contribution.

- The board negotiates an exit agreement and clarifies any post-exit relationship with the departing executive director.

- A committee plans a welcome and orientation for the new executive.

- The new executive and board discuss goals, performance measures, mutual accountability, and communications.

- The board and new executive director agree on a plan for the six-month and annual performance review.

- The board and new executive director set a timeline for updating the sustainability or strategic plan.

Communications Activities It is challenging to be appropriately transparent while avoiding the premature announcement of departure. Finding the balance requires collaborative leadership between the executive, the board chair, and other involved parties. Leaders and consultants with experience in multiple transitions are quite valuable during this part of the process.

- Many factors influence timing and when the departure becomes public. The biggest factor is funder confidence, which relies on a relationship of trust between the executive and funders. Thus, timing may be planned around impending funding decisions, the ability to notify key program officers, and so forth.

- For imminent departures, the sustainability planning session ends with an announcement of a planned departure that launches the transition. In this situation, the communications plan for announcing the departure, the transition timeline, the transition committee leadership, and the committee's initial ideas on the use of outside consulting assistance have all been planned and are part of the report.

Plan Maintenance When the departure is further out than two years, the implementation should include regular review and updating of the plan created in Phase Three. Such review includes an examination of:

- Progress on implementing the sustainability plan recommendations, with revisions as needed

- The readiness of designated backups and progress on cross-training specified in the emergency backup plan

- The succession policy

- Progress in building bench strength and advancing leader development goals and vision

- Progress in completing other preparations determined as essential to a successful planned executive transition

This chapter does not go into detail on the implementation phase of departure-defined succession planning relative to executive transition as it is essentially similar to the Pivot phase in executive transition management, described in Chapter Five. Besides that chapter, organizations preparing for departure-defined succession will want to review Chapter One, which introduces William Bridges's work on change and transition. If your departing executive is a founder or long-term executive, you'll want to read more about the unique challenges and considerations of founder transitions in Chapter Three. Finally, regardless of your role, if you are leading or supporting a nonprofit you care about, you will have feelings about a leadership change. You may find it useful to look at Chapter Two on the emotions and self-care of leadership transition.

Conclusion: Advancing the Leaderful Organization

Departure-defined succession planning advances the leaderful organization. It combines succession and sustainability planning with executive transition management. Timing and circumstances cause it to look quite different from organization to organization.

As noted at the chapter outset, departure-defined succession planning asks the executive and her board and staff leadership team a similar question: What's the highest and best use for the organization of the time between when an executive sets a general or specific departure date and the departure?

Of course, the particulars of the "highest and best use" will vary from one organization to the next. Often, organizations realize that the founder or longtime executive director has had too much work, and they reconfigure the job. They may realize that it's time for the organization to create an institutional identity. They may see the need for new infrastructure, or uncover talent gaps that the current executive's skills had filled.

Here are a few examples of how this type of planning resulted in a more leaderful organization with increased capacity to achieve mission results:

- A large statewide organization went from almost total reliance on an executive and deputy both over the age of sixty to a six-person senior management team aligned around goals and roles.

- A community service organization moved from an identity that was inseparable from that of the founder to an organization with an engaged and visible board and staff leadership team.

- A previously successful organization, which had struggled to raise money for the three years before beginning departure-defined planning, refreshed its mission, broadened its lines of services, communicated the changes to funders, and doubled its annual income.

- An environmental group whose financial system had fallen behind its growth successfully shifted to a new system that gave the board and funders the confidence they were looking for in the financial statements.

If executive transition is highly likely or inevitable for you or your organization over the next four years, departure-defined succession planning is a process and practice you'll want to consider.

REFLECTION QUESTIONS

For the Individual Leader

1. Are you a founder or long-term executive who is beginning to think about how and when to depart from the organization? Or are you a board member or funder who is concerned about the departure of a founder or long-term executive? If yes, what questions or concerns does this chapter raise for you?

2. Are there next actions you need to take as an executive, board leader, or funder to clarify plans for departure? If so, what are these actions and what are the timeline and support needed to complete them?

3. What's the most challenging part of departure-defined succession planning for you personally?

For Executive Directors and Board Leaders of an Organization

1. If you are involved with a founder-led organization or one with a long-term executive:

   a. Does the board chair or executive committee talk with the executive about departure plans and timing?

   b. Are the succession basics in place?

2. If you are facing a founder or long-term executive transition in the next one to four years:

   a. What are the biggest risks your organization faces during the transition? What can you do to reduce their threat?

   b. Does it make sense to consider the departure-defined process described here? If yes, why? If not, why not?

   c. What elements of the departure-defined process seem most needed and appropriate for your organization?

For Funders, Capacity-Building Providers, Association Staff, and Other Supporting Stakeholders

1. Does your organization pay attention to the unique contributions and challenges of organizations led by founders and long-term executives?

2. Are there actions you might consider to increase awareness of the possibilities and benefits of departure-defined succession planning as described here? If so, what are the most important actions and when might you plan to complete these actions?

3. Can you imagine how attention to departure-defined succession planning will improve the effectiveness of organizations you care about and reduce the risks of failed or troubled executive transitions when organizations change leaders?

8

Leader Development and Talent Management

LEADING ORGANIZATIONS PAY ATTENTION to developing both positional leaders *and* staff. Such organizations have moved beyond typical reactive responses to departures of executives, board leaders, or "indispensable" staff.

These organizations have made a commitment to developing a culture where *leader development* is a priority. They invest in training, mentoring, and coaching their managers and staff. Financial resources are budgeted to support individual and manager development. Leaders have performance goals that include their own development as well as their duties to identify and support the development of other leaders. Such organizations are well on the road to what we refer to here as being *leaderful*.

We have described earlier how attention to leader transitions, succession basics (emergency backup planning and the development by the board of a succession policy), and departure-defined succession planning are powerful ways to advance the goal of becoming a leaderful organization. This chapter looks at another aspect of succession planning: *leader development and talent management*. You may also see this third type referred to as "strategic leader development." The terms refer to the same thing: an intentional commitment by the current leaders (sometimes referred to as *positional leaders*) to embracing leader development as critical to expanding organizational capacity to achieve results.

Leader here refers to both positional leaders or managers and other individuals with the potential to contribute significantly to the organization's capacity to meet and exceed goals. *Talent* here refers to all staff and the underlying belief that everyone has the capacity to contribute and lead. The term *talent management* refers to a mission-driven strategy that guides hiring, talent development, performance management, compensation and rewards, and communications for an organization. In larger organizations, leader development tends to focus on managers and potential managers with some attention to broader talent development. In smaller organizations, there is an opportunity to focus on talent development (that is, the entire staff) while setting aside some resources for leader development of executives, managers, or team leaders. *Talent management* is generally a term used in larger for-profit corporations to describe the processes and systems used to ensure the continuity of leadership and talent (managers and staff) that is required to achieve the desired results, but we've adapted it here for the nonprofit context.

All this work is strategic because it is tied to mission and results. An organization's size, mission, and resources influence its approach to leader development and talent management. Since nonprofit organizations do not have excess profits to reinvest like for-profit companies, allocating time and money for leader development is challenging. Given that, the need for a clear strategy and approach is essential. This chapter will help the organization become more strategic in its use of resources to develop leaders and other talent.

For the purposes of our discussion here, what follows will:

- Provide examples of leader development and talent management and their application to different-size organizations

- Offer suggestions on actions individual leaders might take to grow as leaders

- Provide six specific actions for organizations that want to advance leader development

- Introduce in detail the for-profit practice of talent management and suggest how this approach, adapted to the nonprofit organization, fully enlivens the commitment to becoming a leaderful organization

Examples of Leader Development and Talent Management

Juan Vasquez founded a community development organization in the Northeast. For the first ten years, the organization patched together enough resources to support a six-person staff, offer some basic home ownership counseling services, and work on one real estate project of priority to the neighborhood. Juan signed up for a yearlong leadership program for executives involved in community development. Midway through the second weeklong session, Juan realized his organization would never grow without more projects and that he needed a different approach to staffing to accomplish that. Over the next two years, he reorganized his staff and raised money to hire a more experienced real estate project manager and to support training for his staff for this change. He set a goal in the first year of three projects a year, and over the next five years increased the goal to ten projects a year with fifteen to twenty in the pipeline. His organization is now the largest and most productive in the state. Juan attributes this success to the decision to grow and to invest in hiring the people and providing the staff development to enable growth.

Jeanne Jones leads a large human services organization. Her board was concerned about what would happen when she retired. She had been working with her leadership team on a plan to increase the racial diversity of the managers. This had led to discussions of how to grow and develop leaders. Up until then, the agency offered the technical training needed to keep its licenses and comply with state and federal regulations. Jane went back to the board and said the best way to get ready for her retirement was to dramatically increase the investment in leader and management development and training for line staff. The board agreed to support Jeanne and the staff in developing a human capital campaign with a goal of raising $500 thousand a year for the next five years to invest in leader development. It took two years to reach the goal, and the planning happened incrementally. By the third year, key performance measures were improving, management was more racially diverse, and the case for the investment in leader development became simpler each year because it was tied to performance improvements.

Antoine Jackson was the new executive of a successful zoo in the Southwest. He followed a longtime executive who was a great planner and added new attractions every year or two. Antoine had an opportunity to hire three new senior managers because of retirement from the top team who left with the long-term executive. Antoine knew the secret to the zoo's success was the customers' enjoyment of their visit. With the managers he developed a training program for the entire staff focused on how to achieve and sustain 95 percent superior customer satisfaction reviews from customers. It took three years to get from 75 percent to 95 percent. During the recession, the zoo's attendance grew by 30 percent and there were no layoffs. The success of this effort led to the development of a learning institute with offerings for managers and all zoo employees from the increased revenue from the attendance growth.

A foundation in the West was concerned about the number of long-term executives with no succession plans. The foundation executive wrote a letter to the executives saying: "I am thinking about succession planning for myself and am wondering if you are interested in a workshop we are planning to learn about best practices in succession planning." Eighteen of the nineteen executives and their board chairs attended two workshops and worked with a consultant to develop succession plans over the next nine months. Several of these organizations have now successfully transitioned and have used their succession plans to increase attention to developing leaders and looking at where key positions were strengthened through hires or development.

These organizations are among a growing number of exceptional organizations who have experienced the benefit of a leader development culture. Unfortunately, a much larger number of organizations remain in which leader development is either episodic, reactive to external requirements, or doesn't happen at all. These organizations are more likely to have a higher turnover of management and staff and to struggle more with meeting funder and government contract requirements and performance goals. As indicated in earlier chapters, organizations that ignore leader development are more vulnerable when an executive, key manager or staff, or board leader moves on.

What follows begins first with individual leader development and then looks at six organizational actions to advance leader development and talent management.

Leader Development—Personal Commitment and Actions

Being a leader is personal. As individuals we make decisions about how we spend our time, what we want to learn, and what we want to contribute to our families, communities, and society. While the focus of this book is largely how leaders in organizations can advance a leader development culture, such a commitment of necessity has to include a look at our personal growth as leaders.

The nonprofit executive of a Midwest environmental organization attended one of the U.S. service academies. He was fond of sharing that the most important thing he learned about leadership at the Academy was to lead by example. His commitment to learning and growing as a leader was evident to everyone and helped make the possible benefits of growing as a leader real for the organization.

Ideally, you work with an organization that is committed to leader development and offers you learning opportunities and support. Regardless of whether that is true, leader development *starts* with personal decisions and actions. The more engaged you are in leader development, the more likely you will work for an organization that supports leader development in order to advance the organization's work.

What follows is not intended to be exhaustive. It's a menu of choices and a guide to resources to assist leaders and potential leaders in strengthening their commitment to leader development. Here are activities that other leaders have found helpful in their personal leader development:

1. Check your beliefs about leaders and perceptions of yourself as a leader.

2. Develop a personal mission statement.

3. Assess your leadership competencies and goals as a leader.

4. Connect with others to support your learning.

5. Know your blind spots and get help to mitigate them.

Let's explore each.

Check Your Beliefs About Leaders and Perceptions of Yourself as a Leader

Discussions about leadership with grassroots leaders or employees at entry-level positions often reveal a reluctance to see themselves as leaders. This may be true for some managers and persons in formal leadership positions as well. It is challenging to commit to learning to be a leader if you are not sure you want to be one. For others, there may be a belief that leadership requires being smart or having a college degree from a prestigious school. Still others think of leaders as those with a title or responsibility for managing people.

These beliefs can unconsciously limit choices or opportunities. One leader development trainer, Karen Gaskins Jones, introduces the distinction between "formal or positional leaders" and "informal leaders" to expand the ways of thinking about leadership. Organizations typically have formal leaders who are considered leaders because of title or position. These same organizations have individuals who exercise informal influence and are important to getting the mission accomplished.[1]

To expand a leader development culture, first, discussions should focus on perceptions of who is a leader and what leadership requires. The organization needs an expansive definition that does not exclude too many people. This is followed by a commitment of resources for both leader and talent development (for managers and staff). Even when the organization defines *leading* broadly, there may be messages of doubt—what Brigette Rouson in *Embracing Cultural Competency* calls "internalized oppression." This is a "phenomenon in which members of a group adopt a negative view of themselves based on the prejudices of other organizations."[2] Such beliefs can limit the possibilities of personal growth as a leader.

This reflective process on beliefs about leadership can be done as a personal reflection alone or in a group. Changing deeply held beliefs takes time, and the support of a group working on similar issues may be helpful to some leaders.

Develop a Personal Mission Statement

The pace of twenty-first-century life is amazing. Technology and education provide us with so many choices for our time. Leaders feel this stress intensely. People who care passionately about a cause or body of work are impatient for progress and commit themselves with vigor to the work. For both seasoned and emerging leaders, there comes a time when the pace becomes too much and the question is *to what end?*

Like organizations, leaders benefit from a personal mission statement that serves as a rudder to help guide choices and focus. In his classic *The Seven Habits of Highly Effective People,* Stephen R. Covey explains: "The most effective way I know to begin with the end in mind is to develop a personal mission statement or philosophy or creed. It focuses on what you want to be (character) and to do (contributions and achievements) and on the values and principles upon which being and doing are based."[3] Covey compares a personal mission statement to a constitution that changes rarely. It generally takes several drafts to find what works best. Once a leader has that, Covey observes that the mission statement serves as a changeless inner core which makes it much easier to deal with constant change in our environment. Without it, he observes, change can be overwhelming.[4] (For examples of personal mission statements, see the Covey books cited or visit the Franklin Covey Web site [www.franklincovey.com] where you can build your mission statement online.)

Assess Your Leadership Competencies and Goals as a Leader

Perhaps you've heard the story of the centipede that spent so much time thinking about how to walk that he lost his natural ability to do it. Some sages suggest that the unexamined life isn't worth living. The corollary, as demonstrated by the introspective centipede, is that the overexamined life can't be enjoyed. Each leader finds her balance of introspection and "just doing it."

Before diving too deeply into assessing yourself as a leader, you might consider exploring your preferred way of learning. The Web abounds with simple-to-use explanations of three commonly cited learning preferences: auditory (through hearing), visual (through seeing), or tactile or kinesthetic (through touch or experience). There are also many resources that explain the theory of multiple intelligence and its application to learning.[5]

Most communities have a local leadership program, and most community colleges offer courses in leadership. Some tools that leaders use to learn more about themselves include the following:

- *Strengths Finder 2.0.* This is a book and short online test based on research by the Gallup organization. The paradigm shift here is to move away from the heavy focus on weaknesses and to increase attention to understanding your strengths and the strengths of those with whom you work and team. This book is used both for individual learning and for work with teams on how to get the most from their collective talents in achieving the desired results.[6]

- *The Leadership Challenge.* Authors Kouzes and Posner offer what is considered by some to be one of the most evidence-based approaches to leader development. Built around five practices of exemplary leadership (1. Model the way, 2. Inspire a shared vision, 3. Challenge the process, 4. Enable others to act, and 5. Encourage the heart), the fourth edition offers new case examples of the five practices in action. One of the great advantages of this book is that it offers an online 360-degree Leadership Practices Inventory (LPI) that provides feedback and insights about how to grow in the five practices.[7]

- *Leadership Architect Assessment.* Lominger International offers another highly regarded research-based approach to assessing leader competencies and developing a leader and career development plan. Lominger's Leadership Architect assessment is organized around sixty-seven leader competencies and nineteen career stallers and stoppers. For more information about the Lominger products and how to access them in your community, visit www.lominger.com.[8]

- *The Pathfinder.* Author Nicholas Lore offers a unique and holistic approach to leader self-assessments. Believing traditional career planning is too narrowly defined, Lore offers a self-assessment guide that allows the reader to look in an integrated way at how natural talents, temperament, personality and passion, meaning, mission and purpose, and values and rewards combine to produce a path to meaningful and fulfilling work and leadership opportunities. Lore's Rockport Institute (www.rockportinstitute.com) offers information about his Career Choice program that offers testing and coaching around the information found in *The Pathfinder*.[9]

While formal testing may be useful to many leaders, journaling or joining a leader development peer group are equally powerful ways to expand self-awareness of your leader talents and identify any aspirations you might have to grow as a leader.

As noted above there are an abundance of learning opportunities to further hone leader strengths. If you've never participated in a formal leadership program, you might ask yourself why. There is no perfect program. Most leaders find some time away—whether a once-a-week class, a weeklong seminar, or a yearlong program—invaluable in terms of networking, learning, and gaining confidence as a leader. (See Appendix D—also available online—for examples of leader development programs for nonprofit leaders.)

Connect with Others to Support Your Learning

Research indicates that action learning or learning by doing advances leader learning. Ram Charan, in *Leaders at All Levels*, challenges the slow, steady approach to leader mobility and development, particularly for CEO and top executive positional leader development. He describes in detail what he calls the Apprenticeship Approach to leader development, which emphasizes the importance of a mentor and advocate who opens opportunities and the willingness to take measured risks in moving into new assignments that stretch and develop key competencies needed for executive success.[10]

There are many leadership programs from which to choose. Larger urban areas have leadership programs organized by the corporate sector with nonprofit participation. The Leadership Learning Community (www.leadershiplearning.org) provides a summary of programs around the country. Universities and colleges also have programs. The Center for Creative Leadership (www.ccl.org) offers a weeklong program that is well regarded.

If you don't have a mentor, you might consider interviewing a few leaders who do and asking them what they see as the benefits. Mentoring can vary in its purpose and application. Bozeman and Feeney offer one definition of mentoring as "a process for the informal transmission of knowledge, social capital, and the psychological support perceived by the recipient as relevant to work, career, or professional development."[11] In the nonprofit arena, mentoring happens when a seasoned board leader guides a newer board member in leading his first committee or where a manager provides informal support to a first-time supervisor. Some leaders find support and assistance from an executive coach. There are many types of coaches—life coaches, career coaches, and executive coaches, among others. On its Web site (http://www.coachfederation.org), the International Coach Federation provides a simple guide to finding an appropriate coach and a free service to connect you with certified coaches.

As coaching has grown in popularity, there has been a definite shift from coaching being seen as only for the troubled or difficult employee to a tool for all leaders to support leader development. As a leader development tool, coaching may be a helpful tool when change or new behavior is needed or in support of a promotion or stretch assignment. Coaching is also used to assist Baby Boom era managers with the challenges of managing younger workers and adapting to the work ethics and values of a new generation of workers and managers.

A study reported in *Fast Company* (July 8, 2008) in *Coaching: The Fad That Won't Go Away* took a 3-D look at coaching associated with leader development to understand the growing use of this tool. The study involved forty-eight organizations and eighty-six leaders from the perspective of coach, person coached, and the organization. The results were quite persuasive about the perceived benefit to the individual and organization from coaching. Ninety-two percent of those coached said they planned to use a coach again and 63 percent of the organizations intend to increase their use of coaches over the next five years.[12]

Coaching is also growing in use and acceptance as a leader development tool in nonprofit organizations. CompassPoint Nonprofit Services has just concluded an evaluation of its executive coaching program for nonprofit executives with encouraging results. (See www.Compasspoint.org for more details.)[13]

Know Your Blind Spots and Get Help to Mitigate Them

The Lominger Leadership Architect focuses on both leader competencies and career derailers (blind spots that stall or stop development) for a reason. Interim ministers who work with faith-based congregations when they are in the midst of changing leadership have a saying they repeat often to the congregation and to each other: "All pastors have their gifts. And they have their other areas."

All leaders are human and have unique life experiences that shape their approach to leading. Sometimes, overused strengths can become career stallers or derailers. For example, a strength like being determined or dogged becomes a career staller when the board or executive begins to see you as rigid and unable to listen or change. Other times a way of doing something—raising money, handling communication—has worked for a number of years but is not working as well now. The leader committed to learning sees she has a blind spot and needs help to learn some new approaches and aggressively seeks help. The stalled leader ignores the signals and hopes the issue will go away or worse yet gets annoyed at staff and board for continuing to raise the issue.

Each leader finds his own way to get feedback and keep an eye out for habits or behaviors that undermine his role or put support for the leader at risk. The important thing is to make sure you are paying attention and not missing important signals.

In organizations committed to advancing a leader development culture, the individual is not working in isolation to develop her leader development plan. The next section describes ways the organization can support leader development.

Becoming More Leaderful: Paths to Leader Development and Talent Management

Early in my career a wise supervisor suggested I attend a Dale Carnegie introductory course (www.DaleCarnegie.com). I resisted, saying I could only make five of the eight sessions. She replied that would be just fine. When I went, I met a manager of a local McDonald's restaurant. I asked him why he was there. He replied that his boss, the owner of the franchise, sent all his managers to this and other courses. This experience was the beginning of my awareness of the clear link between organizational success and investment in leaders.

Academic and popular research abounds with data and stories that link attention to leader and talent development with organizational success. Jim Collins in *Good to Great* reports that every company that transformed itself from good to great had what he calls *level 5 leaders* who "set up their successors for even greater success." Collins further reinforces the importance of attention to leadership in his emphasis on "getting the right people on the bus" before focusing on vision and strategy.[14]

While this link (results and leadership) is more deeply embedded in the for-profit culture, there are a number of indicators of growing attention by CEOs, managers, and boards in the nonprofit sector to embracing a leader development philosophy. The focus on accountability and results heightens attention to the connection between improved performance by individuals and greater impact for the organization. This evidence comes in a number of forms:

- The recognition by the largest and leading nonprofit organizations of the need to compete to attract and retain skilled employees and leaders, resulting in the formation of a Nonprofit Workforce Coalition

- The shift from the topic of "succession planning" being a scary and taboo topic up until 2005 or so to it being openly discussed and a priority for many boards, executives, and funders

- Publication in 2008 by Grantmakers for Effective Organizations of *Investing in Leadership Volume 2: Inspiration and Ideas from Philanthropy's Last Frontier*, a summary of nonprofit leadership development efforts with case studies[15]

- The growing number of nonprofit management degree and certificate programs supporting the increased investment in leader development

- The growing number of nonprofits developing their own leader development or talent management efforts

The decision to treat leader development and talent management as distinct is an arbitrary one. In reality they are closely related and ideally all part of one focus for an organization. Because both are new to nonprofits and talent management has a different application to midsize and larger organizations than to smaller ones, we will look at them with more distinction than may exist ten years from now.

Many organizations are involved in some form of leader development and have some systems in place to support it. There are usually particular motivations for increasing attention to leader development. The board may be concerned about succession for an aging leadership team or staff. The CEO may have successfully built a solid leadership team and be ready to pay attention to longer-term systems that increase sustainability. The board or CEO may be frustrated by high turnover of key personnel. Funders, members, or other key stakeholders may be raising questions about succession or performance and the viability of the organization.

The following describes the key components of leader development and examples of their application. The fifth action—putting a talent management system with an annual bench strength review in place—is treated in more detail in a separate section. For most larger organizations and many other organizations, adapting a talent management system represents a major step in the paradigm shift to a leaderful organization. Organizations, like individual leaders, succeed by building on the strengths of their existing leader development practices. What counts is a consistent commitment to leader development and talent management systems.

Six Actions to Advance Leader Development

1. Secure CEO, senior management, and board commitment, and establish the specific case for your organization.

2. Put succession basics in place.

3. Align human resources practices to support leader development; strengthen the capacity to manage leader development and talent management.

4. Make leader development a central part of annual operational planning and strategic planning.

5. Put a bench strength and talent management system in place.

6. Expand development and training opportunities for existing and emerging leaders and staff.

Secure CEO, Senior Management, and Board Commitment, and Establish the Specific Case for Your Organization Ideally top leadership commitment is the place to start. This is possible if the CEO and board chair are champions for leader development and can engage the management team and board in discussions about expanding attention to leader development. In reality, the champion may be a senior manager, HR director, or one or two board members who can raise the question but do not have the influence to expand the commitment. In this case it probably will work better to focus on another specific action and incrementally build top leadership support. Because leader development costs will appear to be discretionary spending, resource commitments—time and money— will be episodic and vary widely year to year until there is top leadership support.

Here are examples of how top leaders decided on a focus and commitment to leader development:

The CEO of a large nonprofit had consistently worked to achieve an internal hire rate of 75 percent or higher for key new hires. This meant he was always looking for talent internally and advancing that talent. There was no formal system, and to some the system looked arbitrary and dependent on a relationship with the CEO. When the board began pressing for a detailed succession plan naming his successor, the CEO decided to introduce the leader development approach to succession planning to the board and to make leader development one of six priorities for the new strategic plan. The CEO also attended a workshop for large for-profit companies on succession planning. He learned that best practice required a strong commitment from the CEO and for the CEO to personally spend time on leader development and talent management. This combination of events resulted in the CEO becoming a champion, the organization increasing by 50 percent over three years the resources invested in leader development, and leader development becoming a key performance measure for senior managers.

A seasoned Latina leader became the new CEO of a major nonprofit. Her five senior managers were all white men over the age of fifty. The hiring board was mostly white with two leaders of color. She devoted her first nine months to building relationships and improving results on the board's priorities. Given the age of her management team and the male-dominated culture of the organization, she decided on two first actions. One was symbolic. She began hosting meetings where women in middle management and the male senior managers interacted around business as well as socially. This had never been done before. Simultaneously, she asked the HR director to work with her to put in place emergency succession or backup plans for the senior managers. This analysis of key functions and roles and bench strength gave her the information she needed to discuss with the board the need for two new strategic hires and for making leader development a central part of annual and strategic planning. Over the next three years, she transformed the leadership and culture of the organization to one of full commitment to leader development. A sleepy nonprofit became a leader in its field locally and nationally.

A small community development organization had a ten-year track record of success in the two neighborhoods it served in a Southwest city. The recession reduced its funding support by 40 percent. The executive director had begun his career as a community organizer and knew the power of leader development. She believed that expanding the commitment to leader development could be part of the adaptation to fewer resources and began discussions with the board and staff. Both enthusiastically embraced the idea after she got specific about what this meant in terms of achieving the community's priorities. By expanding and refocusing the roles of both staff and volunteers through an intensive training and mentoring program, the organization increased its results and won back two major funders who supported the new leader development approach.

Put Succession Basics in Place For many organizations, committing to completing the succession basics—an emergency backup plan for executive and senior managers and a board-adopted succession policy—is the least controversial and simplest way to ramp up attention to leader development. It is hard to be against getting ready for an unplanned absence. Most leaders have experienced the sudden absence of a key leader. Done well, where there is a commitment to really look at the key roles and functions of the executive and managers and the implications when there is an unplanned absence, the case for investing in leader development and in some instances key hires or reorganization becomes clear. Chapter Six details how to develop the succession basics as well as providing examples of organizations using the approach.

Here are some examples of how attention to succession basics led to a deeper commitment to leader development:

When the managers of a community health center in New England completed their succession basics, the team decided to organize a leader institute and offer an ongoing series of leader development and technical training for managers and staff. The board agreed to lead a fundraising campaign and event annually with a goal of $100 thousand that would be reserved for the institute and to assist with foundation requests to advance the leader development goal. Because of the ages of the top managers, it was clear to the board and managers that without this commitment the organization would suffer a great loss of capacity and knowledge over the next five years.

A midsize nonprofit concluded after completing the succession basics that it wanted to invest more in its middle manager group. Because of the recession, attendance was down at a highly regarded weeklong leadership program in their region. The CEO negotiated a 50 percent cost discount for ten managers to attend in three cohorts over the next year. Internally she also put together a monthly Leaders' Discussion over lunch that she attended each time and to which she invited any interested middle manager. Morale and retention improved, and the organization exceeded its goals over the next two years.

Align Human Resources Practices to Support Leader Development; Strengthen Capacity to Manage Leader Development and Talent Management

Most small and midsize nonprofits don't have a human resources manager or department, or if there is one, it is a one- or two-person operation. The focus is of necessity often on the basics: payroll, benefits, compliance with regulations, and perhaps annual performance reviews. It is easy for leaders to say that "our staff are our most valued asset," but it is tough to pay for and manage the infrastructure required to fulfill that promise.

For some organizations, particularly those where employee morale is poor, there is high turnover; or where HR is the best place to advance leader development, attention to the HR practices can be a powerful choice. Such an effort might include the following steps:

Define Competency Requirements for Leader Positions. The HR function can take a deep look at current position descriptions and competency requirements and update them in such a way as to support leader development and performance. To begin creating a leader development program, you need to be aware of what competencies you need in your leaders. These will include the current needs as well as those you project you will need in the future. Most organizations approach this by facilitating a discussion of the organization's vision and strategies over the coming three to five years. They then ask people filling current managerial and other leadership positions to revisit their job descriptions, naming the current competencies as well as those they think will be needed over the next three to five years. In sum this process involves:

- Identifying the competencies needed
- Assessing the team to determine what competencies exist
- Identifying competency gaps
- Addressing the competency gaps through leader development or hiring

Leverage performance management processes and policies. In busy organizations, performance reviews can decline to an annual or episodic event with minimal attention. While this may be understandable, the approach misses a powerful leader development opportunity. A commitment to a performance management system and compensation policy that rewards leader development and increased results advances the mission and the sustainability of the organization.

A large advocacy organization CEO realized that the intensity of the organization's work seemed to make it all right to rarely get around to the coaching of new managers or performance reviews. She had a conversation with her three managers about this. All shared their frustration about it and in concept supported the importance. The CEO and managers brainstormed ways to change this behavior. From a long list, they agreed to two actions: they would each dedicate an agreed-upon hour every week to meeting with and coaching the managers. To support one another, they agreed to make it the same time—10 AM every Monday, and if the manager was out on Monday it would be rescheduled for 10 AM the first day she was back. Their second commitment was to pick a time of the year when they had the highest likelihood of focusing on annual performance reviews. They decided on the second week of August and committed to do annual performance reviews that week each year. Over three years, the attention to leader development and morale improved significantly.

Define inclusiveness, cultural competency, and diversity for the organization and clarify practices to support these goals. This is both part of basic human resources and central to talent management. We will address this in both categories. Some organizations have fully developed policies around diversity and inclusiveness; others have informal or implied practices; and others have not considered the question and have no policies. Most organizations work in communities that are becoming more diverse relative to age, race and ethnic background, culture, class, sexual orientation, and mental and physical ability. It is hard to imagine a community that is totally homogenous around all these factors. For this reason, a review of current practices and facts about the organization's culture of inclusiveness and capacity to work in different cultures and with people of many backgrounds seems obvious. However, as pointed out in Chapter Four on diversity, it can be easy to avoid this topic. Discussing what inclusiveness, diversity, and cultural competency mean for your organization is a key step in becoming more leaderful.

A foundation in the Northeast was concerned about the lack of racial diversity among the top leaders of the grantees it supported. The CEO decided that before addressing this issue with grantees, he had better look at practices within the foundation. He discussed this plan with senior managers and the board and got varying degrees of support, from enthusiastic to "Okay, but don't we have more important things to do?" He hired a consultant who specialized in supporting leaders in exploring diversity and inclusiveness and their connection to organizational results. Focus groups were held to explore if there was a connection between diversity and inclusiveness and the goals of the foundation. While the reasons varied slightly (services, fairness, cultural understanding, and so on), all the focus groups agreed there was a connection. With this support, the consultant brought in a partner who specialized in HR practices to support diversity and inclusiveness. The CEO, HR director, and two consultants led a six-month process that resulted in a written diversity and inclusiveness policy and a set of six actions to implement the policy. After six more months of beginning implementation, the foundation CEO convened a lunch of five of the foundation's key grantees and shared what the foundation was doing and engaged them in a conversation about their practices. The CEO concluded the meeting by offering support to the grantees in advancing their diversity and inclusiveness practices. Four of the five asked for help, and the fifth did its own review with a volunteer from the board.

Make leader development a central part of annual operational planning and strategic planning. This seems like an obvious step and yet is easy to overlook. A board and its executive may have frequent conversations about the need to pay more attention to preparing new board leaders and adding needed competencies to the staff or board. Much less frequently do these conversations make it to the annual plan or to performance priorities for the executive or board. Integrating leader development planning into the annual plan increases the odds this activity will get attention. Competition for attention is enormous in most organizations, so making leader development more formal advances the commitment.

Similarly, discussions of vision and values often have to do with leaders and the beliefs that guide the organization. Strategic planning less frequently converts these aspirations into a major strategic objective of leader development and commits time, money, and expected results to this function. During strategic or annual planning, discussions about how becoming a leaderful organization might advance results can help integrate explicit leader development goals into the annual and strategic plan.

A large membership organization that focused on environmental issues decided to combine the board's request for a report on bench strength for the top six positions with integrating leader development into strategic planning. Through participation in the strategic planning, the board and senior staff shaped the new priorities for the organization, and for each priority they did an assessment of the organization's leadership and management capacity to achieve the results. This broader look got integrated into the strategic priorities and made the bench strength discussion with the board much deeper and more meaningful when it occurred nine months after the request.

Put a bench strength and talent management system in place. Further on, this chapter goes into detail about how to develop a talent management system and the benefits. For midsize and larger organizations, this is a crucial piece of the leader development commitment. For smaller organizations, seeing the team of staff, board, and volunteers as a talent management system has enormous potential. Depending on past practices, resources, current leadership, and other factors, talent management may not be the place to start for some organizations. However, to really embrace leader development as a strategy for improved results, it will need to be addressed over time. The talent management discussion is also a powerful tool for advancing organizational goals around diversity and inclusiveness.

Expand development and training opportunities for existing and emerging leaders and staff. For some organizations, this is the obvious and simplest place to advance leader development. Connecting organizational results to training and development helps avoid the perception that training is merely a "feel-good" opportunity for participants. The clearer the focus, the more powerful the results. Options for development include:

- Action learning around a real work project

- "Stretch assignments" for growing leaders

- Offering a cohort of leaders and managers an opportunity to participate in a long-term leader program

- Training in technical skills such as supervision, public speaking, writing, financial management, and collaboration

Leading organizations offer these opportunities to staff either internally or through tuition reimbursement. Focusing on development and training is a good strategy when the organization has an effective HR system and clear goals about which leaders will be developed toward what end.

A number of national organizations have certificate programs to support member organizations in advancing leader development. These initiatives are often a result of discussions between local leaders and national staff about priorities for training and what scale works best for success.

The CEO of a housing organization in the South decided he wanted to improve results around loan production and the rehabilitation of vacant homes. He organized the work so that staff spent 75 percent of the time on loans for six months of the year and 75 percent of the time on rehab for six months. He was fond of quoting Jesse Jackson, who reportedly said: "What I do most, I do best." The CEO, the HR director, and the vice presidents for lending and rehab worked as a four-person team to meet with managers and line staff to determine what training would improve results. They offered intense loan production training along with coaching support during the six months when loan production was a priority. Similarly, when rehab was a priority, they offered intense training and coaching on rehab. The leadership team analyzed the skills needed and which staff could best support what parts of the loan and rehab functions, and organized the work and training around this analysis. By repeating this process annually for three years, the loan production grew by 100 percent, the loan closing time dropped by 40 percent, and the number of completed rehabbed vacant homes grew from fifteen to twenty-five in the first year and to forty in the third year.

Let's shift now from actions that advance leader development to talent management and its benefits.

Talent Management

In 1997, I left a national organization and started a consulting business. From the outset, I recognized I was responsible for developing enough work to pay the bills. While scary at times, I found a rhythm and set a goal of how many hours I needed to work for clients each month and worked toward that goal. As the business grew, I kept a personal goal of "billable hours" or client work as my responsibilities shifted. This approach led to significant ups and downs in terms of work and a fair amount of drama (sometimes in my head only, sometimes in reality) about cash flow.

I worked with several executive coaches, but didn't really get to the heart of this until I began working with a coach who specialized in business development. Over eighteen months, the coach helped me see that the company had grown and I needed to completely rethink my role in the company. My primary role was no longer billable hours; it was business development. I needed to think as strategically about business development as I did about a client's transition challenges. This meant clarifying roles with my business partner and putting in place a number of systems and tactics to support business development. Fortunately, this awakening occurred before the current recession, and we have in place the tools to continue to identify clients in a time of fewer transitions and more focus on survival and sustainability. Without this major shift in thought and behavior, our ability to serve clients might have been seriously threatened.

For nonprofit executives, talent management may be a major thinking and behavioral change, like my awakening about business development. This consideration is essential for larger nonprofits (over $5 million in annual revenue) and potentially useful for all nonprofits. Talent management is most commonly practiced in large for-profit companies. As the discussion that follows indicates, there are elements to talent management that may appear counter to the way many nonprofits operate. Leaders committed to an egalitarian culture where all staff are equal and potential leaders may struggle with terms such as *high potentials* (managers or staff with high potential to grow into leaders or managers or top producers) and *high producers* (managers or staff who are contributing significantly to results and for whom retention and further development is a high priority).

Before deciding what is or is not relevant to any nonprofit or your nonprofit, let's explore the idea in more detail. If there is a direct connection between leader effectiveness and organizational effectiveness, then how well an organization recruits, develops, and retains leaders significantly influences its performance. Talent management is, at its simplest, the process of proactively attending to how an organization is seeking effective leaders and the strategies and processes that support success in recruiting, developing, and retaining great leaders.

While talent management may appear obvious upon reflection, executing the idea is challenging. In Robert Barner's book *Bench Strength,* published by the American Management Association (2006), he observes: "CEOs and senior executives are quickly coming to the conclusion that a distinguishing characteristic of successful organizations is the ability to identify, develop, and deploy exceptional talent."[16]

Barner reports that executives see the leadership challenges growing, and according to a Center for Creative Leadership study, only 24 percent of respondents had a clear plan for developing leadership talent and only 29 percent indicated their organizations ". . . were effective in connecting talent management to the needs of their business units."[17] Another study by a leading human resources consulting company (Accenture) of 264 executives from six countries revealed that while two-thirds rated their ability to develop effective leaders as critical, only 8 percent felt confident in their ability to manage leadership talent.[18]

So talent management is an area where neither the for-profit nor the nonprofit sectors are excelling. Both sectors are acknowledging the increasing importance of leader effectiveness and workforce development. The rest of this section will:

- Further describe talent management as practiced in the for-profit sector

- Suggest possible applications to nonprofits of all sizes with examples

- Offer choices of actions or steps to get started or advance a talent management focus in a nonprofit organization

Talent management goes beyond traditional human resources processes. An organization can excel at how it goes about filling vacancies, offering development opportunities for staff and managing its compensation and benefits in ways that encourage employee retention and totally miss the power of talent management. Without a developed point of view about the link between leaders and results and a strategy for ensuring that the leaders needed now and five years from now are available, human resources is an underperforming asset of the organization. Strengthening the connection between organizational strategy, human resources strategy, and the talent management strategy is critical to increasing effectiveness.

There are inherently competing values within nonprofit organizations amidst the passion for mission, achieving results, and commitment and loyalty to staff. All three are important. The talent management approach argues that effective organizations cannot sacrifice mission results to loyalty to individuals. Nor can the organization make a never-ending commitment to developing leaders, managers, or staff who prove unable to meet the performance requirement for a position.

Many nonprofit CEOs pay attention to the quality of the people on their team. In larger organizations, there is particular attention to the management team. In midsize and smaller nonprofits, the CEO may focus on managers or key positions vital to organizational success. This is the beginning of a talent management approach. The challenge for the CEO is how much to focus on leadership and management. In my experience with hundreds of CEOs from all sizes of nonprofits, attention to leadership and talent pales behind other pressing issues such as fund-raising, board development, or outreach.

Barner suggests that talent management proceeds from a well-considered and clearly articulated strategy that is a ". . . flexible game plan for acquiring, strengthening and deploying an organization's leadership talent to ensure the best long-term competitive advantage for one's organization."[19]

How might such an approach apply to a larger nonprofit organization? Here are some possibilities:

- The executive director commits to making one of his top priorities planning for and developing the leadership and management needed now and in the future. She meets regularly with managers or staff about these needs.

- A consultant, HR director, or senior manager focuses on talent management across the organization. (This is called by some leading organizations the chief talent officer or senior vice president for learning and change and is described in more detail later in this chapter.)

- Quarterly or twice a year, the CEO meets with senior managers one-on-one to discuss their performance, learning goals, and progress in recruiting and developing other leaders and managers in their unit. These discussions would include attention to progress in advancing the organization's commitment to diversity and inclusiveness as a strategy for enhancing results.

- Everyone in the organization would know what competencies are expected of leaders, how the organization supports the development of these competencies, and how the organization rewards those who excel at the recruitment, development, and advancement of outstanding leaders and managers.

A $3 million human services nonprofit CEO had for years supported an internal diversity initiative, offered scholarships for managers to leader development programs, and provided internal training on a quarterly basis for managers and staff. The organization was considered a leader in its field. A board member from the private sector became board chair and began asking about the executive management bench and approach to talent management. At first the CEO thought it was a private sector idea, not relevant to the organization. As she listened over several months, she learned more about it and decided the idea made a lot of sense. She began by finding an HR consultant who had worked with nonprofits on developing a talent management approach. She oriented her senior managers and got their buy-in to adding a discussion of leadership needs and strengths to their monthly meeting. The managers agreed to a 360-degree review process of themselves and to begin looking at middle managers and how to integrate attention to talent into the performance management system. Over a two-year period, the organization hired a chief talent officer and began offering opportunities for managers to advance more quickly and to lead projects and assignments that would speed up their leader development. As these changes were planned, there was much discussion and concern about fairness and not singling out individuals arbitrarily. The CEO, consultant, and chief talent officer were able (after a few false starts and bumps) to put a transparent process in place where all the staff knew the criteria and process by which individuals were selected for additional development support. At the same time, there were opportunities for all staff to continue to learn and grow. Because of this investment, the organization became more of a "go to" agency for government and funders and grew by 15 percent annually during difficult economic times.

A $150 million mental health center was concerned about the "aging out" of its top managers. They commissioned a benchmarking study to see what leading competitors and similar organizations were doing to prepare for change in key leadership positions. They discovered that almost all the organizations surveyed within the past three years had increased attention to training and developing current and future leaders. Recognizing their organization was losing ground, the executive director recommended that the organization invest $200 thousand in creating a leader development and talent management plan. The executive met with five peer organization executives to learn more specifically what they were doing in this area. In the process he developed specific ideas of possible actions and names of people who could help (some board leaders of other organizations and some consultants). Over the next two years, the organization developed one of the best internal leader and management development programs in its field and hired three new senior managers who had track records of recruiting and developing managers. Once the plan was in place, the board fully supported allocating $100 thousand a year for three years from reserves and $300 thousand from operations annually to implement the plan.

Both these executives had to face difficult challenges to make these changes. As they both learned about talent management, they had to decide whether their organization would use terms such as *high performers* and *high potentials*.

In one case the executive decided these terms were too exclusionary. Instead, in every conversation she emphasized the need to wed passion and talent to do our absolute best to achieve results that supported the mission. She made it clear that mediocrity was not acceptable and that managers were expected to find, support, and advance managers and staff who had the required talents and were committed to learning and expanding their contribution. In this process, without knowing it, she embraced what Lance and Dorothy Berger in their book calls "superkeepers." *Superkeepers* are leaders who both make extraordinary contributions and are effective at identifying and developing other leaders.[20] The shift to this value and attention to promoting leaders who excelled at developing leaders increased the number of *high performers* and *high potentials* without using the terms.

In the other case, the CEO made a similar decision about terms. He called the whole effort The XYZ Organization Leadership Advantage and created an internal brand that became known. The branded initiative reinforced attention to leader development as one of the top three priorities for all senior managers. Through Leadership Advantage, the organization developed a three-day workshop on identifying and coaching leaders that all the senior managers attended. From this organization, the CEO had to face the fact that two of his senior managers were not meeting the new standards after nine months of support. In one case the senior manager took on a special project and retired when it was completed. The other manager was supported in seeking employment elsewhere. One of the two managers was the human resources director. In order to make this pivot to the Leadership Advantage, a new leader in HR was required.

Another author, Edward Lawler, also emphasizes the importance of "making people your competitive advantage." He begins by acknowledging the gap between the rhetoric of a CEO saying "our people are our most important asset" and acting like that is true by investing in talent management and leader development.[21]

As funding becomes more competitive and harder to secure, nonprofit organizations of all sizes are forced to define their distinct value to the community. While the term "competitive advantage" is not commonly used to talk about distinguishing features of nonprofit organizations, in reality that is what sets those who are successful in fund-raising apart from those who aren't. Some organizations thrive, some struggle, and others falter and eventually perish. Those that thrive or move back and forth between struggling and thriving (as many do) have effective leaders on the staff and board. Embracing talent management is a way of making more conscious the organization's process of making sure it has the talent it needs.

For talent management to go beyond traditional human resources practice, a nonprofit CEO and organization will want to consider a handful of critical questions summarized here from Barner in *Bench Strength*:

- How does your organization identify senior managers and key talent? Do you most often hire ready-to-go talent from other organizations, or do you develop and promote most of your top leadership talent internally?

- Where does your organization invest most of its time and funds for professional development—on a few senior managers and managers with great potential? On all managers and staff? Or across a larger group of leaders and potential leaders?

- When your organization thinks about bench strength and succession, is your goal to have a stream of specific leaders being groomed for specific positions or a pool of leaders who can fill a number of leadership positions?

- What is your starting point for talent management in terms of when you will need new leaders, and how effective the leaders you have are? Do you build capacity incrementally by strengthening or replacing underperformers, or do you make a major change and recruit a new team of managers simultaneously?

- When your organization recruits for senior leaders, are you looking for the best talent in your mission area, or do you look for the best generalist regardless of experience in your industry?[22]

Addressing and answering questions like these is part of the shift to a talent management strategy. With the required shift in mind-set comes a decision on how to best staff this new approach. For some organizations, this shift begins by reorganizing human resources and orienting the CEO and senior managers to this approach. For others, identifying or hiring a chief talent officer brings focus and expertise to building capacity to effectively hire and develop leaders. Titles vary from organization to organization. In some, the position is vice president or senior vice president/associate director for organizational effectiveness or management development. The important distinction is that there is a person directly responsible to the CEO for serving as a trusted advisor on creating strategies and systems to manage leader and talent development, to attend to current leaders, and to focus on the leader needs of the organization.

Most organizations will need to balance investment in senior managers and staff development. The balance may shift from year to year based on the strategic needs of the organization. The paradigm shift is to recognize the need for the "both/and" approach and to commit to grow the resources and effort over time.

As we think about the possible application of the talent management approach to smaller and midsize nonprofits, leaders face another basic decision about their beliefs about leaders. Some organizations work from an "every person culture" that believes that all people are potential leaders. This results in an assumption that if you find a person with passion for the work of the organization and some skills, she will learn the rest "on the job." Other organizations want to hire only the "best and brightest." These organizations look for smart people and count on them to quickly learn what they need. Regardless of the beliefs about leaders, organizations should define needed competencies and look at how to develop the talent of all those critical to mission achievement—managers, staff, board, and volunteers.

In his book *Leaders at All Levels,* leading business consultant Ram Charan challenges both the "hire the passionate" and "hire the best and brightest" approaches. He argues that chief executive and top leadership positions have unique and demanding requirements. He challenges the slow incremental approach to developing top leaders. Instead, he advocates singling out leaders who show great promise and, with the support of an influential mentor, providing rapid advancement that appropriately stretches and prepares the leader for top leadership.[23]

This point of view challenges how many nonprofit organizations think both about the requirements for leading and the process for preparing leaders. If the sector focused on identifying and providing real leadership opportunities and structured growth to a larger pool of promising leaders, how might organizational effectiveness and results increase? As an example, consider Teach for America alums who move on to become charter school principals and rapidly improve education while in their late twenties or thirties. What if that approach were more systematic and structured across a diverse range of potential leaders?

Smaller and midsize organizations rely on a mix of staff and volunteers to achieve mission results. For these organizations, it is as important to think about the combination of staff and volunteers as the talent system. Then similar discussions are held about such questions as:

- What competencies are critical to the success of our leaders, staff, and volunteers?

- Do we mostly want to grow leaders with the competencies we need, or do we assume a high turnover of staff and volunteers and put our emphasis on effective recruitment and orientation?

- Who is responsible for paying attention to our "talent" and recognizing those making significant contributions, those with great potential, or those whose talents or personal attributes don't fit?

- How does this "talent coordinator" work with the board chair, executive director, and others to ensure continuity of great talent where most needed?

- How do we reward and encourage attention to talent and talent development?

A small museum in the Southwest hired a former private sector executive as its executive director. She brought to the museum a laser focus on the people and skills needed for growth. She spent her first ninety days observing the staff and docents and how the museum provided education and service to customers. She was delighted to learn that both the staff and the docents had deep knowledge of the exhibits and were eager to serve customers. She realized that this capacity was the untapped gold mine of the museum. Next she organized a series of formal and informal conversations with customers and invited staff and docents to participate. Together they learned how much the customers appreciated how knowledgeable the staff and docents were and received suggestions on how to make the museum experience even better. In the second ninety days the executive worked with a team of staff and docents to plan for growth and how to more fully engage and grow the experience and knowledge of staff and docents. Over the next two years, the museum doubled its number of experienced docents in order to meet the growth in visitors. The executive was successful in having a local cable company feature one of the best-known docents as a monthly guest talking about the various exhibits at the museum. The executive developed a cohort of docent and staff mentors, who with the director of exhibits and learning were responsible for the ongoing development of exhibits, staff, and mentors. This attention to talent management including volunteers doubled the museum's income over three years.

A community-based advocacy organization in the Northeast experienced the sudden departure of its executive for health reasons. About six months later, the second most experienced leader moved out of state to be with an aging parent who needed support. The new executive was thirty-four and had worked for three years as a community organizer for the organization. For the first six months the executive and board were scrambling to keep the organization alive and to adjust to the loss of the two longtime leaders. There was grumbling on the board about some of the decisions of the new executive that were different from previous practices. With support from a local foundation, the executive participated in a peer-coaching program with five other executives and a coach. They focused on clarifying how values drove mission and strategy and on connecting this to people and skills. This framework provided the executive a way to communicate with his board and staff. He identified what was sacred and to be preserved from the earlier era, as well as what was going to change. After several months of meetings and a board-staff retreat, there was consensus that the organization could no longer rely on a few leaders. The organization committed to growing the leader capacity of every board and staff member in order to bring about the changes for which they advocated. They changed the lead organizer's title to "coordinator of leader growth." Each organizer and the executive had performance objectives tied to the change goals and to specific outcomes with regard to identifying and supporting the growth of leaders. Working with the current and potential leaders, they developed milestones or indicators of growth in leading that were simple, understandable, and measurable. This organization grew in its success on the issues and in its capacity to articulate its mission and raise funds to support it by focusing on the strategy-people connection.

Launching a Talent Management Program

Some larger organizations may begin with a focus on talent management and have the leader development practices emerge from the talent management planning. For other organizations, particularly smaller and midsize, the discussion may start with leader development and evolve to include talent management's fit. There is no one or perfect way to begin.

What follows are some important steps in launching a talent management program or integrating it into your leader development practices. They include the following:

1. Clarify the mission-strategy-people connection.

2. Empower a work group to develop recommendations on leader development and talent management.

3. Assess the current leader capacity; highlight strengths and growth zones.

4. Develop and implement an annual bench strength and talent review.

5. Finalize an ongoing leader development or talent management action plan.

Clarify the Mission-Strategy-People Connection

This involves a series of conversations that build on current practices and planning process. Some organizations have a regular process for talking about the leadership and talent needed to achieve priority goals now and over the next three years or more. For these organizations, the discussion is an exploration of whether there is anything in the talent management approach that would strengthen current practices. If there is, the action plan is how to explore and advance those elements.

For organizations with less experience making this connection, the executive or a few board leaders with some experience with talent management begin the conversation by focusing on the results the organization is seeking to achieve and the talent and skills required to achieve those results. Once the desired results or talent connection is clarified, the discussion shifts to what we are doing to ensure we have the people and talent required. This often leads to a work group or committee of board and staff working together, or in larger organizations, a group of managers doing work in consultation with a group of board leaders.

Empower a Work Group to Develop Recommendations on Leader Development and Talent Management

The work group may need a skilled facilitator or seasoned talent manager's assistance. For larger organizations, the work group may choose to start by exploring the five talent management strategy questions suggested by Barner and discussed previously. This will provide a picture of current practices. Reviewing the current strategic plan and annual performance goals and strategic priorities provides a way to build on past planning and to explore to what extent talent management and leader development is already embedded in the strategy and goals. This conversation usually results in suggestions on how to strengthen that link.

Once the "to what end" of talent management is clear or clearer, the process of determining what information is needed to advance talent management and leader development begins. Size is a factor here. Larger organizations often begin the conversation with managers. Either through discussions with the management team or facilitated focus groups, there are discussions about what it means to lead and what competencies are required. This covers current perceptions about the clarity of the path for advancement as a leader (that is, is the path transparent and perceived as fair?) and the support available for growth as a leader. It is not unusual for the executive and HR leaders to have a different perception of current practices than other managers and staff. In smaller organizations, these discussions may involve all staff.

These discussions usually result in agreement on what additional data is needed about individual leaders and about the leader development and talent management practices and culture.

Assess Current Leader Capacity—Highlight Strengths and Growth Zones

This process requires the engagement of current organizational leaders. In larger organizations, it may involve a more in-depth leader assessment process, such as a 360-degree assessment. It may be combined with a formal bench strength review and reporting process. In smaller organizations, the process may be less formal and robust, with similar goals. Typically the choice to focus on leader assessment is part of a larger decision to conduct annual bench strength and talent reviews. Some organizations may choose to start with the leader assessment only.

Develop and Implement an Annual Bench Strength and Talent Review Process

This process can be conducted in accordance with periodic reports to the board. It can be led by a trusted human resources director with deep knowledge of the executive and middle managers, by the CEO, by an executive manager, or with the help of an outside consultant. The first step is to clarify the desired results the organization is seeking and the competencies required by its leaders to achieve those results. Then the organization assesses its performance gaps, the kinds of transitions it will need to make, and how it anticipates the leadership will change in the coming years.[24]

Once the organization has clarified its future strategies and required competencies, the CEO, in consultation with his HR advisors and executive team, chooses the best approach to leader assessment—for example, using 360-degree leader assessment. This may be tied to a performance review (often preferred by the HR field) or not, depending on the CEO's sense of what works for the organization.

For example, when the organization lacks a history of meaningful performance reviews, or when managers mistrust the organization's motives, some CEOs opt to start with an informal leader self-assessment. In this form, all managers complete a self-assessment and may choose (or not) to share the results with their supervisors. The advantage of this approach is that it fosters a culture of learning and leader development. The disadvantage is that it makes getting useful information for the bench strength review more complex—at some point, the organization is going to need to conduct another assessment to determine the strength of its managerial cadre.

Defining competencies is also an important and complex task. Because of the challenge of integrating this approach well and within the resources of the nonprofit, some CEOs turn to a human resources consultant to put the leader assessment and bench strength review in place the first time. This is particularly helpful for organizations where the human resources director has led more traditional human resources functions and has not been a partner to the CEO in assessing and planning for needed leadership. This assistance also provides an independent view of the decision about whether to link the assessment process formally to the performance review system.

In deciding whether and how to advance a talent management system with a bench strength review, nonprofit executives might consider a key research finding by Lance Berger and the organizing principles of the *Talent Management Handbook.* He writes, ". . . successful companies either articulate or intuitively focus on three outcomes":

1. The identification, selection, development, and retention of Superkeepers. Superkeepers are a very small group of individuals who have demonstrated superior accomplishments, have inspired others to attain superior accomplishments, and who embody the core competencies and values of the organization.

2. The identification and development of high-quality replacements for a small number of positions designated as key to the current and future success of the organization.

3. The classification of and investment in each employee based on his or her actual or potential for adding value to the organization.[25]

While many nonprofit executives would not use the same language as Berger, and may even disagree with his point of view, it is hard to refute the link between mission results and talent. An organization focused on *mission* requires an approach to developing staff and leaders that is consistent with its values and its commitment to its mission. The belief that passion for mission is sufficient or that all employees and leaders are equally skilled and should be treated equally simply flies in the face of reality. While the term *superkeepers* may feel repugnant, in reality most organizations rely on a small number of leaders to empower and advance the development of other leaders.

Once the bench strength review is completed, the person or team in charge of the process analyzes which managers are ready now, ready in one to three years, and ready in three to five years to advance to a specific key leadership position or into more generalized expanded management.

BENCH STRENGTH REPORT EXAMPLES

The following are examples of ways organizations track and report bench strength for key leadership positions. Additional tools for supporting talent management and bench strength review are found in Appendix D (also available online).

For some nonprofit leaders, terms such as *high potentials* and *high performers* grate against the values of inclusion and equity. The bench strength review and talent management approach invites leaders to recognize the importance of mission results and pay attention to the leaders and staff who are contributing the most to those results. An organization may choose other descriptions or terms to identify leaders or staff contributing significantly. However it is important to be proactive to ensure that the organization has the talent it needs to achieve its mission and that leaders are working from their strengths and growing. The following tools assist with that process within an organization.

Example 1. Key Position Bench Strength Summary

This is a simple tool that summarizes findings after a bench strength review. For key leadership positions, indicate whether there is an individual for interim short-term replacement or permanent replacement who is:

1. Identified and ready
2. Identified and getting ready
3. Not identified or not ready

With this framework, you can create a simple chart that might look something like this:

POSITION	INTERIM REPLACEMENT	PERMANENT REPLACEMENT
Executive Director	Identified and ready	Not identified/ready
Comptroller	Identified/getting ready	Not identified/ready
Director of Operations	Identified and ready	Identified and ready

Example 2. Readiness Needs

This example provides more details on the specific people and steps needed to get ready.

Position: Chief Operating Officer

Interim replacement: Identified and ready Jane Doe

Permanent replacement(s): Identified and getting ready

A. JANE DOE, DIRECTOR OF PROGRAMS

When ready: 1–2 years

Strengths: Knowledge of programs, management of small unit, work with one board committee, prior work as executive director of small nonprofit

Areas for growth: Financial management, managing larger operation and more direct reports, increased interaction with board on budget, planning, and technology

Stretch assignments: Will lead the annual budget development process with senior managers and board

Professional development: Join COO roundtable at state association and attend local leadership program for high-performing executives

B. ELLEN JONES, COMPTROLLER

When Ready: 3–4 years

Strengths: Knowledge of finances and budget, work with board finance committee, previous experience as program manager with a sister organization

Areas for growth: Managing programs and senior managers, broader role with board, writing and public speaking

Stretch assignment: Colead the strategic planning process with director of development

Professional development: Leadership and management courses, Toastmaster or similar public speaking practice, and writing coaching from the director of communications related to the writing of routine communication (e-mails) and reports

Note: This process is repeated for other leadership positions. These reports are reviewed every six months (sometimes more frequently) by the CEO and are part of the talent management system led by human resources or a chief talent officer.

Talent management reports vary somewhat depending on organizational trust, culture, and how the reports are used. A typical report would include the following types of information for each manager or employee included in the process:

- Current position and date entered that position
- Prior positions and tenure
- Key goals and accomplishments last year
- Priority areas for development action plan
- Possible new assignments or stretch goals to support development goals
- Coaching or mentoring opportunities or suggested training programs
- Readiness for other leadership positions and time frame

This process results in consensus among the CEO and trusted advisors about the *high performers* and *high potentials* in the organization. Most for-profit companies do not disclose who is on what list or in what category. However, leaders who are singled out for special assignments or given above-average opportunities for professional development know who they are. And leaders denied those opportunities also often recognize that fact. Nonprofit organizations utilizing the corporate talent management approach must know how transparent to be. Some nonprofits use open, competitive processes for selecting leaders for special attention and investment. For organizations with a high value on equity and openness, this transparency aligns with the culture. Don't let your current culture block the process as described here; adapt it to fit your values.

The benefits of the bench strength approach include:

- Consistent and more effective attention to leadership and talent by the CEO and top leadership

- Increased capacity to respond to changing trends and required competencies in leadership

- Improved capacity to reposition the organization quickly and effectively

- Increased morale because there is a stated commitment to leader development and a known path and process for advancement

- Ability to incorporate diversity and inclusiveness goals into leader development methods and in strategic hiring

- Increased retention of the most critically needed leaders because of the attention paid to their performance and growth

- More flexibility and capacity to fast-track younger leaders with demonstrated ability

For smaller nonprofits, creating a talent development plan for all employees (and relevant board leaders and volunteers) is a logical way to adapt this approach and achieve some of the benefits above.

Small to midsize nonprofit organizations may find a benefit in blending a commitment to leader development with a plan for more focused attention to leader requirements and leader advancement. Whether the activities are called *leader development* or *talent management* or something else is not important. What is important are the leader and organizational behaviors that advance results through attention to leaders.

Some boards of nonprofits have a leader development or talent management approach for board succession. The nominating or governance committee has a process and agreement within the board that the vice chair will become chair and that the outgoing chair will serve on the executive committee for one year. This is thoughtful planning for board chair continuity based on a set of skills and competencies required to be board chair. Boards should look for similar thoughtfulness in their staff.

Finalize an Ongoing Leader Development or Talent Management Action Plan

This concluding step, completed by the CEO, board, and appropriate staff, incorporates leader development and talent management into the organization's culture. For larger organizations, the plan may include an annual bench strength review and an ongoing leader and executive development program. For smaller organizations, the plan may mean focusing on one or two areas that will have the most impact, such as staff training in a critical core competency, an initiative focused on volunteer improvements, or board development, among many choices.

Depending on fit with the organization's culture and priorities, other possible actions include:

- Defining or refining a shared definition of *leader* for the organization

- Clarifying the competencies desired for staff and volunteer leaders

- Adapting current human resources and volunteer management practices to advance leader development and talent management

- Agreeing to focus on talent management, designating a person to lead the work, and allocating the funds to accomplish it

- Increasing the resources for leader and talent development and agreeing on a process for connecting leader development to performance measures and to organizational measures of success

- Annually reviewing progress and refining talent management goals and strategy

In deciding on an annual plan and commitment, leaders may choose to collaborate with other nonprofits in efforts that are better done at a larger scale. Such a collaboration might focus on back office human resources functions, leader development workshops and learning, executive or peer coaching, or joint marketing at job fairs to improve efficiencies in hiring and developing leaders and expand access to "ready to go" talent.

Conclusion: A Critical Leadership Strategy

Whether in collaboration with several organizations or within your own organization, attention to talent management is a critical leadership strategy.

Berger, in *The Talent Management Handbook,* summarizes a study by his company to identify ". . . the factors that most contributed to the creation and sustenance of organization excellence." He notes, ". . . six human resources conditions had to be met. These conditions were: a performance-oriented culture, low turnover (particularly in premium employees), high levels of employee satisfaction, and a cadre of qualified replacements, effective investment in employee compensation and development, and the use of institutional competencies (success factors) in employee selection and performance evaluation processes."[26]

Achieving and sustaining organizational excellence is not easy. Many for-profit companies struggle to pay sufficient attention to leader development and talent management and to the processes described above. The nonprofit advantage in pursuing such excellence is the passion for mission results. Organizations that demand results will increasingly embrace leader development and talent management. The best organizations already are.

REFLECTION QUESTIONS

Leader Development

For the Individual Leader

1. Do you think of yourself as a leader? Why? Why not?

2. How has your perception of yourself as a leader changed over the past five to ten years? What experiences or learning have shaped or influenced your current point of view?

3. Reflecting on this chapter, what is your next action to continue to grow as a leader?

For Executive Directors and Board Leaders of an Organization

1. Does the organization support and invest in leader development? If so, in what ways?

2. What are the benefits and challenges of current leader development efforts?

3. Given what you know and have read, what are the two or three actions you want to consider to advance leader development?

For Funders, Capacity-Building Providers, Association Staff, and Other Supporting Stakeholders

1. Does your organization invest in or support leader development in organizations it works with and cares about? If so, in what ways? If not, have you considered it? What are barriers?

2. Given what you have read, how might you be most supportive to organizations you are involved with when the organization is actively working to expand leader development? Please be as specific as possible.

3. What systems or alliances might increase the impact of leader development if you think that is important to do?

Talent Management

For the Individual Leader

1. As a leader, what are your strengths in proactively building and sustaining the talented leaders the organization needs for optimal advancement of priority goals?

2. In what ways, if any, might you aspire to pay more attention to talent management and the recruitment and development of the leaders the organization needs?

3. Have you read anything in this chapter about talent management that causes you to want to reflect more or explore any aspect of the topic? If so what would you like to explore or learn more about?

For Executive Directors and Board Leaders of an Organization

1. How does the organization pay attention to talent management? What are the processes and procedures that support talent management now?

2. Do you think more attention to talent management would advance mission results? If yes, in what ways? If no, why not?

3. Given what you know and have read, what actions are you considering or committing to that will advance the talent management system in the organization?

For Funders, Capacity-Building Providers, Association Staff, and Other Supporting Stakeholders

1. What perspective does your organization bring to talent management within your own organization? With the organizations you work with or support?

2. Given what you have read, how might you be most supportive when your organization is actively working to increase its effectiveness at talent management? Please be as specific as possible.

3. Are there collaborations or networks of which your organization is a part where a discussion of talent management and leader development to advance goals might be appropriate? If so, will you bring the topic up and lead the discussion?

9

Many Paths to a Leaderful Organization

WELL-LED ORGANIZATIONS MAKE A BIGGER DIFFERENCE
in the world than their mediocre counterparts. Such organizations
adapt more quickly to changing conditions and are often looked to by
funders and peers to point the way and to develop and model promising and
innovative practices. Well-led organizations consistently have the resources to
meet their current goals and are on their way to attracting more resources
to increase impact. These organizations are clear about the results they intend to
have in the world, continuously measure progress in reaching these results,
and learn from their experience.

Do such organizations exist? For sure. There are many organizations
that achieve these aspirations for periods of time under a particular team
of leaders. It is more challenging to consistently stay well led. The practices
described in the previous chapters offer a road map that increases the likelihood of an organization staying well led and effective.

These practices are ways to increase the possibility of sustaining outstanding
leaders over time. Organizations who sustain excellent leaders over multiple
transitions and decades have a *leader development culture*. They are what we
call in this book *leaderful*. As more organizations become more leaderful, our
campaign for increased results through attention to leader transitions and
leader development grows.

˙ng effective leaders is not an accident. It requires a commitment
˙eas and practices. No organization is perfect at these practices.
˙˙ and commitment to pay attention to leader transitions and
˙˙velopment that distinguishes organizations on their way to leaderful
from those who are not.

A national organization based in the Midwest made attention to leader
development and succession one of four priorities in its 2006 strategic plan.
In 2007, managers and staff enthusiastically launched a series of actions
aimed at building the core leadership competencies identified in the process.
In late 2008, downturns in funding required a slowdown of the plan implementation. The management team agreed to focus on activities that had the
greatest benefit to the organization and refocused some of the action learning
for emerging managers to focus on new approaches to fund-raising. By late
2009, the organization's finances were beginning to improve, and the leader
development activities were back on the timeline established in the strategic
plan. CEO and management support and discussions by board and staff as
part of the strategic planning made it possible for this organization to continue to advance its leader development goals despite economic barriers.

This chapter offers examples of what organizations do to sustain attention to leader transitions and leader development. It also provides suggestions
on actions, commitments, and habits for the individual, organization, and
supporting stakeholder that will advance the leader development culture.

Promising Practices

By now we are hoping the case for attention to leader transitions and leader
development is clear. The benefits that are possible from these practices include:

- More clarity about results and the competencies and systems needed
  to achieve the results

- Less disruption and loss of capacity when a key leader moves on

- Quicker adaptation to changing demographics and needs through
  proactive attention to planning for and managing leader transitions
  and how inclusiveness and diversity advance mission and results

- Extraordinary opportunities for organizational change and growth during leader transitions

- A more focused and engaged board that is aligned with the executive and staff on mission, goals, and priorities

- A more engaged and effective workforce and management team

- A management team that fits current and future needs in leadership and is always expanding leader capability throughout the management team and organization

There are four practices that, in the author's experience, speed up progress on the path to a leaderful organization. They include the following:

1. Moving toward consistent commitment and support from the CEO and board

2. Picking a place to start that builds from strength and is doable

3. Attending to an incremental organizational change process

4. Protecting the time and money required for success

Let's look at these practices and their application.

Consistent Commitment and Support from the CEO and Board

For many CEOs and board leaders, attention to leader transitions and development is squishy and the results are not very measurable. A national association for years had a debate within its senior management team about whether to develop a leadership program. Those for it saw it as a no-brainer. Effective leaders will increase results. Those on the fence or against it were not so sure. They believed in the connection between leaders and results, but were less convinced that with their resources they could influence this connection.

This debate or lack of it occurs in many organizations. Sometimes the hesitation to commit to investment in leaders is never articulated. The topic never gets past the first few sentences. Here are some ways CEOs and board leaders have deepened their commitment and expanded support:

- A trusted board leader with personal experience in a company that emphasizes leader development introduces the idea to an interested and skeptical nonprofit CEO. She invites the CEO to attend a talent management session at her company and to meet with other managers there. The CEO sets aside a day and attends the session and has coffee with three managers. Seeing and hearing the ideas in action make it real for the CEO and show her how to get started. She engages her senior managers and the board personnel committee, and the planning for implementation of a leader development program begins.

- A CEO is beginning to think about retirement and leader succession. He attends a workshop on CEO succession and decides he needs to pay more attention to bench strength among his managers. He asks people he met at the workshop for names of consultants who might guide him and the organization. He invites his COO and CFO to join him in interviewing and selecting the consultant. One year later there is both a leader development program for managers and a reorganized performance review system that rewards managers who develop managers and leaders.

- A younger CEO sees how there is a logjam of talent in her organization. There are younger people with untapped potential and more seasoned managers who have had limited opportunity to lead and grow. She makes leader development and the opportunity to take on stretch assignments and new projects a top organizational priority. Through an open process of rotating special assignments and providing mentoring and coaching support to managers selected for these assignments, she expands the opportunities over three years for four seasoned middle managers and three younger first-time managers.

- A floundering organization is put in the hands of an interim CEO and a task force of a few board leaders and respected community leaders with a stake in the survival of the organization. The interim CEO and task force decide that money and leaders is the path to a better future. Identifying staff and board leaders for two new projects that are the core business of the organization and a fund-raising team to secure investments for these projects and the leader development required to support them provides a path for an organizational turnaround and a much more capable leader team.

- A human resources director with experience with talent management in a Fortune 500 company slowly educated the CEO about it. The CEO slowly convinced the senior management team and the board to make attention to leadership a strategic priority. It took six months to gain the CEO, senior management, and board commitment. Within two years from that commitment, the organization had put the succession basics in place and completed its first bench strength review of managers as part of a new talent management system.

Pick a Place to Start That Builds from Strength and Is Doable

Because time and resources are so constricted in most nonprofits, your choice of where to start is critical. False starts or attention to the "leader fad of the month" can distract and prevent real progress. Think about your strengths, the level of commitment of the CEO and board, and pick a place to start that builds on that strength and is the right size to have a high likelihood of success. Sometimes the strength is a board or staff member with expertise and a willingness to be supportive (and not intrusive or demanding). In other cases the strength is a system or practice that is already working. It might be as simple as a monthly management session devoted to sharing successes and lessons learned, or a performance management system that encourages career planning and leader development. For some organizations strength is one or more funders who are committed to the success of the organization and are open to supporting investments like succession planning and leader development.

While a big vision is helpful in the long run, if the first effort is too ambitious and gets bogged down or is seen as not working or irrelevant, future efforts will have a harder time. Here are some possible discrete places to start depending on your strengths and organizational context:

- *Succession basics.* When in doubt, the easiest place to start with the least resistance is the emergency backup planning. There is little resistance other than the time required to pay attention to unplanned absences. As noted in Chapter Six, this process opens up other discussions about bench strength and cross-training of managers and staff.

- *CEO education.* Most CEOs like to understand where change might lead. Working with an HR consultant or attending a workshop assists the CEO and other decision makers in adapting these practices to the organization's needs and situation.

- *Board-CEO work group.* In some situations, the CEO and a few board leaders may decide to work together to explore what sustainability means. The CEO may be approaching retirement age and may want to begin to engage the board in succession planning. Or the organization may be poised for growth and the leaders want to ensure that any growth is sustainable, pays attention to leader development opportunities, and contributes to long-term capacity. This work group may meet regularly for a few months and then serve as an ad hoc sounding board, or it might be part of the formal committee structure.

- *Coaching or mentoring.* Some organizations get started by offering access to a coach or mentor. This offer may be part of the performance management process or independent of it depending on the circumstances. Important considerations are the selection of coaches and mentors, selection criteria, and what if anything the supervisor is told about the experience.

- *Book clubs and peer support groups.* A regular session to discuss a book that advances leader development is a simple first step. *Eight Habits* by Stephen Covey, *The Leadership Challenge* by Kouzes and Posner, and *Cultural Competency* by Patricia St. Onge et al. are among the many possibilities. Some organizations convene periodic meetings of peers (as defined by role in the organization, race, generation, or other similarity) and connect leaders who share a desire to learn together.

- *Next-generation leaders.* Organizations where the basics are in place or where there is a lot of untapped potential among younger managers and staff may opt to begin with a focus on next-generation leaders. The term is intentionally vague and might apply to younger leaders or leaders new to management or both. The key here is clarity about goals, selection criteria, and process and what the benefits are to the individual and the organization.

- *Bench strength review.* In larger organizations where the basics are in place or there is a lot of change happening or expected among key managers, a more detailed look at bench strength is a great first step to moving to a more formal talent management system. Typically, there is an outside consultant or an HR manager with experience in bench strength to assist in guiding this process. In smaller organizations who look at staff, board, and volunteers as their talent, a similar bench strength process can be a helpful step. This is a big commitment and needs to be made carefully.

Attend to an Incremental Organizational Change Process

When choosing among these (or other) options, pay attention to the organizational change process required to move *incrementally* to a leader development culture. While there may be a commitment to becoming leaderful, there are always competing priorities. There will be times when leader development appears to be a low priority that can be put on hold. Experience shows that the danger is that once put on hold, it never gets *off* of hold.

Given the ever-shifting nature of organizational priorities, there are two big challenges to pay attention to: how to stay focused and how to decide on the right path for change for your organization. Both of these challenges are overcome by:

- Selecting a trusted and empowered leader for the effort who can convene and influence the managers needed for success, has a budget, and is committed to the agreed-upon goals

- Using an outside consultant or resource person who understands organizational and leader development and change and is knowledgeable about the culture and work of the organization

- Building into the monthly and annual calendar key events and requirements that advance the leader development goals

The path is not always a straight line. There are often parallel processes that involve in different ways senior managers, the CEO and board, the human resources department, all managers, and all staff. A trusted guide reduces the risks of derailment due to a lack of attention to an important stakeholder or element required for success.

Protect the Time and Money Required for Success

This starts with the consistent commitment of the CEO and board. In hard times, when salaries are frozen, staff may be laid off, and budgets trimmed, leader development is at risk. CEO commitment does *not* mean protect the budget for leader development no matter what. It does mean creatively exploring what is possible in the current circumstances. Over time as the benefits are clear to more managers and the board, there will be more champions and more creative ideas about how to expand the time and money available to support the development of a leaderful organization. Some organizations set aside a percentage of a certain type of income. Other organizations involve the staff and board in one or two events a year and dedicate the proceeds to the leader development effort. Still other organizations seek out individual donors who know the importance of leader development and ask for annual or one-time support for this purpose. Still other organizations seek corporate sponsors for training and other leader development events, or scholarships for managers to attend leadership or management training.

While money is often cited as the biggest barrier, time is often harder to get on a consistent basis. Organizations that are becoming more leaderful develop habits that make the time commitment less of a struggle. Among these practices are the following:

- The CEO and senior managers annually attend at least one learning event of two to five days and encourage their managers to do the same.

- The organization organizes by itself or with other peer organizations or an association a series of educational opportunities for managers and staff. Managers and staff are encouraged to participate and rewarded for the increase in skills and value to the organization.

- Once or twice a year there is time (one day up to three days) set aside for learning and celebrating the work of the organization.

- The CEO and senior managers calendar and attend monthly performance review meetings with direct reports and make progress in leader development a routine part of these conversations.

- The CEO and board chair meet quarterly to review goals and progress, and leader development is part of the goals and report.

- The performance review system is a priority, and reviews are completed and submitted on time with useful support from the human resources professional or department.

- There are quarterly meetings of a bench strength team with CEO participation in all or a portion of the meeting to hear progress and an annual bench strength report to the board that includes updating the emergency backup plans and succession policy.

Many Paths, Many Champions

There are indeed many ways to advance the leaderful organization. Each requires a leader or champion. We call this *the leaders' way.* It is simultaneously a path and a way of being as a leader.

Throughout our journey, we've paid attention to three types of actions: individual, organizational, and supporting stakeholders. We conclude with a return to how each of us as leaders can act on our own and collectively speed up the positive results from our work through attention to leader transitions and development. For our sector to be more leaderful, many of us will need to lead the way. Here are some actions leaders have shared:

As an Individual

- Invest in personal leader development. Work with an executive coach, attend the weeklong program of the Center for Creative Leadership or a university program, and complete a 360-degree leader assessment. Do whatever is next to advance your self-awareness and skills as a leader.

- Review your self-care and resiliency rituals (see Chapter Two). Burned-out, frustrated leaders struggle to lead. What do you need to do to take better care of your body, mind, and spirit? Commit to doing it and ask a friend to support you in your commitment.

- Join a group of other leaders for learning or support. Leading can be lonely work. Make sure you are not isolated. Find a peer group that interests you and become involved.

- Write. Journaling is a powerful tool for clarifying complex decisions and issues. It is also a useful way to share ideas if you are so inclined.

- Coach. Share what you've learned by volunteering as a coach to a new executive or someone outside your organization.

- Volunteer more or volunteer less. If you have never been on a board, find one that interests you and try it. If you are on too many boards and feel ineffective, pick the one or two that most meet your goals of contributing and networking and consider resigning from the rest.

As an Organization

- Check your fundamentals. Make sure you are clear about your mission and the results you are working toward.

- Have the succession conversation. Talk with your CEO about her plans and about whether there are emergency backup plans and a succession policy.

- Define leadership. Involve the staff, managers, and board in a series of conversation to clarify the leader competencies required for organizational success and how to advance those competencies.

- Invest in leader development. Quantify in dollars and hours the current investment in leader development and set a goal for increasing that commitment.

- Build leader development and transitions into annual planning. Make sure that you attend to any leader transitions and leader development in the annual and strategic planning processes with written goals and measures of success.

- Pay attention to diversity and inclusiveness. Diversity fosters creativity and better results. How is your organization doing in inviting and engaging as leaders people of different ages, race and ethnic backgrounds, and life experiences? What is the next action?

- Embrace transition management. Every time a manager or employee leaves, pay attention to what will increase the odds of a good ending with the organization for that leader and a great beginning for the successor. Build systems to support good endings and beginnings.

- Consider succession basics or a bench strength review. Pick the action from the menu provided here that makes the most sense and commit to a start date and a date to have completed an initial process. Persist until you succeed.

As a Supporting Stakeholder

- Walk the talk. Embrace these practices for your organization and be a champion for building leaderful organizations.

- Have the conversation. Ask your grantees, members, or clients about their leader transition and leader development practices. Ask how you can be supportive of their efforts.

- Make leader development a priority. Advocate for overt attention to leader development for the organization and its work with grantees, members, or clients. Explore what peers who are leaders in this work are doing and look for ways to deepen your commitment and collaborate with others.

- Provide a safe place and independent convener. Support CEOs and leaders in developing for themselves and their peers safe places where there can be frank and open conversation about personal and organizational leader development issues. Where requested, pay for an independent facilitator to help organize and facilitate planning and the sessions.

- Provide funds and time. Create legitimacy by convening on leader development topics and give money to support travel and learning or make it easy financially for grantees or members to participate in workshops, peer learning sessions, and so on.

- Write and speak. Share your successes in supporting leader development and encourage peers to do the work and share successes.

Enjoy the Leader's Way—and Grow the Campaign

America's nonprofit organizations are an amazing testimony to innovation, compassion, and commitment. So much love and good gets shared every day in every community through our individual and collective efforts. Think of the added benefits as we become more intentional about leader transitions and leader development and a more leaderful world. The possibilities are stunning. Let the change process continue with the next action by each of us. May our collective actions fuel a campaign that benefits many. Together we are making the world more just, caring, and sustainable.

Appendixes

Note: These Appendixes, with the exception of sections C1 and C2 of Appendix C, are also available online at www.josseybass.com/go/tomadams, using the password *professional*.

Executive Transition Management Tools and Worksheets

A1. Executive Transition Management Process Overview

Figure A1.1. Executive Transition Management Process Overview

Source: ETM 2.0. Copyright © TransitionGuides, 2004-2009.

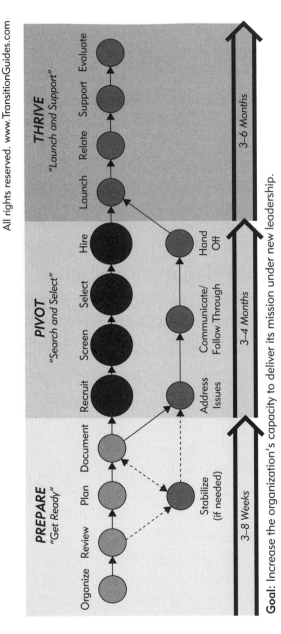

Goal: Increase the organization's capacity to deliver its mission under new leadership.

Outcomes:

- A new executive in place who fits current and future leadership needs of the organization.
- Transition issues have been addressed or are in a resolution track.
- Board and staff are prepared to work effectively with the new executive.
- Board and executive agree on priorities, roles, expectations and performance measures.

Figure A1.2. The Executive Transition Management Prepare, Pivot, and Thrive Model

Source: ETM 2.0. Copyright © TransitionGuides, 2004–2009.
Version 10, 02/17/09. All rights reserved. www.TransitionGuides.com

PREPARE

Organize—Get the Team Ready for Transition and Search

- Ensure that a board-level transition and search committee is appointed and given their charge.

- Make certain that the executive leadership needs are addressed for the transition period, for example, provide coaching for the departing executive director, place an interim executive director (if needed), or ensure that the internal acting executive director has the appropriate skills and authority to do the transition work, not just the caretaking work.

- Craft the initial timeline and work plan for the entire ETM process.

- Plan for a positive ending with the current executive director.

- Hold a project launch meeting with the transition and search committee to review the timeline and project responsibilities and create a definition of success.

- Craft a communications plan for informing all key stakeholders of the board's plan for managing the transition.

Review

- Conduct an organizational review that looks at the organization's strengths, challenges, direction, and priorities, including leadership interviews, staff and board questionnaire, document review, and a stakeholder questionnaire or interviews.

Stabilize—Stabilize Situation (If Needed)

- Address the critical uncertainties and presenting issues—those that have an immediate and direct effect on the organization's viability and its readiness to hire, or prove so distracting that the board cannot give its full attention to the organizational review and transition planning process.

Plan

- Hold a "Strategy and Leadership Review" session or otherwise ensure that the board is clear about the organization's strategic direction and implications: the attributes sought in new executive director, any "pivots" or key changes for the organization (including the board), the twelve- to eighteen-month leadership priorities, and the organizational constraints to be addressed before the new executive director is hired.

Document

- Develop the search plan and collaterals: multipage position profile, one-page position announcement, ad copy, outreach lists, compensation research, and so on.
- Summarize the results of the "Strategy and Leadership Review" session, including the organizational preparation and change management work to take place parallel to the search.

PIVOT

Recruit

- Recruit a strong and diverse candidate pool.

Screen

- Screen résumés and conduct vetting interviews with promising candidates.

Select

- Hold résumé review meeting with the search and transition committee.
- Conduct interviews.
- Arrange for staff/senior staff to meet with semifinalists.

Hire

- Secure board ratification of the choice.
- Confirm employment agreement with the finalist.

Address Issues (Simultaneously with Search and Selection)

- Ensure diligent teamwork to address the top-level organizational constraints and other changes that will set the stage for the new executive director's success.

Communicate/Follow Through

- Keep staff appropriately informed during the search and transition.
- Facilitate stakeholders' (primarily board and staff) movement through the emotional, political, and other issues that accompany a leadership transition, for example, separation from the departing executive director and anxieties about what the future holds.

Handoff

- Plan the arrival and orientation of the new executive director.
- Ensure a good handoff between the departing and arriving executive directors.

THRIVE

Launch

- Ensure that an appropriate announcement has been made and the handoff plan has been executed. In addition hold a post-hire planning meeting with the board chair and the new executive director.

Relate

- Work with the new executive director in developing leadership goals and a ninety-day entry plan.
- Facilitate the board-executive social contracting process that affirms or builds consensus about priority goals, respective roles, and expectations.

Support

- Encourage the new executive director and clarify his or her professional development and support needs. Support him or her in addressing those needs.

Evaluate

- Ensure that a plan is developed for monitoring performance and conducting periodic evaluations, including both executive and board evaluations.

- Hold a project closure meeting with the board or transition committee chairs to review the ETM project outcomes and accomplishments.

A2. The Interim Executive Advantage: An Overview of the Benefits

The use of an interim executive director can have a variety of benefits that enable a nonprofit to transform the uncertainty of the transition period into an opportunity to create a solid platform for organizational growth.

An Objective Review

The capacity-building advantages of an interim executive director include an objective review of administrative systems and a resulting plan for upgrades.

The interim executive director will affirm what is right about the operations of the agency. However, he or she is also uniquely free to "speak the truth" to the board and managers about what is dysfunctional in order to identify the barriers to full programmatic achievement on behalf of clients. Some of the analysis results from reviews with internal personnel. Other important perspectives are gained in talking with funders and peer agencies. The candor with which recommendations for change are made should always be accompanied with respect for the efforts of the previous executive.

Specialized Skills and Expertise

The interim executive director works with managers to develop short-term solutions for removing major organizational barriers. Longer-term strategies may require the next permanent executive's involvement. Interim directors bring the wisdom and techniques accumulated in their own nonprofit careers to this process. Some characterize their role in this regard as taking care of problems rooted in the past so that the newly hired executive can focus on the future.

Source: Excerpted from Wolfred, T. "Interim Executive Directors: The Power in the Middle." San Francisco: CompassPoint Nonprofit Services and The Annie E. Casey Foundation, 2005.

Creating Separation

The skilled interim leader also facilitates the agency's necessary separation from the ways and means of the previous CEO. Staff and board are given forums in which to acknowledge the departed executive's gifts and achievements, talk about what they would like to see maintained and what might have been done differently—sometimes accompanied by passions that had been bottled up—and outline which skills and attributes they'd like to see in their next executive.

These activities—and the passage of time—bring added distance from the presence and tenure of a strong executive director, creating a more welcoming environment for the new leader.

Facilitating a Fresh Vision

The interim executive director engages all key stakeholders in scripting a fresh and exciting vision for the agency's future. With the new vision in hand, the board can sharpen its profile of the next executive and better focus its recruiting efforts.

A Mentor Who Knows the Ropes of the Organization

If the next executive is a first-timer, which is frequently the case with small to midsize agencies, the interim executive director can be invaluable in mentoring the rookie executive director. For example, all candidates placed in interim executive director positions by CompassPoint have previously served as nonprofit CEOs and can guide the professional development of new leaders.

Avoiding the Rush to Hire

Beyond taking advantage of the power of the neutral zone, having an interim in place simply allows the board to take the time needed to recruit a strong pool of candidates. If employing an interim is not considered when an executive director leaves on short notice, too many boards become anxious and rush the hiring process.

The board may skip key recruitment steps and choose a less-than-ideal candidate. Too often, the result is a failed executive tenure—and another leadership transition not too far down the road.

A Cost-Effective Strategy

The agency's budget line item allocated for the executive salary, plus taxes and benefits, can be applied to the interim executive's compensation. Calculated as a per-hour rate, the compensation for an interim can be much more than the agency would typically pay its executive. Interims can command the higher rate because they are veteran executives who are immediately ready and prepared to meet the needs of an agency. However, most interims can be hired for less than a forty-hour week—typically twenty to thirty hours per week.

While the hourly rate is higher, the total cost need not be much higher than the funds already allocated for the permanent executive's salary. Additionally, interim executive directors generally do not receive the normal agency benefits (paid vacations, sick leave, insurance, and so on), which also reduces costs for the hiring agency.

A3. Where to Find an Interim Executive

There is a growing cadre of trained nonprofit interim executives across the country. With support from The Annie E. Casey Foundation and local funders, CompassPoint Nonprofit Services has trained several hundred interim executives based on their extensive experience in managing an interim executive program.

For more information about interim executive directors as a capacity-building strategy, see the article in this Appendix, "The Interim Executive Director Advantage: An Overview of the Benefits," and The Annie E. Casey Foundation monograph *Interim Executive Directors: The Power in the Middle* (http://www.transitionguides.com/resources/docs/IED_final.pdf).

For examples of interim executive programs see the following:

- CompassPoint Nonprofit Services
  (http://www.compasspoint.org)

- The Support Center of New York
  (http://www.supportcenteronline.org/training.php)

- Executive Service Corporation (Chicago)
  (http://www.esc-chicago.org/services-programs/
  organizationaltransformation.html)

- Executive Consulting for the Nonprofit Sector, Inc.
  (http://www.interimexecutive.org/html/training.htm)

A4. Sample Transition Timeline

Event	Responsible Party	Date
Resignation notice—chief executive gives ninety days' notice	Chief executive	Sept. 1
Board/chief executive discuss departure	Board and chief executive	Sept. 1–7
Board appoints transition committee	Board chair	Sept. 7
Transition committee holds organizing meeting	Transition committee	Sept. 10
Transition committee plans departure announcement	Transition committee/PR consultant	Sept. 10–14
Board chair meets with staff	Board chair	Sept. 14
Organization announces departure publicly	Board chair with staff support	*To be determined*
Transition committee holds planning session with staff	Transition committee chair	Sept. 22
Board holds strategic review and leadership planning meeting	Board	Sept. 27
Transition committee holds meeting to develop job profile and search plan	Transition committee	Oct. 9
Transition committee launches search	Transition committee	Oct. 12
Transition committee holds check-in meeting(s)	Transition committee	*To be determined*

(Continued)

Sample Transition Timeline *(Continued)*

Event	Responsible Party	Date
Transition committee holds résumé review meeting	Transition committee	Nov. 28
Transition committee holds round one interviews	Transition committee	Dec. 8
Transition committee holds second planning session with staff	Transition committee chair	Dec. 10
Semifinalists visit office and meet with staff	Semifinalists	Week of Dec. 10
Executive committee holds round two interviews	Executive committee	Dec. 18
Board meets to ratify selection	Board	Dec. 21
Executive gives notice to current employer	—	Dec. 30
Transition committee plans on-boarding process	Transition committee	Jan. 2
Organization announces new executive	Transition committee	Feb. 1
New executive starts work	—	March 1
New executive and board embark on orientation/ post-hire process	Various members of the executive committee and management staff	Mid- to late March
Chief executive completes ninety-day plan	Chief executive	Early to mid-April

Event	Responsible Party	Date
Board chair engages with chief executive in ninety-day check-in review	Board chair chief executive	Mid- to late June
Executive committee conducts six-month evaluation of executive	Executive committee	Mid- to late December
Executive committee conducts annual performance evaluation of executive	Executive committee	Mid- to late March of the following year

A5. Sample Chief Executive Ninety-Day Entry Plan

Building Relationships

Staff

- Meet with each staff member (individually or in teams) within my first two weeks.

  - Assess their perspectives and evaluation of our organization.

  - Impart my management, mission philosophy, and key expectations.

  - Hold the first monthly all-staff meeting by March 31.

Board Members

- Hold face-to-face or phone conversations with each member of the board within the first thirty days.

  - Ask about their specific expectations for my first twelve to eighteen months.

  - Inquire about any concerns.

  - Discuss their sense of the vision for our organization's future.

Key Donors

- Plan joint visits with the former CEO by February 15 (if agreed).

- Introduce self to relevant senior-level county and city staff by March 15.

- Complete joint visits with donors by March 31.

- Initiate individual conversations with at least three donors per week until the development director position is filled, then six to eight per week.

Source: Copyright © TransitionGuides, 2004–2009. (Also found in Tebbe, D. *Chief Executive Transitions: How to Hire and Support a Nonprofit CEO.* Washington, D.C.: BoardSource, 2008. Don Tebbe is the executive vice president of TransitionGuides.)
Note: This plan assumes that the start date is January 1st.

- Recruit table captains and sponsors for the benefit breakfast by March 31.

- Meet with other close-in stakeholders (collaboration partners, peer organizations, and so forth).

- Visit each program sponsor by March 31.

- Redundant Work with board leaders and senior staff to arrange introductory meetings with other community stakeholders important to the organization's success.

- Meet with county board chair and all commissioners covering our service area by March 31.

Developing an Understanding and Assuming Appropriate Responsibility for the Organization's Operations

Programs

- Receive briefings from key staff regarding the programs they direct by February 1.

- Review key grant agreements by February 1.

- Meet with all significant grantors by March 31.

Finances

- Review current financial statements (profit and loss, balance sheet, and cash-flow projections) by February 1. Review at least monthly thereafter.

- Ensure signatories on all accounts are up-to-date by February 1.

- Meet in person with the accountant and treasurer at least once each month.

- Meet with the finance committee by February 15 and at least monthly thereafter. Provide updated budgetary information to key staff on a weekly basis by March 1.

- Provide a strategy to the finance committee to address equipment upgrades by the committee's March meeting.

Fund-raising (see "Donors" under "Building Relationships")

- Assess skill requirements and develop a plan for filling the vacant development director position by February 15; hire a development director by March 15.

- Assess the overall development resources by February 28.

- Develop a plan to address donor acknowledgment issues by March 1.

Marketing and Communications

- Develop a media plan to include news articles and coverage of major events by February 15.

- Consult with the executive committee on the agenda for the March board meeting.

- Distribute a monthly chief executive update to the board beginning on March 1.

- Review current marketing materials by March 15.

- Develop a process for evaluating possible changes in the Web site by April 1.

- Demonstrate support for the board of directors.

- Maintain personal contact with all board members at least once per month.

- Return all messages and phone calls within twenty-four hours.

Building the Organization's Capacity

Take the initiative and develop a plan to lead the board to formulate and implement its vision in regard to:

- Relocating and expanding the office

- Shaping the "next leap" in services, for example, expanding our meals program, and so forth

- Broadening the base of major donors

- Implementing a planned giving initiative

Personal Learning Goals and Support Needs

- Participate in a new executive program.

- Seek professional training in board relations, especially regarding building donor support and the tension between governance and management.

- Identify and hire an executive coach.

- Participate in an executive peer support program.

Finding and Choosing a Consultant

B1. When to Use and How to Find a Consultant

The size, culture, and needs of your organization will dictate when and how to find an appropriate consultant. One purpose of this book is to make access to these practices more available and provide nonprofit leaders with the knowledge and tools to support leader transitions, succession planning, and leader development with limited or no outside assistance. There are situations in which experience indicates that organizations benefit from the outside expertise and facilitation role of a consultant. What follows offers some suggestions about:

1. When to hire a consultant

2. Where to find a consultant

3. How to assess and select a consultant

When to Hire a Consultant

There are many factors that influence what an organization can do alone and when outside help is useful. The capacity of board and staff, access to pro bono assistance, and money are all factors. Experience shows that a growing number of funders appreciate the importance of attention to leader transitions, succession, and leader development and will invest in the related costs. Ideally, goals, internal capacity, and the facilitation and technical expertise required will inform the decision of whether to seek consultant assistance.

Here are some broad guidelines for different types of situations.

When a Founder or Long-Tenured Executive Plans to Leave in the Next Six Months to Four Years In this case, an outside perspective is most likely needed to assist the board and founder in clarifying roles in the transition planning and search process and in facilitating that process. Typically the founder is too close to see the whole picture, and long-term relationships may limit new perspectives or points of view that might arise. If the organization has access to a pro bono human resource or organizational development consultant or staff person in a large firm, that person may be able to provide some of the outside independent facilitation and consulting assistance. Appreciating the unique role of the founder and of a nonprofit executive are important to deliberations when securing a consultant or internal assistance.

Routine Executive Transitions For more routine executive transitions, if a board member has the time and facilitation skills and access to support to handle résumés and candidate communications, the board may be able to handle the transition or limit the use of a consultant to facilitation of a board-staff planning session or recruitment and outreach. If one or more leaders with those skills, time, and resources is not available, the use of a transition and search consultant is recommended. Without outside help, the board runs the risk of burning out key leaders and staff, which negatively affects the next executive. (For an excellent review of the use of consultants for executive transition, see Tim Wolfred's book, *Managing Executive Transitions*, pp. 131–134.)

Emergency Backup Plan and Succession Policy Development For work on an emergency backup plan and succession policy, again a skilled facilitator from the board or a local resource can guide the executive and board through this process. It is possible to put the succession basics in place without consulting assistance. The benefit of working with a consultant who has experience in nonprofit succession planning is the ability to take the process deeper and more quickly advance the leader development practices and culture. Where there is a need to strengthen communication on this topic between the executive and the board, facilitation by an outside consultant is encouraged.

Cultural Competency and Diversity Concerns In situations where an organization is focused on cultural competency and age, race or ethnic diversity, and inclusiveness, a person with experience and facilitation skills who is trusted is quite important. This person may be from the organization, a volunteer, or a consultant.

The Development of a Talent Management System For larger organizations that want to move into a talent management approach, some outside assistance from a consultant with experience in this process is suggested. Talent management processes can easily get sidetracked, and leaders can feel disrespected. The process needs to be carefully planned and thoughtfully executed.

Leader Development Plans Efforts to advance leader development often are staff driven. If there is limited staff time or expertise available internally, some outside assistance may be needed. As the leader development effort matures, a consultant or local leader development trainer may be helpful in adding depth and breadth to the effort and ensuring that leader development is tied to organizational goals and results.

Where to Find a Consultant

In larger communities, management support organizations (organizations that provide technical assistance and training to nonprofit organizations, such as Third Sector New England, CompassPoint Nonprofit Services, the Support Center, and others around the country) or universities may provide consultants or referrals. The Alliance for Nonprofit Management (www.allianceonline.org) provides a listing of consultants who provide various forms of nonprofit capacity building. The Organizational Development Network is a national membership organization of consultants with expertise in organizational development. In some communities, there are local chapters of this network. Local United Way organizations, community foundations, foundations that support capacity building, and statewide nonprofit associations are all possible sources for information on consultants.

Depending on where you are located, you may or may not have access locally to trained and experienced consultants in executive transition management and nonprofit succession planning. If you don't, think about your situation and how much experience is needed given the complexity of your transition or leader planning. National organizations such as TransitionGuides provide services across the country and have refined, cost-efficient ways to use Webinars and conference calls to do much of the work off-site where needed.

How to Assess a Consultant

If your organization has used consultants, you may already have found your way to assess how a consultant fits in with your culture and to determine how much she or he needs to know about your mission area and the distinct work of your executive and staff. You also have given thought to what cultural competency and diversity appreciation means for your organization and how to factor that into assessing consultants.

If you have not worked with a consultant before or only infrequently, you may want to interview two or three organizations who have. This will help your organization clarify your goals in seeking consulting assistance and increase the odds of your locating an appropriate consultant. Clarity about mutual expectations is key to good contracting between an organization and a consultant. The following steps will assist you in assessing consultants and their fit with your needs:

1. Write down the results you want to achieve and any assumptions you have about the steps or process to achieve the goals. State as clearly as you can what the organization will do or provide and what you want the consultant to do or provide.

2. Clarify the type of consultant you are seeking and identify networks or consultants with that expertise.

3. Identify two to four consultants and interview each by phone to determine interest cost or fee, and their expertise and experience in the area of work, and to ask for written information about the consultant or firm.

4. Invite two or three consultants to meet with you and others in the organization about the goal and process and request a written proposal. (If the consulting project is large, you may send a request for proposal to selected consultants and ask for the proposal before you interview them.)

5. Develop interview questions, a protocol, and the criteria that will guide your selection. Make sure the questions get at the values or key questions, including experience with the area of work, cultural competency and connection to organizational values, and other important considerations.

6. Check references and compare fees among consultants and with other organizations that have used consultants for similar work.

7. Select someone, begin, and check in on how it is going for the person after thirty days or at the first milestone, throughout the project, and at the conclusion.

Succession Planning Tools and Samples

C1. Sustainability Audit

CONFIDENTIAL MEMORANDUM

TO: Executive Director and Executive Committee, ABC Nonprofit
FROM: CONSULTANT
DATE: September 15, 2009
SUBJECT: Results of the Sustainability Audit

The following report is based on our sustainability audit of ABC Nonprofit conducted during August 2009. Allow us to begin this report by expressing our profound appreciation for the work of ABC Nonprofit and its executive director. What you have accomplished on behalf of children over the past twenty-nine years has been truly heroic. In addition to the struggles that you faced as advocates for children and providers of critical services, you also faced down many funding and organizational challenges over the years. The result is an organization that has not only survived but thrived, amassing

---

Note: This sample sustainability audit report was developed by TransitionGuides. It is abbreviated here because of space considerations.

a tremendous track record of accomplishments as well as respect and goodwill among funders, partner organizations, and constituents.

The Stance of This Report

In our experience, most nonprofits are underresourced and as a consequence almost always grow asymmetrically. Typically, any new resources are directed toward the programs or mission work with the business or program support aspects of the organization, such as governance, staffing, and systems, playing catch-up. It is when the organization reaches a certain "pinch point" in one or more of these business or program support areas that there is a realization that your program growth has eclipsed your organization's capacity in one of these key support areas.

ABC Nonprofit has reached some pinch points in several areas. This report identifies some critical challenges that the organization should address as part of its sustainability planning work. The report is not intended as a critique of the current leadership or its decisions. Rather, it is intended to be an objective look at key factors that contribute to sustainability, to identify the challenges, and to offer associated actions and recommendations to address those challenges. In short, the goal is to provide the information base and recommendations to further the sustainability of ABC Nonprofit.

The Information Base for This Report

The information base for this report was acquired through the following means:

- A document review of key organizational documents, including the current strategic plan and progress reports as well as the fund development plan

- A financial review that covered income and expense statements as well as balance sheets and other key financial reports for the past five years

- A board survey that included a board self-assessment

- A questionnaire completed by the senior management team

- In-depth interviews with the executive director and members of the senior management team

- Interviews with external stakeholders including funders and former board members

The report is organized around the four areas critical to the sustainability of any organization: business model and strategy, leadership, resources, and culture.

Business Model and Strategy

ABC Nonprofit is principally a government-funded entity (currently 77 percent) that advocates for children and provides some direct services principally to low-income children in [*geographic area*]. Recent client satisfaction surveys as well as the interviews and questionnaires conducted as part of this audit indicate strong consensus about the value of ABC Nonprofit's programs among constituents and donors alike.

As discussed further in the Resources section below, the organization has plans and has taken steps toward diversifying its funding.

The board and senior management surveys and interviews indicated some disconnect between board and staff about organization priorities and the level of emphasis on resource diversification. More fundamentally, a disparity in views exists about who is ABC Nonprofit's primary customer (who is most directly affected by ABC Nonprofit's work on an ongoing basis), with some seeing it as the children, others seeing as the families, and still others seeing it as the funding sources.

Recommendation

- Implement a mechanism to ensure greater alignment between the board and senior management about the primary customer, strategic direction, and priorities. For example, as part of the sustainability planning, consider conducting a strategy review session that involves the board and senior management.

Leadership

ABC Nonprofit has, by all reports, a very strong and respected management team, and an experienced, charismatic, long-term executive director. The organization has a flat structure in which the program directors have been given a significant amount of autonomy. The executive director, senior management team, and board leadership all agree that the executive director is stretched too thin trying to keep up with the demands of advocacy, external relations, internal management, and fund development. The organization does not have emergency backup plans for the executive director or members of the senior management team. The current strategic plan is silent on staffing and staff development.

The board represents a diverse cross-section of community leaders; however, the board survey indicated an opportunity for better orientation of new board members and some board development opportunities, particularly regarding their role in fund development. Currently, ABC Nonprofit does not have a committee charged with board development.

Recommendations

- Develop emergency backup plans for the executive director position and the members of the senior management team, which address how key functions will be backed up in the event of an unexpected absence of a staff member and how individuals providing the backup will be cross-trained.

- Develop a board-adopted succession policy that addresses how the board will manage a transition in the chief executive position, whether that transition is unexpected or planned.

- Appoint a board committee on governance or a board development committee. Have them work with the board leadership to digest the results of the board self-assessment conducted as part of this audit, and create and implement a board development plan.

- Implement a more robust process to orient new board members about the width and breadth of the organization, the role of the board, and specific expectations for individual board members.

- Invest new resources in strengthening the team in key areas, allowing the executive director to offload some activities. As part of the sustainability planning process, revise the strategic plan to address future staffing needs and outline a plan for the development of current staff to meet those needs, as well as identify positions where external hires will be made.

- Consider accelerating the plan to hire a director of development as discussed in the *Resources* section that follows.

Resources

In 2005, 82 percent of ABC Nonprofit's income was from just three government sources. Today that figure is 77 percent, but still from the same three government sources, with nearly 45 percent from one source. The 2007 strategic plan envisioned the organization being supported by a broader array of funders, including private foundations and individuals. Progress has been made toward the diversification and private-funding goals, but results have been short of the objectives outlined in the strategic plan. Organizational leaders including the executive director are in agreement that the major constraint to their fund development program is that too many of the duties fall on the shoulders of the executive director.

The organization's history as a sponsor of government-funded programs that emphasize service provision and grant/program compliance is a strength. The organization has real competencies in this area that could be tapped to secure other government grants, thus achieving some diversification in revenues, albeit still in the government domain.

The five-year financial review reveals relatively positive trends in income growth, a modest growth in expenses, and increasing margins that have been applied to the financial reserves. Reserves have grown significantly over the past five years, but still fall short of the ability to cover ninety days of operations, the minimum recommended benchmark.

Recommendations

- Continue progress on the development of the financial reserves.
- Accelerate the plan to hire a director of development to expand the number of "heads and hands" devoted to fund-raising and allow

the executive director's energies to be devoted to more strategic engagement on fund development.

- Create a robust fund development strategy(ies) to more fully address the goal of revenue diversification and create an expanded fund development plan to fulfill that strategy(ies).

- Consider resource diversification by building off the organization's grant fulfillment competencies and expanding its government grant portfolio to draw on funders other than its current sources.

Culture

ABC Nonprofit has a vibrant, results-oriented culture and an evolving view of itself. The board culture is changing through the addition of new board members. Previously, the board composition and culture emphasized programmatic compliance. With the implementation of the 2007 strategic plan, board members have been brought on with an eye toward resource development capacity.

The organization's portfolio of supporting customers, particularly funders, is evolving. These new supporting customers, especially individuals and private sector funders, have different values and expectations than the organization's previous supporting customers, which were a few government grant sources. As a consequence, the discourse within the organization is evolving. Where central management conversations had been about adherence to grant objectives, those conversations are being displaced by conversations about the achievement of outcome goals.

The leadership recognizes that some emerging tensions are inherent in the culture change associated with the greater emphasis on private sector fund-raising. Beyond recognition, action is needed to alleviate those tensions and manage the transition.

Focused on a limited set of supporting customers, ABC Nonprofit's external messages historically have been directed at program clients, not on attracting private sector funders and individual donors. The organization has made great progress in developing its key message points from a donor perspective, but could benefit from engaging a good communications consultant to unify the team around the organization's value proposition and core messages to the external world.

Recommendations

- Consider and manage the tensions associated with organizational culture change. Encourage open discussion, particularly among the management team, about the impact of this change. Encourage team members to read and discuss *Managing Transitions* by William Bridges. Consider outside facilitation, if warranted.

- As the sustainability planning team considers the discussion of the primary customer recommended above, include a parallel process to catalog supporting customers; closely consider complementing and competing interests and what those customers value about the organization's services.

- Foster open discussion among the management team, and encourage the development of unified messages about the organization's value and contributions to the world. Consider engaging a communications consultant to sharpen the focus in the organization's external messages, developing crisp, outcome-oriented messages about the organization's value.

- Consider communications training for everyone to empower board, staff, and volunteers to be able to make a compelling case for supporting the organization.

Conclusion and Next Actions

ABC Nonprofit is a respected and effective provider of services and advocates for children. ABC Nonprofit's overreliance on a handful of government funding sources, particularly in today's climate, leaves it extremely vulnerable, especially given the fact that one of those funding sources accounts for nearly 45 percent of the organization's revenues. The executive director, board leadership, and management team have expressed a strong commitment to furthering the sustainability of the organization. Toward that end we recommend the following next actions:

- Implement "succession basics," putting in place emergency backup plans for the executive director and members of the senior management team. Develop a board-adopted succession policy outlining how turnover in the executive director position will be managed in case of an unexpected or planned departure of the incumbent.

- Appoint a sustainability planning committee comprised of the executive director plus two or three members of the senior management team and augmented by one or two board members.

- Charge the sustainability planning committee with the task of revising the strategic plan to be aligned with the recommendations above.

We appreciate the opportunity to have contributed to the sustainability of ABC Nonprofit's mission and great works. We look forward to continuing to work with you as you develop and implement the sustainability plan.

C2. Sustainability Audit Questions (Executive Transition Management Focused)

1. Actions to ensure clear strategic direction and priorities:

   a. Are the mission, vision, and values for the organization clear and agreed to by the board and staff?

   b. Is there a current and up-to-date strategic plan or agreed-upon strategic priorities and goals? If not, what actions are needed to update them and build consensus?

   c. Are the history and values that have made the organization successful clear? Is there any change expected in values or important ways of doing the work under a new executive? Are there nonnegotiables a new executive will not change?

   d. Are there new opportunities or expected changes in the environment or resources that necessitate a review of strategic priorities? If so, what are they and what actions are needed?

2. Actions to ensure that the executive director position is a doable job as structured:

   a. Is it reasonable to expect one person to carry out the same duties with similar results as the executive?

   b. Do any functions need to be reassigned to make the position doable? If so, which ones?

   c. Looking ahead twelve to twenty-four months, is there any change in the duties of the executive (new projects, major fundraising campaign, and so on) that will influence the job? If so, how do these changes influence whether the job is doable as structured?

   d. Are there critical skills or competencies that are essential to the success of the next executive? If so, define.

Note: Each report is tailored to the specific needs of the organization. This report provides examples of the areas typically covered. The example is based on work by CompassPoint Nonprofit Services and TransitionGuides.

e. Will the compensation package offered to a new executive increase to attract the candidates desired? If this is likely, by how much, and how will that increase be funded?

f. Which of the executive's functions have backup and which do not? What are the options for addressing the areas where there is no backup?

g. Does the executive have an executive assistant or adequate support? Will the new executive consider the support available reasonable? If not, what changes are needed and what is the cost implication?

3. Actions to increase funding sustainability:

a. Do the board and executive managers understand the mix and amount of funding required to meet operating expenses?

b. Do the leaders know how much financial reserve the organization has?

c. Do the leaders know how much the new executive will be expected to raise and by when? Is this reasonable?

d. What percent of current funding is dependent on or directly tied to the relationships of the current executive? How can other leaders develop relationships with those funders?

e. What actions are needed to hand off relationships and to increase funder confidence and ongoing commitment to the organization?

4. Actions to sustain effective management team and staff:

a. Are there emergency backup plans for all managers?

b. Are there managers or staff whom the organization cannot afford to lose during the executive transition? If so, who and why?

c. Are there managers or staff who seem likely to leave before or within six to twelve months of the executive's departure? If so, who?

     d. Does the management team (or staff) have a track record of working together collegially as a team? If not, what is the status and what actions are recommended?

     e. How would you characterize the culture of the organization and staff morale? How might or should the culture and morale change under new leadership?

5. Actions to support the infrastructure required for sustainability:

     a. What systems are effective and will serve the organization well over the foreseeable future?

     b. How dependent is financial oversight on the executive director? Is the staffing appropriate for financial oversight and reporting for this size and type of organization and its future growth? If not, what actions are recommended and what is the cost implication?

     c. Are there other areas of the organizational infrastructure (human resources, information technology, resource development, communications and marketing, and so on) where there are aspirations for improvements? If so, what are they and which improvements need to occur before the new executive arrives?

6. Actions to ensure board capacity and success in managing the transition:

     a. Does the board routinely do a board self-assessment? Is there a governance committee or other board committee responsible for board development? If not, what actions are suggested?

     b. What is the current balance of responsibility between the board and the executive (for example, in budgeting, planning, annual performance review, fund-raising, and so on)? How will this balance need to change with a new executive director?

     c. Does the board have the leadership and time resources to lead the transition and work with the new executive? If not, what changes are needed?

    d. Does the board have a clear understanding with the executive about her role during the transition? Will the executive have any role after her successor begins? If so, what, and what say does the new executive have in this decision and its continuation?

    e. How will the board provide oversight to the new executive and hold him accountable?

7. Any other actions?

    a. Are there other actions required to increase the sustainability of the organization? If yes, please specify.

Leader Development and Talent Management Tools and Samples

D1. Examples of Leader Development Learning Opportunities

There are many programs and organizations that provide leadership development learning opportunities. The following are examples to help you explore what works best for you.

Organizations

- Leadership Learning Community:

http://leadershiplearning.org/leadership-resources/leadership-program-directory

This site provides a comprehensive listing of leadership program offerings by audience and type.

- Center for Creative Leadership: www.ccl.org

Source: Copyright © TransitionGuides 2007–2009. All rights reserved. www.TransitionGuides.com.

The Center offers a flagship one-week leadership development program and numerous other offerings, as well as contracts to provide training at your organization.

Major Universities

Most of the major universities have a leadership and management program. Many local universities and community colleges also offer leadership courses and programs. Among the better-known university programs are the following:

- Harvard Business School
  - Advanced Management Program: www.exed.hbs.edu/programs/amp
  - Executive Education and Management Training Program: http://www.exed.hbs.edu
- Stanford Graduate School of Business
  - Executive Education Program: www.gsb.stanford.edu/exed /programs.html
- Yale School of Management
  - MBA for Executives Program: http://mba.yale.edu/mba-e/default .asp
  - Chief Executive Leadership Institute: www.ceoleadership.org
- Wharton School of the University of Pennsylvania
  - Executive Education Program: http://executiveeducation.wharton .upenn.edu
  - Center for Leadership and Change Management: http:// executiveeducation.wharton.upenn.edu
- Massachusetts Institute of Technology
  - Sloan School of Management: http://mitsloan.mit.edu

Nonprofit Management Degree and Certification Programs

- Seton Hall University: http://academic.shu.edu/npo/list.php? sort=name

Provides an alphabetical listing of over 292 colleges and universities, by state and by degree.

Community Leadership Programs

- Community Leadership Association: http://www.claweb.org

Provides hundreds of diverse community leadership organizations at the local, state, and national levels with thousands of individual graduates and others interested in community leadership development.

- Council of International Programs USA: http://www.cipusa.org /community_leadership.asp

Comprises local nongovernmental organizations, educational institutions, businesses, and government.

D2. Talent Management Tools
Sample Talent Management Comparative Matrix

Employee Name	Title	Eligible Key of Position?	Leader Color?	Gender	Annual Salary	Performance Ratings (last 3 yrs)	Recent Leader Development Training/ Experience	High Performer?	Why High Performer?	High Performer?	Why High Potential?	High Potential?	Why High Potential?	Comments
		Y/N		M/F		Scale of 5		Y/N	Comments	Y/N	Comments	Y/N		
Jones	Assoc. Dir.	COO	Y	F	75 K	4, 4.2, 4.4	CCL	Y	Consistently exceeds expectations	Y			Thrives w/new challenges Quick Learner	
Smith	Comptroller	CFO	N	M	68 K	4.1, 4.5, 4.3	MBA	Y	Balances numbers and results	Y			Continuously expanding financial & program capability	

Source: Copyright © TransitionGuides 2007–2009. All rights reserved. www.TransitionGuides.com.
Note: This tool is intended to provide a snapshot of a group of managers or leaders. It is completed by the human resources director or person in charge of the talent management process with input from appropriate managers and supervisors.

Sample Talent Management Summary Matrix

Employee Name	Strengths	Development Areas	Performance Rating	Retention Risks	Progression Assignments	Readiness Level 1—Now (6 mo.) 2—Soon (18 mo.) 3—Later (18+ mo.)	Other Considerations
Jones	1. Management 2. Hiring and coaching staff 3. Program expertise	1. Budget and staff 2. Raising money	4.3	High Has had two offers	Program manager Associate director COO	2	Compensation adjusted to meet competitive offer Eager to start and move up
Smith	1. Accounts payable 2. Audit prep 3. Bank relations	1. Manage and prepare budget 2. Develop staff 3. Board communications	4.4	Low	Accounts payable Comptroller CFO	2	Support for MBA and to move up appreciated

Source: Copyright © TransitionGuides 2007–2009. All rights reserved. www.TransitionGuides.com.

Note: This tool is also used to summarize a group of managers relative to readiness to move to another position by looking at key development factors.

Helpful Inventories

The following are self-assessment tools or inventories to guide your personal and organizational leader development. Focus on the areas or questions where you want to grow or suspect you might have a blind spot that is holding you back. The inventories are intended first as a personal learning tool. Where useful, leaders in an organization may use the inventories for planning and collective learning.

E1. Leader's Personal and Professional Inventory

The goal of this inventory is to help you think through where you've been and where you'd like to go as a leader in your career.

1. A look at the facts:

   a. My age and generational cohort

   b. Years in this role or position

   c. Years at this organization

   d. Years in nonprofit leadership

   e. Years in workforce

   f. Define current leader position

Source: Copyright © TransitionGuides 2007–2009. All rights reserved. www.TransitionGuides.com.

g. Define past leader positions (summarize or pick the most instructive, if helpful)

h. Race or ethnicity

i. Career goal (if defined)

j. Retirement goal

k. Where I consider home

l. Where I live now

m. Preference(s) for where I live and lifestyle (urban, rural, beach, suburban, and so forth)

2. My experience as a leader:

a. Proudest moments or high points

b. Strengths as a leader

c. Darkest moments or low points

d. Derailers or annoyances

e. Estimated remaining years in this position

3. My leader development experiences:

a. What has supported your growth as a leader?

b. What has inhibited or limited you?

c. Transition *beginnings:* How have you experienced beginnings in different positions? Any patterns?

d. Transition *endings:* How have you experienced endings in different positions? Any patterns? Any patterns from how you handle endings in your personal life?

4. My satisfaction as a leader and attention to self-care:

a. Do you feel you are making a difference in your organization or community (or both)? How?

b. Are you satisfied with the time you spend with this organization? Why or why not?

    c. Is this role a good fit for you?

    d. Do you want to grow more as a leader? If so, is there opportunity for you to grow?

    e. Do you enjoy the staff and board with whom you work?

    f. How long do you want to be in your current position?

    g. Are you taking care of your physical health? How?

    h. Are you taking care of your emotional health? How?

    i. Are you satisfied with the alignment of your personal values and your daily work?

    j. Do you have the time you need to attend to your family, friends, or the community life that brings you personal fulfillment?

Finally, take a moment to consider your answers to these questions. Write out a statement—for your eyes only—that describes your sense of where you should go next in life and your goals and action plan for the next three to six months. (See section E5, p. 322, for a place to make action planning notes.)

E2. Questions About the Organization

These questions can be answered by the executive, managers, and board leaders. They can be discussed or not as appropriate in the working relationship. To keep it simple, the questions are set up with a five-point scale. However, there is no meaningful "tally" of results for you. The best approach is to give your response, and then think through the reasons why.

Please rank how you feel about the organization on a scale of 1–5: (1–Very Positive, 2–Positive, 3–Neutral, 4–Negative, 5–Very Negative)

a. Clarity of mission and hoped-for results: _____

b. Clarity of annual goals and success milestones: _____

c. Readiness of the organization for a planned executive transition: _____

d. Readiness of the organization for an unplanned executive transition (emergency or otherwise rapid transition): _____

e. Readiness of the organization for a board chair transition (planned or unplanned): _____

f. The way that leaders are selected: _____

g. The commitment to inclusiveness of people of different backgrounds and points of view: _____

h. The way the organization prepares and nurtures current and future leaders: _____

i. The organization's "bench strength" of leaders and potential leaders: _____

j. The way the organization raises its resources: _____

k. The way the organization uses and manages its resources: _____

l. The performance of the executive: _____

m. The performance of the board: _____

n. The quality and effectiveness of the board-executive relationship: _____

o. The overall health of the organization: _____

E3. Diversity Inventory

Our population is becoming increasingly diverse, and most organization development experts (including this author) agree that attention to diversity is critical to maintaining competitive advantage and mission success. Plans for leadership development and transitions should therefore include extra attention to diversifying the organization in ways that will help it achieve these advantages.

This inventory has two parts. The first part helps you examine the makeup of your organization and its constituents. You can answer this part with qualitative guesstimates, or you can dig in and get the facts. The second part is designed to spur discussion.

Organizational Racial, Age, and Gender Diversity

This inventory is intended to provide a factual look at the organization's current and projected future reality relative to racial or ethnic, age, and gender diversity. Answer the following with guesstimates of *high, low,* or *don't know;* or get the actual statistics if you have access to them. Make any summary observations in the action planning notes section that follows.

a. Racial or ethnic diversity of the people served (current and future trends)

b. Racial or ethnic diversity of the essential stakeholders (funders, contractors, or others to whom we have obligations) (current and future trends)

c. Racial or ethnic diversity of the government in the communities served or the funding agencies (current and future trends)

d. Racial or ethnic diversity of the board of the organization

e. Racial or ethnic diversity of the top leaders of the organization

f. Racial or ethnic diversity of all the staff of the organization

g. Age diversity of the people served (current and future trends)

h. Age diversity of the essential stakeholders (current and future trends)

i. Age diversity of the government in the communities served or the funding agencies

j. Age diversity of the board of the organization

k. Age diversity of the top leaders of the organization

l. Age diversity of all the staff of the organization

m. Women in top board leadership

n. Women in top staff leadership

o. Attention to inclusiveness of people with different physical or mental abilities, sexual orientation, and so on

Attitudes About Diversity

The second part of the inventory helps spur thought and discussion once you've assessed the organization's diversity. These questions can be answered by the executive, managers, and board leaders about the entire staff with special attention to the leadership cadre. To keep it simple, the questions are set up with a simple *agree*, *disagree*, or *not sure* response. The best approach is to give your response, and then think through and discuss the reasons why you have responded this way. Please answer the following questions with *agree*, *disagree*, or *not sure:*

a. Attention to cultural competency and diversity is important to leading.

b. In our organization, white leaders have opportunities and privileges that are not available to or as easily available to leaders of color.

c. Diversity of backgrounds and opinions enhances creativity and effectiveness.

d. Generational differences are important to understand and to pay attention to in leading an organization and developing leaders.

e. Younger leaders are valued and encouraged in our organization.

f. Race and ethnicity is personal and not relevant to leadership planning or organizational life.

g. Race discrimination is largely a historical phenomenon in America. Race relations and equity have improved dramatically.

h. When we think about diversity, we think about it in broad terms (race, ethnicity, age, gender, sexual orientation, disability, and so forth).

i. We have a long history of attending to diversity in our organization.

j. Attention to diversity should be a value for the organization regardless of its costs or strategic benefits.

k. Attention to diversity is a strategic decision with a goal of maintaining competitive advantage and mission success.

E4. The Leader's Emotional Check-in Barometer

Use the following list to reflect on how you feel about your leadership role in this organization today. Feelings are not facts and are neither right nor wrong. They are a guide or indicator of what is going on and clues to actions we might want to consider.

Instructions: Each set of emotions is set up to provide a choice. The point is to gauge where on the feeling continuum you are today relative to this leadership position. Your feelings may and most likely will change. You can return to this barometer and look at your patterns over time and how your feelings change. You can also use it to shape and adjust your personal and professional goals. Place a check on the line at a place that best expresses your feelings today, as indicated below.

Engaged	X	Withdrawn
Peaceful	X	Angry
Calm	X	Anxious
Satisfied	X	Agitated
Fulfilled	X	Frustrated
Accepting reality	X	Avoiding reality
Vibrant	X	Depressed

E5. Action Planning Notes and Commitments

Based on your reflections in the previous sections, use this section to make some notes about possible actions and commitments you would like to make. Take some time to think about your commitments. Action plans without commitment yield limited results. Making too many commitments leads to frustration and less success. Commitment means to entrust, to pledge for safekeeping, to pledge oneself to a particular course. Change and transition are paths that require commitment; getting ready for transition is part of this commitment.

Actions I am considering to increase my leader satisfaction or advance my leader or career goals:

Actions I am considering to increase the effectiveness of this organization:

Commitments I am considering (list any possible commitments):

Commitments I am making, why, and the benefit I expect:

My goals over the next year:

My action plan for next three to six months:

Support I will need and where I plan to obtain this support:

How I will review progress and define success:

NOTES

Chapter 1

1. Kreinin Souccar, M. "Financial Crisis Will Kill Nonprofits." *Crain's New York Business.com*, Nov. 19, 2008. [http://www.crainsnewyork.com/article/20081119/FREE/811199976].

2. Masaoka, J., and Wolfred, T. *Leadership Lost: A Study on Executive Director Tenure and Experience.* San Francisco: Support Center for Nonprofit Management, 1999.

3. Illinois Arts Alliance Foundation. "States of the Arts: Career Conditions of Nonprofit Arts Professionals in Chicago." Section A of *Succession: Arts Leadership for the 21st Century.* Chicago: Illinois Arts Alliance Foundation, 2003.

4. Salamon, L. M., and Sokolowski, S. W. *Employment in America's Charities: A Profile.* Baltimore, Md.: Johns Hopkins Center for Civil Society Studies, Johns Hopkins University, 2006.

5. Ibid., p. 3.

6. Cornelius, M., Corvington, P., and Ruesga, A. *Ready to Lead? Next Generation Leaders Speak Out.* San Francisco: CompassPoint, 2008.

7. Ibid., p. 11.

8. Ibid., p. 4.

9. Collins, J., *Good to Great.*

10. Masaoka, W., *Leadership Lost.*

11. Bell, J., Moyers, R., and Wolfred, T. *Daring to Lead 2006: A National Study of Nonprofit Executive Leadership.* San Francisco: CompassPoint Nonprofit Services, 2006, p. 3.

12. Cornelius, Corvington, and Ruesga, *Ready to Lead?* p. 4.

13. The Bridgespan Group. *Finding Leaders for America's Nonprofits.* Boston: Bridgespan Group, 2009, p. 4. [http://www.bridgespan .org/finding-leaders-for-americas-nonprofits.aspx].

14. In 2001, The Annie E. Casey Foundation initiated work in their Leadership Unit to better understand the threat of executive transition to their grantees. A survey of grantees in 2002 revealed that 85 percent of the executives intended to leave their position in the next seven years. Over the next four years, this finding and a concern about the aging leadership of key grantees led the Foundation to invest in field research, dissemination, and services to their grantees. Consultative sessions were held with executives, board leaders, and consultants to better understand the issues. A decade earlier NeighborWorks America (then the Neighborhood Reinvestment Corporation) was concerned about high executive turnover among its one-hundred-member network of community and housing development organizations. NeighborWorks launched a five-year Community Development Leadership development project with support from the W.K. Kellogg Foundation, which resulted in early tracking of executive turnover and the initial work on executive transition management. The author led both

projects and draws from the experience in this section and in the chapters on executive transition management and succession planning. See Hinden Rothman, D., and Hull, P. "Executive Leadership Transition: What We Know." *The Nonprofit Quarterly*, 2002, *9*(4), 1–5.

15. Bell, Moyers, and Wolfred, *Daring to Lead 2006*.

16. Ostrower, F. "Nonprofit Governance in the United States: Findings on Performance and Accountability from the First National Representative Study." Washington, D.C.: The Urban Institute, 2007.

17. Raelin, J. A. "We the Leaders: In Order to Form a Leaderful Organization." *Journal of Leadership and Organizational Studies*, 2005, *12*(2), 18–30.

18. Bridges, W. *Managing Transitions: Making the Most of Change.* Reading, Mass.: Addison-Wesley, 1991.

19. Center for Applied Research [http://www.cfar.com/Documents/hbrcamp.pdf].

Chapter 2

1. Bridges, W. *Managing Transitions: Making the Most of Change.* Reading, Mass.: Addison-Wesley, 1991, p. 3.

2. Ibid., pp. 4–6.

3. Perls, F. S. *Gestalt Therapy Verbatim.* Lafayette, Calif.: Real People Press, 1969.

4. Redington, E., and Vickers, D. *Following the Leader: A Guide for Planning Founding Director Transition.* Leadership Report, no. 1. Columbus: Ohio: The Academy for Leadership & Governance, 2001.

5. Cooperrider, D. L., and Whitney, D. *A Positive Revolution in Change: Appreciative Inquiry.* San Francisco: Berrett-Koehler, 2005.

6. Ibid., p. 16.

7. Goleman, D. *Emotional Intelligence: Why It Can Matter More Than IQ.* New York: Bantam Books, 1995.

8. Mayer, J. D., and Salovey, P. "What Is Emotional Intelligence?" In P. Salovey and D. Sluyter (eds.), *Emotional Development and Emotional Intelligence: Implications for Educators.* New York: Basic Books, 1997, pp. 3–31.

9. Mayer, J. D. "Emotional Intelligence Information: The Four Branch Model of Emotional Intelligence." [http://www.unh.edu/emotional_intelligence/ei%20What%20is%20EI/ei%20fourbranch.htm]. Aug. 2004.

10. Ibid.

11. Mayer and Salovey, "What Is Emotional Intelligence?" p. 12.

12. Ibid., p. 13.

13. Mayer, "Emotional Intelligence Information."

14. Mayer and Salovey, "What Is Emotional Intelligence?" p. 14.

15. Kübler-Ross, E. *On Death and Dying.* New York: Simon & Schuster, 1997.

16. Ibid.

17. For more information on Alcoholics Anonymous and the Twelve Steps see http://www.aa.org/.

18. The Hazelden Publishing Company offers a number of general meditation books that are derived from Twelve Step practices: http://www.hazelden.org/web/public/startedmeditationbooks.page.

19. Carnegie, D. *How to Stop Worrying and Start Living.* Ed. by Dorothy Carnegie. New York: Simon & Schuster, 1984, pp. 3–13.

20. For more information on Al-Anon/Alateen, visit their Web site at http://www.al-anon.alateen.org/.

21. Beattie, M. *Codependency No More: How to Stop Controlling Others and Start Caring for Yourself.* Center City, Minn.: Hazelden, 1992.

22. Fraser, B. "Resiliency in Nonprofit Leadership Transitions: Three Kinds of Rituals That Really Work." *Leadership Guide,* March 2009, pp. 4–7. [http://www.transitionguides.com].

23. Siebert, A. *The Resiliency Advantage: Master Change, Thrive Under Pressure, and Bounce Back from Setbacks.* San Francisco: Berrett-Koehler, 2005.

24. Loehr, J. E., and Schwartz, T. *The Power of Full Engagement: Managing Energy, Not Time, Is the Key to High Performance and Personal Renewal.* New York: Simon & Schuster, 2003, p. 166.

25. Fraser, "Resiliency in Nonprofit Leadership," pp. 4–6.

Chapter 3

1. Independent Sector. *The New Nonprofit Almanac and Desk Reference: The Essential Facts and Figures for Managers, Researchers, and Volunteers: In Brief.* Washington, D.C.: Independent Sector, 2001, p. 7. [http://www.independentsector.org/PDFs/inbrief.pdf].

2. Independent Sector. *The New Nonprofit Almanac and Desk Reference: The Essential Facts and Figures for Managers, Researchers, and Volunteers: Overview and Executive Summary.* New York: Jossey-Bass, 2002, p. xxviii. [http://www.independentsector.org/PDFs/NAExecSum.pdf].

3. Bell, J., Moyers, R., and Wolfred, T. *Daring to Lead 2006: A National Study of Nonprofit Executive Leadership.* San Francisco: CompassPoint Nonprofit Services, 2006, p. 5.

4. Ibid.

5. McLaughlin, T. A., and Backlund, A. N. *Moving Beyond Founder's Syndrome to Nonprofit Success.* Washington, D.C.: BoardSource, 2008, p. x.

6. Ibid.

7. Ibid.

8. Ibid.

9. Stevens, S. K. "Helping Founders Succeed." *Grantmakers in the Arts Newsletter,* 1999, *10*(2), 1–6.

10. Block, S. R., and Rosenberg, S. "Toward an Understanding of Founder's Syndrome: An Assessment of Power and Privilege Among Founders of Nonprofit Organizations." *Nonprofit Management and Leadership,* 2002, *12*(4), 353–368.

11. Ibid.

12. Adams, T. *Founder Transitions: Creating Good Endings and New Beginnings.* Executive Transitions Monograph Series, no. 3. Baltimore, Md.: The Annie E. Casey Foundation, 2005.

13. Redington, E., and Vickers, D. *Following the Leader: A Guide for Planning Founding Director Transition.* Leadership Report, no. 1. Columbus: Ohio: The Academy for Leadership & Governance, 2001.

14. With support from The Annie E. Casey Foundation, TransitionGuides developed the two-day Next Steps workshop for founders and long-term executives. The workshop has been offered annually in Baltimore and San Francisco since 2003 with three hundred executives attending. Over two hundred additional executives have attended the same workshop hosted by other funders and nonprofit sponsors.

15. Mark Leach in his 2009 study "Table for Two: Can Founders and Successors Co-Exist So Everyone Wins?" offers examples and lessons from organizations where the founder stayed in a new role. This study is available on the Management Assistance Group Web site at www.managementassistance.org.

Chapter 4

1. Throughout this chapter, I use *racial diversity* to refer to diversity related to either race or ethnicity.

2. Page, S. E. *The Difference: How the Power of Diversity Creates Better Groups, Firms, Schools, and Societies.* Princeton: Princeton University Press, 2007.

3. The Annie E. Casey Foundation. *Race Matters Initiative: Unequal Opportunities for Health and Wellness.* Baltimore, Md.: The Annie E. Casey Foundation, 2006, p. 2.

4. Pease, K., and others. *Inclusiveness at Work: How to Build Inclusive Nonprofit Organizations.* Denver: The Denver Foundation, 2005. [http://www.nonprofitinclusiveness .org/definitions-inclusiveness-and-inclusive-organizations].

5. St. Onge, P., Rouson, B., Applegate, B., Asakura, V., Moss, M. K., and Vergara-Lobo, A. *Embracing Cultural Competency: A Roadmap for Nonprofit Capacity Builders.* Saint Paul, Minn.: Fieldstone Alliance, 2009, p. 7.

6. Ibid.

7. Page, *The Difference*, pp. 313–338.

8. St. Onge, P., Rouson, B., Applegate, B., Asakura, V., Moss, M. K., and Vergara-Lobo, A., *Embracing Cultural Competency*, p. xxiv.

9. Berthoud, H., and Greene, R. D. "A Multi-Faceted Look at Diversity: Why Outreach Is Not Enough." *The Journal of Volunteer Administration,* 2001, *19*(2), 2–10.

10. McIntosh, P. "Unpacking the Invisible Knapsack." An excerpt of Working Paper #189 from *White Privilege and Male Privilege: A Personal Account of Coming to See Correspondences Through Work in Women's Studies.* Wellesley, Mass.: Wellesley College Center for Research on Women, 1988. The working paper has a longer list of privileges.

11. Grantmakers in Health. "We the People: Key Demographic Trends in the United States." Paper presented at the GIH annual meeting, Seeing the Future with 20/20 Vision, Washington, D.C., March 2009, p. 2.

12. U.S. Census Bureau News. "An Older and More Diverse Population by Midcentury." Press release. Suitland, Md.: U.S. Census Bureau, 2008.

13. U.S. Census Bureau. *General Population and Housing Characteristics: 1990, Montgomery County, MD.* Suitland, Md.: U.S. Census

Bureau, 1990. [http://factfinder.census.gov/servlet/QTTable?_
bm=n&_lang=en&qr_name=DEC_1990_STF1_DP1&ds_
name=DEC_1990_STF1_&geo_id=05000US24031].

14. Kachura, M. *More in the Middle Initiative—Dashboard
Report: Analysis and Metrics of Baltimore City's African American
Middle Class.* Baltimore, Md.: Associated Black Charities,
2008. [http://www.abc-md.org/wp-content/uploads/2009/03/
dashboardreport.pdf].

15. Holder, E. "Remarks as Prepared by Attorney General Eric Holder."
Paper presented at the Department of Justice African American
History Month Program, Washington, D.C., Feb. 2009.

16. Ayira, Adar A., Bell McKoy, D., and Adams, T. H. "Progress and
Possibility: Racial Diversity in Baltimore's Nonprofit Leadership."
Unpublished draft. Baltimore, Md.: Associated Black Charities with
TransitionGuides, 2007.

17. La Piana, D. *The Nonprofit Strategy Revolution: Real-Time Strategic
Planning in a Rapid-Response World.* St. Paul, Minn.: Fieldstone
Alliance, 2008.

18. Table 4.1 is interpretive and includes a mix of terms that generational
members may use to define themselves as well as terms others may
apply to them.

19. Kim, H. S., and Kunreuther, F. *Up Next: Generation Change
and Leadership of Nonprofit Organizations.* Executive Transitions
Monograph Series, no. 4. Baltimore, Md.: The Annie E. Casey
Foundation, 2005.

20. Kim, H. S., Kunreuther, F., and Rodriguez, R. *Working Across
Generations: Defining the Future of Nonprofit Leadership.* San
Francisco: John Wiley & Sons, 2008.

21. Kim and Kunreuther, *Up Next*, p. 3.

22. Cornelius, M., Corvington, P., and Ruesga, A. *Ready to Lead? Next
Generation Leaders Speak Out.* San Francisco: CompassPoint, 2008.

23. Kim, Kunreuther, and Rodriguez, *Working Across Generations,* pp. 9–15.

24. Brinckerhoff, *Generations,* p. 197.

25. A good resource to refer to would be the following: Fellner, K., Keleher, T., and Ortiz, E. *Work with Me: Intergenerational Conversations for Nonprofit Leadership.* Washington, D.C.: National Council of Nonprofits, 2007.

26. Nonprofit Workforce Coalition Diversity Committee. *Workforce Diversity and Inclusion Compact.* Kansas City, Mo.: Nonprofit Workforce Coalition, 2009. [http://www.humanics.org/atf/cf/%7BE02C99B2-B9B8–4887–9A15-C9E973FD5616%7D/Diversity%20and%20Inclusion%20Compact%20Launch%20Packet%20to%20Members%208–5–09.pdf].

27. Bangs, R. L., and Constance-Huggins, M. *Diversity Within and Among Nonprofit Boards in Alleghany County.* Tropman Report, no. 8. Pittsburgh, Pa.: University Center for Social and Urban Research, University of Pittsburgh, 2003.

28. Brinckerhoff, *Generations,* pp. 90–92.

29. Kim, Kunreuther, and Rodriguez, *Working Across Generations,* p. xvi.

30. Funder awareness and action are growing, as shown by sessions or materials by Grantcraft, Philanthropic Initiative for Racial Equity, Grantmakers for Effective Organizations, and the Diversity in Philanthropy Project.

31. Mark, M., and Pearson, C. S. *The Hero and the Outlaw: Building Extraordinary Brands Through the Power of Archetypes.* New York: McGraw-Hill, 2002.

32. Berger, D., and Berger, L. *The Talent Management Handbook: Creating Organizational Excellence by Identifying, Developing, & Promoting Your Best People.* Madison, Wis.: McGraw-Hill, 2004.

33. Brinckerhoff, *Generations,* pp. 52–54.

34. Ibid.

35. Ibid.

36. Terry, A. S. *Next Generation and Governance: Report on Findings.* Washington, D.C.: BoardSource, 2008.

37. Covey, S. *The 8th Habit: From Effectiveness to Greatness.* New York: Free Press, 2004.

38. Kim, Kunreuther, and Rodriguez, *Working Across Generations,* pp. 168–173.

Chapter 5

1. Tebbe, D. *Chief Executive Transitions: How to Hire and Support a Nonprofit CEO.* Washington, D.C.: BoardSource, 2008, pp. 12–13.

2. Ibid, pp. 12–15.

3. Two excellent new books that describe the ETM process in great detail are the following: Tebbe, D. *Chief Executive Transitions: How to Hire and Support a Nonprofit CEO.* Washington, D.C.: BoardSource, 2008; Wolfred, T. *Managing Executive Transitions: A Guide for Nonprofits.* Saint Paul, Minn.: Fieldstone Alliance, 2009.

4. Hinden Rothman, D., and Hull, P. "Executive Leadership Transition: What We Know." *The Nonprofit Quarterly,* 2002, *9*(4), 1–5.

5 CompassPoint Nonprofit Services. *CompassPoint Executive Transitions Program: Client Longitudinal Survey.* San Francisco: CompassPoint Nonprofit Services, 2001, pp. 2–8. Survey report prepared by Nancy Frank & Associates, Oakland, CA.

6. Hull Teegarden, P. *Nonprofit Executive Leadership and Transitions Survey 2004.* Silver Spring, Md.: Managance Consulting, 2004.

7. Bell, J., Moyers, R., and Wolfred, T. *Daring to Lead 2006: A National Study of Nonprofit Executive Leadership.* San Francisco: CompassPoint Nonprofit Services, 2006, p. 5.

8. Information on the emotions surrounding change and transition can be found in Chapter Two.

9. Tebbe, *Chief Executive Transitions,* pp. 3–9.

10. Neighborhood Reinvestment Community Development Leadership Project, 1994.

11. For new executive directors, this book is an excellent resource: Carlson, M., and Donohoe, M. *The Executive Director's Survival Guide: Thriving as a Nonprofit Leader.* San Francisco: Jossey-Bass, 2003.

12. Hull Teegarden, P. *Nonprofit Executive Leadership and Transitions Survey 2004.* Silver Spring, Md.: Managance Consulting, 2004, p. 7.

13. For more information on executive social contracting, see http://www.transitionguides.com.

Chapter 6

1. Bell, J., Moyers, R., and Wolfred, T. *Daring to Lead 2006: A National Study of Nonprofit Executive Leadership.* San Francisco: CompassPoint Nonprofit Services, 2006, p. 3.

2. Tim Wolfred of CompassPoint Nonprofit Services developed the first emergency succession (backup) plan template. Karen Gaskins Jones and TransitionGuides refined this template and developed a workbook for an emergency backup plan with a CD-ROM available through www.transitionguides.com.

3. Denice Hinden of Managance Consulting developed the first succession policy template, which we have refined with practice.

Chapter 7

1. There are a number of organizational assessment tools and approaches. To inform the work of TransitionGuides, my partner Don Tebbe does a periodic review of these tools. His summary of these organizational assessment tools and a more recent review of organizational sustainability literature is found at www.transitionguides.com.

Chapter 8

1. Gaskins Jones, K. "Preparing an Organization to Sustain Capable Leadership." *The Nonprofit Quarterly,* 2007, *14,* 69–71.

2. St. Onge, P., Rouson, B., Applegate, B., Asakura, V., Moss, M. K., and Vergara-Lobo, A., *Embracing Cultural Competency: A Roadmap for Nonprofit Capacity Builders.* Saint Paul, Minn.: Fieldstone Alliance, 2009, p. 151.

3. Covey, S. R. *The Seven Habits of Highly Effective People.* New York: Simon & Schuster, 1990, p. 106.

4. Ibid., p. 108.

5. You can learn more about the theory of multiple intelligence by visiting the Web site run by its creator, Howard Gardner, at http://www.howardgardner.com/index.html. There is also an audio recording of a conversation between Howard Gardner and Daniel Goleman, author of *Emotional Intelligence: Why It Can Matter More Than IQ* (see Chapter Two of this book), and other social intelligence luminaries at http://www.morethansound.net/wired-to-connect.php.

6. Rath, T. *StrengthsFinder 2.0.* New York: Gallup Press, 2007.

7. Kouzes, J. M., and Posner, B. Z. *The Leadership Challenge, 4th Edition.* San Francisco: Jossey-Bass, 2007.

8. Eichinger, R. W., and Lombardo, M. M. *Career Architect Development Planner 4th Edition.* Minneapolis, Minn.: Lominger International, 2007.

9. Lore, N. A. *The Pathfinder: How to Choose or Change Your Career for a Lifetime of Satisfaction and Success.* New York: Simon & Schuster, 1998.

10. Charan, R. *Leaders at All Levels: Deepening Your Talent Pool to Solve the Succession Crisis.* San Francisco: Jossey-Bass, 2008.

11. Bozeman, B., and Feeney, M. K. "Toward a Useful Theory of Mentoring: A Conceptual Analysis and Critique." *Administration & Society,* 2007, *39*(6), 719–739.

12. Bolt, J. "Coaching: The Fad That Won't Go Away." *Fast Company*, July 2008. [http://www.fastcompany.com/resources/learning/bolt/041006.html].

13. Harder+Company Community Research. *Executive Coaching Project: Evaluation of Findings.* San Francisco: CompassPoint Nonprofit Services, 2003. [http://www.compasspoint.org/assets/6_execcoaching.pdf].

14. Collins, J. *Good to Great: Why Some Companies Make the Leap . . . And Others Don't.* New York: HarperCollins Publishers, 2001, p. 39.

15. Enright, K. P. *Investing in Leadership, Volume 2: Inspiration and Ideas from Philanthropy's Latest Frontier.* Washington, D.C.: Grantmakers for Effective Organizations, 2006.

16. Barner, R. *Bench Strength: Developing the Depth and Versatility of Your Organization's Leadership Talent.* New York: AMACOM, 2006, p. 1.

17. Ibid., p. 2.

18. Ibid.

19. Ibid., pp. 3–4.

20. Berger, D., and Berger, L. *The Talent Management Handbook: Creating Organizational Excellence by Identifying, Developing, & Promoting Your Best People.* Madison, Wis.: McGraw-Hill, 2004, p. 4.

21. Lawler, E. E. III. *Talent: Making People Your Competitive Advantage.* San Francisco: Jossey-Bass, 2008, p. xv.

22. Barner, *Bench Strength,* pp. 74–75.

23. Charan, *Leaders at All Levels.*

24. Barner, *Bench Strength,* pp. 43–66.

25. Berger, *Talent Management Handbook,* p. 4.

26. Ibid., p. 3.

The following resource guide contains books and articles referenced in *The Nonprofit Leadership Transition and Development Guide.* It is updated periodically and is found on the TransitionGuides Web site (www.transitionguides.com).

Resource Organizations

Alliance for Nonprofit Management
1899 L Street, NW, 17th Floor, Washington, D.C. 20036
(www.allianceonline.org) (202) 959–8406

American Society of Association Executives
1575 I Street, NW, Washington, D.C. 20005–1168
(www.asaenet.org) (202) 626-ASAE

BoardSource
1828 L Street, NW, Suite 900, Washington, D.C. 20036 (www.boardsource.
org) (202) 452–6262

CompassPoint Nonprofit Services
706 Mission Street, Fifth Floor, San Francisco, CA 94103 (www.compasspoint.
org) (415) 541–9000

The Council on Foundations
1828 L Street, NW, Washington, D.C. 20036 (www.cof.org) (202)
466–6512

The Foundation Center
1001 Connecticut Ave., NW, Suite 938, Washington, D.C. 20036
(www.fdncenter.org) (202) 331–1400

Independent Sector
1828 L Street, NW, Washington, D.C. 20036 (www.indepsec.org) (202)
223–8100

Nonprofit Risk Management Center
1001 Connecticut Avenue, NW, Suite 900, Washington, D.C. 20036
(www.nonprofitrisk.org) (202) 785–3891

TransitionGuides
1751 Elton Road, Suite 204, Silver Spring, MD 20903
(www.transitionguides.com) (301) 439–6635

Recommended Readings
Executive Transition and Executive Transition Management

Adams, Thomas H. *Executive Transition Management: Capturing the Power
of Leadership Change.* Executive Transition Monograph Series, no. 1.
Baltimore, Md.: The Annie E. Casey Foundation, 2003.
An overview of the executive transition management process with case
examples of its application.

Adams, Thomas H. *Stepping Up, Staying Engaged.* Executive Transition Monograph Series, no. 5. Baltimore, Md.: The Annie E. Casey Foundation, 2006.

Bonavoglia, Angela, and Anne MacKinnon. *Executive Transitions: Grant Makers and Nonprofit Leadership Change.* New York: GrantCraft, 2006.

Bridges, William. *Managing Transitions: Making the Most of Change.* Reading, Mass.: Addison-Wesley, 1991.
Classic on the difference between change and transition and why a good beginning requires a positive ending and a confusing in-between period—an easy and important read for leaders of transition.

CompassPoint Nonprofit Services. *CompassPoint Executive Transitions Program: Client Longitudinal Survey.* San Francisco: CompassPoint Nonprofit Services, 2001, pp. 2–8. Survey report prepared by Nancy Frank & Associates, Oakland, Calif.

Gilmore, Thomas. *Making a Leadership Change: How Organizations and Leaders Can Handle Leadership Transition Successfully.* New York: Author's Choice Press, 2003.
Classic description of leadership transitions; thoughtful and detailed.

Hinden Rothman, Denice, and Paige Hull. "Executive Leadership Transitions: What We Know." *The Nonprofit Quarterly,* 2002, *9*(4), 1–5.
An excellent summary of over ten years' research and learning about executive transition management.

Hinden Rothman, Denice, and Don Tebbe. "Managing Executive Leadership Transitions in Nonprofits." *The Public Manager,* 2003, *32*(2).

Tebbe, Don. *Chief Executive Transitions: How to Hire and Support a Nonprofit CEO.* Washington, D.C.: BoardSource, 2008.

Leadership Guide [www.transitionguides.com].
Quarterly e-newsletter on nonprofit executive succession and transition.

Weisman, Carol, and Richard Goldbaum. *Losing Your Executive Director Without Losing Your Way.* San Francisco: John Wiley & Sons, 2004.

A great step-by-step guide to the executive transition process with a lot of examples and humor.

Wolfred, Tim. "Stepping Up: A Board's Challenge in Leadership Transitions." *The Nonprofit Quarterly,* 2002, *8*(4).
A clear and persuasive case for why and how boards can exercise a unique and key leadership role in making their organization's leadership transition positive and successful in advancing the organization's mission.

Wolfred, Tim. *Managing Executive Transitions: A Guide for Nonprofits.* Saint Paul, Minn.: Fieldstone Alliance, 2009.

Executive Transition Departing Executives and Founders

Adams, Thomas H. "Departing? Arriving? Surviving and Thriving: Lessons for Seasoned and New Executives." *The Nonprofit Quarterly,* 2002, *8*(4).
A frequently turned-to resource for incoming and departing executives that provides a process overview and role options for the executive.

Adams, Thomas H. *Founder Transitions: Creating Good Endings and New Beginnings.* Executive Transitions Monograph Series, no. 3. Baltimore, Md.: The Annie E. Casey Foundation, 2005.

Backlund Nelson, Addie, and Thomas A. McLaughlin. *Moving Beyond Founder's Syndrome to Nonprofit Success.* Washington, D.C.: Boardsource, 2008.

Bangs, Ralph L., and Monique Constance-Huggins. *Diversity Within and Among Nonprofit Boards in Alleghany County.* Tropman Report, no. 8. Pittsburgh, Penn.: University Center for Social and Urban Research, University of Pittsburgh, 2003.

Block, Stephen R., and Steven Rosenberg. "Toward an Understanding of Founder's Syndrome: An Assessment of Power and Privilege Among Founders of Nonprofit Organizations." *Nonprofit Management and Leadership,* 2002, *12*(4), 353–368.

Linnell, Deborah. "Founders and Other Gods." *Nonprofit Quarterly,* 2004, *11*(1), 8–17.

A well-written article with many examples that puts the founder's challenge in an organizational life-cycle context.

Redington, Emily, and Donn Vickers. *Following the Leader: A Guide for Planning Founding Director Transition.* Leadership Report, no. 1. Columbus: Ohio: The Academy for Leadership & Governance, 2001. A thirty-three-page booklet that provides a concise and thoughtful presentation of the work of founders in "letting go" and "preparing the way."

Stevens, Susan Kenny. *In Their Own Words: The Entrepreneurial Behavior of Nonprofit Founders.* Long Lake, Minn.: Stagewise Enterprises and Maryland Nonprofits, 2002. A comprehensive study of nonprofit founder executives with an extensive review of nonprofit founders in comparison to small business entrepreneurs.

Executive Transition Incoming Executives

Carlson, Mim, and Margaret Donohoe. *The Executive Director's Survival Guide: Thriving as a Nonprofit Leader.* San Francisco: Jossey-Bass, 2003. Two seasoned executive and transition consultants answer the questions nearly every new executive director faces—a great resource for the new executive.

Gabarro, John. "When a New Manager Takes Charge." *Harvard Business Review,* 1985, *63*(3), 110–123. Study of the take-charge process of fourteen for-profit executives, detailing the process and trends in how the change occurred. A helpful guide for executives thinking about an organizational change process.

Linnell, Deborah, Zora Radosevich, and Jonathan Spack. *The Executive Directors Guide: The Guide for Successful Nonprofit Management.* Boston: United Way of Massachusetts Bay, 2002. A practical introduction to the key work of an executive director, developed by the Third Sector New England in conjunction with United Way of Massachusetts Bay.

Watkins, Michael. *The First 90 Days: Critical Strategies for New Leaders at All Levels.* Boston: Harvard Business School Publishing, 2003.

Succession Planning

Barner, Robert. *Bench Strength: Developing the Depth and Versatility of Your Organization's Leadership Talent.* New York: AMACOM, 2006.

Cohn, Jeffrey, Rakesh Khurana, and Laura Reeves. "Growing Talent as If Your Business Depended on It." *Harvard Business Review,* 2005, *83*(10), 62–70.

Gaskins Jones, Karen. "Preparing an Organization to Sustain Capable Leadership." *The Nonprofit Quarterly,* 2007, *14,* 69–71.

Illinois Arts Alliance Foundation. *"States of the Arts: Career Conditions of Nonprofit Arts Professionals in Chicago." Section A of Succession: Arts Leadership for the 21st Century.* Chicago: Illinois Arts Alliance Foundation, 2003.

Kesner, Idalene, and Terrence Sebora. "Executive Succession: Past, Present & Future." *Journal of Management,* 1994, *20*(2), 327–372.

Kets De Vries, Manfred. "The Dark Side of CEO Succession." *Harvard Business Review,* 1988, *88*(1), 56–60.
Highlights the emotional and psychological forces at play in leadership transitions and how these can sabotage successions. The issues identified include fear of death, loss of power, choosing an insider versus an outsider, the changes in group and power dynamics, the tendency to romanticize the past, and the potential to place unrealistic expectations on a new executive.

Orellano, Tim, and Janice Miller. *Succession Planning: Lessons from Kermit the Frog.* Little Rock, Ark.: The Human Resources Team, 1997.

Rechtman, Janet. "Legacy and Letting Go." *Board Member,* 2000, *9*(9). [http://www.boardsource.org/Membership.asp?mode=archive&ID=457] The article frames the issues of executive transition by talking about the importance of articulating one's legacy, honoring legacies, and letting go of power.

Rothwell, William. *Effective Succession Planning: Ensuring Leadership Continuity and Building Talent from Within.* New York: AMACOM, 1994.

Siebert, Al. *The Resiliency Advantage: Master Change, Thrive Under Pressure, and Bounce Back from Setbacks.* San Francisco: Berrett-Koehler, 2005.

Sonnenfeld, Sandi. "When the CEO Can't Let Go." *Harvard Business Review,* 1995, *73,* 24–40.
Case study of the successful, long-time CEO of Coltrane Farm Equipment and Manufacturing facing retirement, based on a for-profit corporation; many of the issues are relevant to founders of successful nonprofits.

Sustainability Planning

Center for Civic Partnerships. *Sustainability Toolkit: 10 Steps to Maintaining Your Community Improvements.* Sacramento, Calif.: Center for Civic Partnerships, 2001.

La Piana, David. *The Nonprofit Strategy Revolution: Real-Time Strategic Planning in a Rapid-Response World.* St. Paul, Minn.: Fieldstone Alliance, 2008.

Langford, Barbara Hanson, and Margaret Flynn. *Sustainability Planning Workbook.* Washington, D.C.: The Finance Project, 2003.

Mattocks, Ronald. *Zone of Insolvency: How Nonprofits Avoid Hidden Liabilities and Build Financial Strength.* Hoboken, N.J.: John Wiley & Sons, 2008.

Ralser, Tom. *ROI for Nonprofits: The New Key to Sustainability.* San Francisco: JohnWiley & Sons, 2007.

Tebbe, Don. *Building a Sustainable Organization.* Silver Spring, Md.: TransitionGuides, 2009. [www.transitionguides.com]

York, Peter. *The Sustainability Formula.* New York: TCC Group, 2009. [www.tccgrp.com/pdfs/SustainabilityFormula.pdf]

Diversity

The Annie E. Casey Foundation. *Race Matters Initiative: Unequal Opportunities for Health and Wellness.* Baltimore, Md.: The Annie E. Casey Foundation, 2006.

Ayira, Adar, Diane Bell McKoy, and Thomas H. Adams. "Progress and Possibility: Racial Diversity in Baltimore's Nonprofit Leadership."

Unpublished draft. Baltimore, Md.: Associated Black Charities with TransitionGuides, 2007.

Berthoud, Heather, and Robert D. Greene. "A Multi-Faceted Look at Diversity: Why Outreach Is Not Enough." *The Journal of Volunteer Administration,* 2001, *19*(2), 2–10.

Brinckerhoff, Peter. *Generations: The Challenge of a Lifetime for Your Nonprofit.* Saint Paul, Minn.: Fieldstone Alliance, 2007.

Fellner, Kim, Terry Keleher, and Elisa Ortiz. *Work with Me: Intergenerational Conversations for Nonprofit Leadership.* Washington, D.C.: National Council of Nonprofits, 2007.

Grantmakers in Health. "We the People: Key Demographic Trends in the United States." Plenary address at the GIH annual meeting, Seeing the Future with 20/20 Vision, Washington, D.C., March 2009, p. 2.

Holder, Eric. "Remarks as Prepared by Attorney General Eric Holder." Paper presented at the Department of Justice African American History Month Program, Washington, D.C., Feb. 2009.

Kachura, Matthew. *More in the Middle Initiative—Dashboard Report: Analysis and Metrics of Baltimore City's African American Middle Class.* Baltimore, Md.: Associated Black Charities, 2008. [http://www.abc-md.org/wp-content/uploads/2009/03/dashboardreport.pdf].

Kim, Helen, and Frances Kunreuther. *Up Next: Generation Change and Leadership of Nonprofit Organizations.* Executive Transitions Monograph Series, no. 4. Baltimore, Md.: The Annie E. Casey Foundation, 2005.

Kim, Helen, Frances Kunreuther, and Robert Rodriguez. *Working Across Generations: Defining the Future of Nonprofit Leadership.* San Francisco: John Wiley & Sons, 2008.

McIntosh, Peggy. "Unpacking the Invisible Knapsack," excerpt of Working Paper #189 from *White Privilege and Male Privilege: A Personal Account of Coming to See Correspondences Through Work in Women's Studies.* Wellesley, Mass.: Wellesley College Center for Research on Women, 1988.

Nonprofit Workforce Coalition Diversity Committee. *Workforce Diversity and Inclusion Compact.* Kansas City, Mo.: Nonprofit Workforce Coalition, 2009. [http://www.humanics.org/atf/cf/%7BE02C99B2-B9B8–4887–9A15-C9 E973FD5616%7D/Diversity%20and%20Inclusion%20Compact%20Launch%20Packet%20to%20Members%208-5–09.pdf].

Page, Scott E. *The Difference: How the Power of Diversity Creates Better Groups, Firms, Schools, and Societies.* Princeton, N.J.: Princeton University Press, 2007.

Pease, Katherine, and others. *Inclusiveness at Work: How to Build Inclusive Nonprofit Organizations.* Denver: The Denver Foundation, 2005. [http://www.nonprofitinclusiveness.org/definitions-inclusiveness-and-inclusive-organizations].

St. Onge, Patricia, Brigette Rouson, Beth Applegate, Vicki Asakura, Monika K. Moss, and Alfredo Vergara-Lobo. *Embracing Cultural Competency: A Roadmap for Nonprofit Capacity Builders.* Saint Paul, Minn.: Alliance for Nonprofit Management, 2009.

Terry, Alexis S. *Next Generation and Governance: Report on Findings.* Washington, D.C.: Boardsource, 2008.

U.S. Census Bureau. *General Population and Housing Characteristics: 1990, Montgomery County, MD.* Suitland, Md.: U.S. Census Bureau, 1990.

U.S. Census Bureau. *Profile of General Demographic Characteristics: 2000, Montgomery County, MD.* Suitland, Md.: U.S. Census Bureau, 2000.

U.S. Census Bureau News. "An Older and More Diverse Population by Midcentury," press release. Suitland, Md.: U.S. Census Bureau, 2008.

Emotional Intelligence and Appreciative Inquiry

Beattie, Melody. *Codependency No More: How to Stop Controlling Others and Start Caring for Yourself.* Center City, Minn.: Hazelden, 1992.

Carnegie, Dale. *How to Stop Worrying and Start Living.* Ed. by Dorothy Carnegie. New York: Simon & Schuster, 1984. (Originally published 1948.)

Cooperrider, David L., and Diana Whitney. *A Positive Revolution in Change: Appreciative Inquiry.* San Francisco: Berrett-Koehler, 2005.

Covey, Stephen. *The 8th Habit: From Effectiveness to Greatness.* New York: Free Press, 2004.

Fraser, Brian. "Resiliency in Nonprofit Leadership Transitions: Three Kinds of Rituals That Really Work." *Leadership Guide,* March 2009, pp. 4–7. [http://www.transitionguides.com].

Goleman, Daniel. *Emotional Intelligence: Why It Can Matter More Than IQ.* New York: Bantam Books, 1995.

Kübler-Ross, Elisabeth. *On Death and Dying.* New York: Simon & Schuster, 1997.

Loehr, Jim E., and Tony Schwartz. *The Power of Full Engagement: Managing Energy, Not Time, Is the Key to High Performance and Personal Renewal.* New York: Simon & Schuster, 2003.

Mayer, John D. "Emotional Intelligence Information: The Four Branch Model of Emotional Intelligence." [http://www.unh.edu/emotional_intelligence/ei%20What%20is%20EI/ei%20fourbranch.htm]. Aug. 2004.

Mayer, John D., and Peter Salovey. "What Is Emotional Intelligence?" In Peter Salovey and David Sluyter (eds.), *Emotional Development and Emotional Intelligence: Implications for Educators.* New York: Basic Books, 1997, pp. 3–31.

Mohr, Bernard J., and Jane M. Watkins. *Appreciative Inquiry: Change at the Speed of Imagination.* San Francisco: Jossey-Bass/Pfeiffer, 2001.

Perls, Frederick S. *Gestalt Therapy Verbatim.* Lafayette, Calif.: Real People Press, 1969.

Siebert, Al. *The Resiliency Advantage: Master Change, Thrive Under Pressure, and Bounce Back from Setbacks.* San Francisco: Berrett-Koehler, 2005.

Leader Development and Talent Management

Barner, Robert. *Bench Strength: Developing the Depth and Versatility of Your Organization's Leadership Talent.* New York: AMACOM, 2006.

Berger, Dorothy, and Lance Berger. *The Talent Management Handbook: Creating Organizational Excellence by Identifying, Developing, & Promoting Your Best People.* Madison, Wis.: McGraw-Hill, 2004.

Bozeman, Barry, and Mary K. Feeney. "Toward a Useful Theory of Mentoring: A Conceptual Analysis and Critique." *Administration & Society,* 2007, *39*(6), 719–739.

Charan, Ram. *Leaders at All Levels: Deepening Your Talent Pool to Solve the Succession Crisis.* San Francisco: Jossey-Bass, 2008.

Eichinger, Robert W., and Michael M. Lombardo. *Career Architect Development Planner 4th Edition.* Minneapolis, Minn.: Lominger International, 2007.

Enright, Kathleen P. *Investing in Leadership, Volume 2: Inspiration and Ideas from Philanthropy's Latest Frontier.* Washington, D.C.: Grantmakers for Effective Organizations, 2006.

Harder+Company Community Research. *Executive Coaching Project: Evaluation of Findings.* San Francisco: CompassPoint Nonprofit Services, 2003. [http://www.compasspoint.org/assets/6_execcoaching.pdf].

Kouzes, James M., and Barry Z. Posner. *The Leadership Challenge, 4th Edition.* San Francisco: Jossey-Bass, 2007.

Lawler, Edward E. III. *Talent: Making People Your Competitive Advantage.* San Francisco: Jossey-Bass, 2008.

Lore, Nicholas A. *The Pathfinder: How to Choose or Change Your Career for a Lifetime of Satisfaction and Success.* New York: Simon & Schuster, 1998.

Raelin, Joseph A. "We the Leaders: In Order to Form a Leaderful Organization." *Journal of Leadership and Organizational Studies,* 2005, *12*(2), 18–30.

Rath, Tom. *StrengthsFinder 2.0.* New York: Gallup Press, 2007.

Other Resources

Allison, Mike, Jan Masaoka, and Tim Wolfred. *Leadership Lost: A Study on Executive Director Tenure and Experience.* San Francisco: Support Center for Nonprofit Management, 1999.

Bell, Jeanne, Richard Moyers, and Tim Wolfred. *Daring to Lead 2006: A National Study of Nonprofit Executive Leadership.* San Francisco: CompassPoint Nonprofit Services, 2006.

The Bridgespan Group. *Finding Leaders for America's Nonprofits*. Boston: Bridgespan Group, 2009, p. 4. [http://www.bridgespan.org/finding-leaders-for-americas-nonprofits.aspx].

Collins, Jim. *Good to Great: Why Some Companies Make the Leap . . . And Others Don't*. New York: HarperCollins Publishers, 2001.

Gripe, Alan. *The Interim Pastor's Manual*. Louisville, Ky.: Geneva Press, 1997. This manual is grounded in the practice of interim ministry in the Presbyterian Church (U.S.A.), but its clear discussion of the interim process will be useful to many others. Of particular help is Gripe's discussion of the five tasks of the interim pastor.

Independent Sector. *The New Nonprofit Almanac and Desk Reference: The Essential Facts and Figures for Managers, Researchers, and Volunteers: In Brief*. Washington, D.C.: Independent Sector, 2001. [http://www.independentsector.org/PDFs/inbrief.pdf].

Independent Sector. *The New Nonprofit Almanac and Desk Reference: The Essential Facts and Figures for Managers, Researchers, and Volunteers: Overview and Executive Summary*. New York: Jossey-Bass, 2002. [http://www.independentsector.org/PDFs/NAExecSum.pdf].

Salamon, Lester M., and S. Wojciech Sokolowski. *Employment in America's Charities: A Profile*. Baltimore: Johns Hopkins Center for Civil Society Studies, Johns Hopkins University, 2006.

INDEX